PLAY 'RED WING'!

A FAMILY'S ODYSSEY THROUGH EUROPE AND THE OLD WEST

by

Stan Welli

authorHOUSE®

AuthorHouse™
1663 Liberty Drive, Suite 200
Bloomington, IN 47403
www.authorhouse.com
Phone: 1-800-839-8640

First published by AuthorHouse   10/29/2007

ISBN: 978-1-4343-4458-8 (sc)
ISBN: 978-1-4343-4457-1 (hc)

Library of Congress Control Number: 2007908247

Printed in the United States of America
Bloomington, Indiana

This book is printed on acid-free paper.

CONTENTS

PART ONE:
THE EARLY YEARS, 1862-1906

PART TWO:
HOME IN OKLAHOMA, 1906-1920

PART THREE:
THE LATER YEARS, 1920-1938

ACKNOWLEDGMENTS AND
BASIS FOR THE STORY

I was born to a family that valued its history. Over the years that history, with its anecdotes, music, and humor, served my family well, especially during hard times and tragedy. With *Play 'Red Wing'!*, an oft-repeated song request, I have attempted to capture that spirit.

I relied heavily on my family as primary sources, especially the recollections of Katherine Welli Keiter, my great-aunt, and George Welli III, my father. They were born at Goodwell, Oklahoma in 1906 and 1914, respectively. Marylou Welli Helsel and Rosa Mae Welli Hemphill also provided excellent insight, especially into the later years — the 1930s. And in 1982 Rosa sat down with my great-aunt Katherine to record her memories. She also persuaded my father to write his boyhood recollections.

This family history was supplemented with information from newspapers of the day, various historical associations, historical markers and monuments, and several visits to places where my family lived. I also reviewed original military and immigration records at the National Archives and map records at the Library of Congress in Washington, D.C.

Ken Turner, Ph.D., Custodian of Collections at the No Man's Land Historical Society was helpful and enthusiastic, which kept me motivated to complete the book. I also owe gratitude to several public libraries whose reference facilities were invaluable to my research, including those in Guymon, Oklahoma; Pratt, Kansas; Aurora, Illinois; and Youngstown, Ohio.

Special thanks go to my daughter Susan Welli and my friend Shelley Bishop for an initial review of the manuscript. Special thanks is also due my son Mike Welli for his deft touch in bringing new life to the family photos, many of them 100 or more years old. I'm also grateful to Jeanine Welli, Mike's wife, for her skill in transcribing my interviews of Katherine Keiter. Thanks also to my brothers Larry Welli and Earl Welli. Their research and recall provided key information, often at just the right time when I was stumped.

Books or movies about the Old West often portray musicians as nameless, faceless individuals lost in the background. This book helps tell their story. The musicians in this saga played for pure enjoyment in barns, ranch houses, homesteads, or town halls at dances lasting all night long. During the nineteenth century and early twentieth century, those Saturday dances were, for many people, the most important social events of their lives and were the glue that held fledgling communities together through good times and bad.

Although the story is biographical, I've written it with dialog and a few fictitious characters, thus "fictionalizing" it. This permits better character development and story continuity without detracting from the family history. The reader, however, may wonder how to separate fact from fiction. The wise counsel of an author from earlier times may be helpful. In the foreword to her novel *Cimarron*, published in 1929, Edna Ferber said: "Only the more fantastic and improbable events in this book are true . . . In many cases material entirely true was discarded as unfit for use because it was so melodramatic, so absurd as to be too strange for the realm of fiction . . . Anything can have happened in Oklahoma. Practically everything has." The same logic applies to *Play 'Red Wing'!*

The Generations

First	John Welli	1820-1887
Second	George Welli, Sr.	1864-1950
Third	Mathias Welli	1891-1949
Fourth	George Welli III	1914-2002
Fifth	Stan Welli	the author

PART ONE:

THE EARLY YEARS,
1862-1906

INTRODUCTION

The eighteenth and nineteenth centuries and the early years of the twentieth century were times of heavy migration. People moved to avoid military conscription or religious persecution, to escape debts, or to find employment. Sometimes their motives were more esoteric, such as seeking a healthier climate or fulfilling the need for a "fresh start." For still others, it may have been to satisfy an adventurous spirit, find riches, or cheat the hangman. This was true in both Europe and the United States. In America, westward expansion and migration was considered part of fulfilling President Thomas Jefferson's manifest destiny.

CHAPTER 1
WESTWARD

The Rock Island train rumbled over the Kansas prairie at a steady, distance-eating pace toward the Oklahoma Territory. For the third time since 1862 the Welli family was making a long move. It was late spring 1906 and George Welli, Sr. was headed west to claim homestead land.

Seated across the aisle from his father, fifteen-year-old Mathias "Mat" Welli stared out the window, fascinated by the passing scenery. For the brown-haired youth with blue eyes, this long trip beginning in Youngstown, Ohio was a fine adventure. Passing through Ohio, Indiana, and Illinois was interesting but it didn't prepare him for what he saw after the Rock Island train they boarded in Chicago took them on the last leg of this long journey. Farther and farther south and west sped the train, through Kansas towns named Herington, McPherson, Hutchinson, and Pratt. These were like towns in Ohio, with lots of people, horse-drawn buggies, and wagons on the streets and buildings three stories tall. He even saw an automobile in Hutchinson.

Pratt, Kansas, midway between Wichita and Dodge City, seemed a gateway. From there on west the rolling land abruptly changed to vast tabletop high plains. The area was occasionally broken by moderate ravines and bluffs near the rivers. Here, the fields of waving wheat and the prairie grass sometimes gave way to low, gray-green bushes and strange-looking, dark green plants. Growing in clumps, they had dozens of long, slender leaves with sharp, spear-like ends. Once in a while, small whirlwinds carried dust and sun-parched grass or weeds in a revolving column high into the air. These would move rapidly across the prairie until out of sight. *Strange country,* thought Mat, shaking his head. Except near the rivers, the plains were treeless, stretching from horizon to horizon in overwhelming grandeur. It looked lonely, almost to the point being frightening, but at the same time, breathtaking.

Through the shimmering heat waves, Mat saw a few scattered farms and ranches. Suddenly he saw a group of ranch buildings near the horizon. Maybe his eyes were playing tricks on him. He looked again. Now the buildings were floating *above* the horizon. "Father, look out the window, quick!" he exclaimed, reaching across the aisle and shaking him by the shoulder.

Half-asleep, George muttered "What's wrong, Mat?"

Mat pointed out the mysterious sight. "You can see blue sky under those buildings!" He jumped across the aisle to an empty seat behind his father and continued staring.

George nodded. Then, shaking his head, "Strange country," he muttered to himself. The words were muffled and lost in his heavy, drooping, old country mustache. After five years in America he still had the look of a European, slender but tough and wiry, nearly six feet tall with piercing blue eyes, a hawk nose, and prominent cheekbones. He topped things off with a short-billed cap, a favorite of many men, especially immigrants.

Strange country indeed. But it was what the doctor in Youngstown had ordered. The rhythmic sounds of the fast-moving train helped drown out any other sounds or thoughts. *You have to move to a higher, dryer climate. Otherwise, you won't live another six months. And throw that pipe away. Stay just as far away from tobacco as possible.* The doctor's diagnosis had played out over and over in George's mind ever since their train left Youngstown. *Moving so far to such desolate country, it must work. It has to work! My darling Anna and the children back in Youngstown; how would they make it without a man to earn the living? Mat is old enough to go to work. He would have to support his mother and the younger children. But even if I do live, can I support the family? I don't know anything about farming in America. And where we're going is what some people call semiarid country. That must mean you get only half the rainfall you need. Ha! I'll have to tell Joe Udry that when he meets us in Goodwell.*

The passenger car rocked and swayed as the train hurried on. As George dozed off, Mat remained against the car's window, his gaze still fixed on the distant horizon.

"Must be somethin' awful scary out there! Are Indians after us or is a gang of train robbers fixin' to hold us up?"

Mat turned to see the conductor's smiling face. The wrinkles around the older man's eyes enhanced his smile, complementing the silver hair showing below his cap. "Sir, look at those buildings out there!"

The conductor looked out the window and then chuckled. "Son, you've just seen your first mirage."

"You mean it's just my imagination, my eyes playing tricks on me?"

"No, not that kind of mirage. Those buildings exist but they just ain't nearly as close as they seem to be. What you see is a reflection. Most likely they're some 30 miles away. Sometimes in this part of the country, when the weather is just right, you see some real funny things in the sky. Those buildings are way past Dodge City."

"Dodge City? Are we going there?"

"This branch of the Rock Island doesn't go through Dodge, but right now we're about 20 miles south of it. I take it you heard of Dodge."

"Golly, yes! I read about it in books. Is it still a wild place?"

"Until about twenty years ago it was the wildest town in the West. It was on the Santa Fe Trail and was the headquarters for lots of buffalo hunters. There was an army post just outside town where Col. George A. Custer's Seventh Cavalry was stationed. With all the mule skinners, bull whackers, hunters, and soldiers around, it was wild even before the Texans began driving longhorns there."

Mat was somewhat taken aback. "All that *before* the cattle drives even began?"

"Yes sir! The cowboys really took a liking to the place 'cause it was more 'Western' than say, Abilene or some of the other Kansas cow towns. All those young bucks around, most of them with money, made for quite a brew. When a trail herd hit town, those cowboys wanted whiskey, women, a card game, and a place to sleep off a wild night. And most of them carried guns, so there were plenty of shootings. Some of the cowboys called Dodge City a place where you could break all Ten Commandments in one night."

Mat's eyes widened. "You been there?"

"Many times," replied the conductor. "I was a buffalo hunter after I got out of the army."

"What made Dodge City change?"

The old conductor chuckled again. "Well, when you get right down to it, a little bug made it change."

"A bug?"

"Yep, a bug. A tick, really. The longhorns carried ticks that spread Texas fever. It didn't hurt *them* but the disease was fatal to cattle in Kansas. It could wipe out whole herds pronto. Nothing saved them once they got sick. Because of the fever, Kansas set up a quarantine line that kept the trail herds out of the eastern half of the state. So, Dodge was the only town where they could drive cattle. Finally, in about 1885, Kansas extended the quarantine boundary all the way west to the Colorado line. And that ended Dodge City's days as a major cow town. You say you read books about it? In school?"

"No, books you buy at the store for a dime. I have one in my grip." Mat pulled his battered valise from under the seat, took out the treasured novel, and handed it to the conductor.

"Well, well, well, *Buffalo Bill's Best Shot*. By Mr. Ned Buntline. Seen it before, it's a pretty good one. But some of those other books really stretch the truth about the West."

Mat's mind was still on the cattle drives. "How did the Texans get them to market after Kansas closed off the whole state?"

"This railroad, the Rock Island, kinda' saved the day. The line went to Liberal, Kansas, only about five miles from No Man's Land. It's part of Oklahoma Territory now, the panhandle. They laid new track down to a settlement called Tyrone. So, the cattle drives went there instead of Dodge City until about 1901. Tyrone became the end of the line for them. By '01 the railroads had extended their lines into most parts of Texas so there wasn't as much need to make the long drives."

"That's really interesting. Say, we're slowing down."

"Yep, we're coming into Meade, Kansas. We make a stop to pick up passengers and maybe let some off." The conductor got up and moved toward the door. "Look closely when we stop. You might see a stagecoach."

The whistle sounded in long, plaintive bursts. The train slowed even more, finally stopping at the depot with a lurch. Mat peered out the windows. He saw three well-dressed women get on the train. But no stagecoach — was the conductor joshing him? Soon the train gave a short whistle and, with another lurch, started inching out of the station. A few miles outside town Mat saw a sod house with grass growing on the roof and pointed it out to his father. George nodded and smiled, remarking that it resembled the ones at home in southern Austria-Hungary.

Later the conductor came into the car. "Sorry there was no stagecoach. It usually comes up to Meade from Beaver, Oklahoma to make connections with the Rock Island. But the depot agent said they had a big rain down that way. The trail from Beaver runs through some rough country and he has to cross the Cimarron River so he's probably runnin' very late."

"I suppose I'll get to see one some time since we're going to be living out here."

"Where you from?"

"Ohio. We're going to Goodwell to homestead."

"Why are you leaving Ohio?"

"My dad has to move to a better climate. He speaks German and Hungarian but very little English so I got to come with him."

"I've heard him coughing. Other folks have moved out west for the same reason and it helped them. Goodwell is a new town, just about three years old. They have a fine water well there.

"The Oklahoma Panhandle is lonely country. And until they made it part of Oklahoma Territory, it was one really wild place. Years ago the government made some bad mistakes when they were resetting the northern border of Texas. They ended up with a strip of land 167 miles long and 34 miles wide that wasn't part of any state or territory."

Mat knew about boundaries. He'd lived in Europe where some changed frequently, usually after a war. But this was hard to understand. Besides, he was finding that a railroad passenger car was an uncomfortable place in the Kansas heat.

"Sir, excuse me for interrupting, it's getting awful hot in here."

"We can open that window a little and let in some breeze. But you may get smoke from the engine, too."

"Does it always get this hot out here?"

"This is only May, wait 'til summer comes. It gets so hot that when a dog chases a rabbit they both just walk!"

Mat laughed heartily at the thought.

The conductor showed him how to open the window. "Well now, where were we?"

"That big strip of land, what was it called?"

"It had several names: the neutral strip, public lands, public domain. At one time the folks there called it Cimarron Territory and tried to make it a state. Once, a judge ruled that no man could own land there. So, people started calling it No Man's Land. That name stuck but some of us still call it the strip. But it had no law because there wasn't any government. The place became a hideout for murderers, thieves, bushwhackers, and robbers. It got so bad the folks who lived there formed vigilante committees and they started hanging most of the crooks they caught. Why, there's a story about one young man, not much older than you, that they hanged twice."

Again, Mat's eyes widened. "How could they hang him twice?"

Seeing he had a captive audience, the conductor took off his cap and settled in the seat beside Mat. The train was half-empty and there was lots of time for stories.

"Well, this boy stole a horse. That's always been a hangin' offense. There weren't any trees around so they were going to hang him in a barn. They put the noose around his neck, threw the end over a rafter, and tied it to a post. Then, they pulled the stool he was standing on out from under him. But they'd left the rope too long and he was able to touch the floor with his toes. There was a big discussion. Some said they had carried out the sentence by hanging him. Others said that wasn't good enough. He had to be hanged by the neck until dead. So they shortened the rope and hanged him a second time. The strangest thing is that this was the son of one of the men on the vigilante committee! Well, when the word got around about that, things got much better in the strip. There still wasn't any law but there was a lot more order."

This story was like those Mat read in the dime novels. "I guess we'll really be living in the West."

"Yep, you'll be right in the middle of things. There are parts of the Old West all around the strip just like the points on a compass."

"Besides Dodge City what else is close to Goodwell?"

"Well, on the compass Dodge is to the northeast. Off to the southeast is Fort Sill, in Oklahoma Territory. Old Geronimo, the Apache chief, and quite a few other Apaches are there as scouts for the army."

"He's still alive?"

"Yes, but he is gettin' up in years, and so are some of the others. Now, up to the northwest in Colorado is where Fort Bent used to be. That was headquarters for the Bents' trading company. Kit Carson operated out of there."

"What's west of Goodwell?" Mat wondered aloud.

"Santa Fe, over in New Mexico Territory, is to the west and so is Fort Union. There was a good scrap near there during the Civil War at a place called Glorieta Pass. I was in it. This was at a time when I wasn't too much older than you. We had been living up near Denver City where my pa and I mined silver. There was talk about some people trying to drag Colorado and the southwestern territories into the Confederacy."

"Why did they want to do that?"

"Because of the gold and silver. The Confederates needed it to back up their paper money. In the fall of '61 Colorado started raising a Union force so I joined up. I was in the First Regiment, Colorado Volunteer Infantry. I thought I'd get to see some different country and

I sure did. I was in one of the three companies commanded by Major John Chivington they sent down to Fort Wise in southeastern Colorado Territory.

"After winter set in, we got orders to move to New Mexico and reinforce the Union army. We marched over to old Fort Bent on the Arkansas River. There, we got news that the Confederates had moved into New Mexico and captured a place called Val Verde. And so it started. Us making forced marches south through snow and gettin' bad news all along the way. Joined by the other companies of the regiment, we crossed over Raton Pass into New Mexico. We thought we'd get to rest. But a courier from Fort Union rode into camp saying the Confederates had captured Albuquerque and Santa Fe and were fixin' to attack Fort Union."

"Does that mean you were too late?"

The train began passing over rough track and the passenger car rocked and swayed violently. The conductor walked back several rows to where the three women were sitting. "Sorry for the bumpy ride, ladies. This stretch of track is going to need repairs real soon. Folks shouldn't have to be shook up like they were riding an ordinary wagon on some mountain trail."

Returning to Mat he resumed his story, "No, we weren't too late. As tired as we were, we got up and pushed on, taking only our guns and blankets. After awhile, we and our pack horses had to stop from sheer exhaustion. We took a short rest, and then pushed on; marching through a blizzard, a sand storm, and a dust storm in the two days more it took to reach Fort Union."

"Did you get to rest up then, or did you have to start fighting right after you got there?"

"We were resupplied and got regulation uniforms and arms after we arrived. But after a couple of weeks of doing nothing but drill we were getting pretty bored. They soon took care of that! We went out in a reconnaissance in force, which means looking for a fight. Well, we found a good one the very first day at Glorieta Pass. The major had us outflank the Confederates and we took thirty prisoners."

"On the third day the battle got real interesting. Col. Slough and the rest of the regiment set off to attack the Confederates in the pass. Meanwhile, Major Chivington's group circled around by a rough mountain trail to the south until we came to the west end of the pass. There, we could look down on the Confederate camp and their supply trains more than a thousand feet below. Getting up to that ridge was tough but getting down was worse. We used ropes, leather straps, even our guns to help each other get down the first half of the cliff. Then, we just leaped, crawled, and slid the rest of the way. There were only a few guards so it was a quick fight. We spiked their cannon, destroyed the ammunition, burned eighty-five wagon loads of supplies, and took their horse herd. All that damage made them give up their campaign in New Mexico.[1] Those Confederate boys had a long, hungry walk back to El Paso."

The train rumbled on, once again on smooth track. "Quick, take a look," said the conductor, pointing out the window.

Mat turned in time to see a group of large rabbits. "They're huge! And they have black tails, instead of white like the ones in Ohio."

"Those are jackrabbits. They grow big out here and can they ever run."

"Are they any good to eat?"

"A young one isn't bad if you're hungry. Full grown, they're tough and stringy. An old-timer once told me any critter who runs that fast ain't fit to eat."

The train moved on, ever closer to the Oklahoma Territory. "How much longer before we leave Kansas?" Mat asked.

Pulling out his watch, the conductor squinted at the dial. "About twenty-five or thirty minutes. We get to Liberal in about twenty minutes and make a short stop. It's in the southwest corner of Kansas. When we leave Liberal, we'll be only five miles from Oklahoma Territory."

"There's one compass direction you haven't said anything about yet. What's south of the strip?"

"You're a sharp lad, got a good mind for keeping track of things. What's south? Why, you got the whole state of Texas," the conductor drawled with a broad smile. "But pretty close to Goodwell, less than a day's ride away, is a place in the Texas Panhandle called Adobe Walls. There was a famous battle there thirty years ago. Twenty-eight buffalo hunters and one white woman held off 700 Comanches, Kiowa, and Southern Cheyennes for several days. Finally, old Quanah Parker, the Comanche chief, decided to give up the battle because he'd lost too many braves. The buffalo hunters lost only four men."

"Were you there? How could only twenty-nine people hold off 700?"

"I was a buffalo hunter myself those days. I wasn't there but I knew some of the hunters who were. They were in three sod buildings that had good, thick walls and roofs. When the attack first started, the Indians got in real close and the hunters had to fight them off with pistols and Winchester rifles. But the Indians pulled back because of heavy losses. Once they did that, the buffalo hunters could start using their Sharpe's to fire at them."

"Is that the buffalo gun?"

"Right. It's the one most of us hunters used to shoot buffalo. The Sharps .50 caliber could kill a full-grown animal at 800 yards and was accurate up to three quarters of a mile. Some even had telescopic sights. Well, once the buffalo hunters unlimbered those guns, the Indians pretty much had to stay back. They always had lots of respect for the

Sharps because of its long range. They called it the 'shoot today, kill tomorrow gun.' Most buffalo hunters called it the Big Fifty."

"Anyhow, one day became two, then three. The Indians were still there and had the buildings surrounded. Finally, a young hunter named Billy Dixon spotted a group of chiefs astride their ponies on a ridge east of the buildings. He fired his Big Fifty and darned if he didn't pick one of them off. That ended the siege as the Indians decided to leave. Later, some army surveyors used their equipment to measure Billy's shot. It was well over 1500 yards!"

"Could someone find arrowheads or other signs of that battle?"

"Nah, probably not. Even if you found the right place, you probably wouldn't see anything except cattle. Or rattlesnakes."

"Rattlesnakes?"

"Yep, that's another thing that grows big out here, poisonous rattlers. Their bite can kill. Yes sir, a snakebite is the last thing you want if you're miles away from a doctor. So, always keep a sharp eye out for them. Wear boots and be careful where you walk. And don't ever reach into a hole in the ground, a clump of grass or sagebrush, or anyplace around a building foundation without checking first. Sometimes you can hear their rattles. It sounds a little like someone scratching a drumhead or shaking an Indian rattle."

"Anything else?" Mat's concern showed.

"There's one more thing. Out here we got a saying: 'A man's never too busy to kill a rattlesnake.' The next time you meet, he might see you first and you sure wouldn't want that."

Mat was silent for a while. He looked out the window as the train continued to cross the seemingly endless Kansas prairie.

"Oh, there's something I left out of the Adobe Walls story that you may find interesting. Billy Dixon was good friends with another young buffalo hunter by the name of William Barclay Masterson. He also gave a fine account of himself in that battle."

"Bat Masterson? The famous marshal at Dodge City?"

"One and the same. I'll bet you've read stories about him."

"I sure have but I didn't know he was a buffalo hunter. Is he still around?"

"Yes, but he's about as far away from here as you can get and still be in this country. He works as a reporter for a newspaper in New York City."

"Really?"

"Yep, I've always wondered how a man could live out here so many years and then move to a big, crowded city. They say he's good friends with President Teddy Roosevelt."

"I've been in New York. It's a big place."

"What were you doing there?"

"We moved here from Austria-Hungary four years ago. Our ship docked there."

"I see," nodded the conductor. "Then you got a good look at it."

"But Bat Masterson, how did he get to know the president?"

"Well, Mr. Roosevelt loves the West. He spent a lot of time up in Dakota, living on a ranch. But he's been in these parts, too. Just last year he was hunting wolves down in the Texas Panhandle on Billy Dixon's ranch, a little way south of Adobe Walls."

"He was hunting with him?"

"Call it chance, but things like that seem to happen a lot out here. Mr. Roosevelt always liked the frontier life and the rugged folks who live in the West. I figure sometime in his travels he must have met Bat Masterson. Remember those two Indian chiefs we talked about?"

"Geronimo and Quanah Parker? Sure."

"Well, last year there was a big parade in Washington when Teddy Roosevelt was inaugurated President. Both of those chiefs marched in that parade."

"To remind him of this part of the country?"

"That may be. That may be. Times are changin' and some day the Old West will be just a memory. It may not be as wild as it once was, but it's still a mighty tough place to live. You'll find that out, soon enough."

For a while the two rode in silence, Mat nearly overwhelmed by all the new information, the older man by his memories. After this long pause, he said, "Say young man, I notice you carry a harmonica in your shirt pocket. Are you pretty good with it?"

"I'm just learning. I know 'My Old Kentucky Home' by Stephen Foster," Mat replied. "And I almost know 'Buffalo Gals.'"

"Well now, that's just all right. By gravy, you'll do mighty fine out here. In two or three years you'll be a good-looking young man. You speak good English; you dress well and know how to make music. Out here folks can't get together much. So they always want to dance to the music, not just listen. Learn some songs they can dance to and you'll be mighty popular. Mark my word. Now I gotta go." Getting up, he announced, "Folks, we're coming into Liberal, Kansas."

George, Sr. sat up as the train began slowing down. Turning to Mat, "You sure had a long conversation. What were you talking about?"

"He was telling me about this area where we're moving. It was really interesting."

"Yes, it must have been. My father often told me about a big move they made years before I was born. Their reasons were much different from ours. They didn't want my older brothers to have to serve in Chancellor Bismarck's army. So, one day the family loaded up everything in the wagons and moved from Prussia all the way to the far southern part of Austria-Hungary."

CHAPTER 2
BLOOD AND IRON

"The great questions of the day will not be settled by means of speeches and majority decisions . . . but by blood and iron."

Otto von Bismarck, Chancellor of Prussia, September 29, 1862

"It's madness! Madness, I tell you!" John Welli was usually in good spirits after a trip to Berlin, but not this time.

"What's wrong, John?" asked Mary, worried about his news from the city. Most of the time it was interesting, even entertaining. Clearly, today's would be different.

"We have an ambitious chancellor. After only two months in office he's going to unite Prussia with the other German states. And he wants military conscription to help do it!"

"Oh? Really? What has happened?"

John sat down at the kitchen table, took off his cap, and sighed. He managed a weary smile for Mary, his loving wife of so many years. Her dark brown hair had the first touches of gray, but with it and her brown eyes so full of merriment, she was still one of Bernau's prettiest *hausfraus. "Braumeister* Heinz and I went to Berlin for supplies and new barrels. After they loaded our wagon, we sat down with Kurt Mueller, the man who owns the supply house. He told us all this."

"*Herr* Mueller, he always seems to know so much."

"He's an important businessman and he's well educated. He told us that the government issued a formal order telling young men to register for military service. *Herr* Mueller has seen the order and it's in the newspapers. He said that Prussia has had enough heroes. He's worried because most of his workers are young. He would lose them to the army if there's a big call-up."

"*Ja*? What did *Herr* Mueller mean, 'enough heroes'?"

"I asked what he meant and he told us about Prussia's past. Fifty years ago in the war with France, there was a battle in Belgium near a place called Waterloo. Field Marshal Blucher rescued the English from certain defeat by Napoleon's army. Afterwards, Blucher always referred to himself as the 'Savior of Europe.' And before him, there was Frederick the Great. But their 'heroism' cost the lives of thousands of young Prussian men."

"I see. Now they will again take them into the army?"

"Yes! And we have sons who will soon be old enough. Christian already is and Valtina and young Johnny will be in only a few years. Only little Maria doesn't have to worry. We should have had all daughters."

Mary smiled, touching John's work-hardened hands. They matched his stern look, complementing his high cheekbones and his luxurious full mustache. Then, glancing at her expanding midriff and the crucifix on the wall, she said, "But we accept all babies the Lord gives us, right John?"

"That's right, little *muter*," he smiled. "Tomorrow is Sunday. After mass we can talk about this some more."

Walking home after church the next morning, they were enthralled by the bright, late November sunshine. It wasn't a time to talk of problems. The chill in the air warned that winter would soon grip all of Northern Europe; right now it was invigorating. "Close up your jackets," Mary urged the children. It was a glorious autumn day, the quiet broken only by children's laughter, the rustle of falling leaves, and the occasional clip-clopping of horses' hooves and the rumble of carriage wheels on cobblestone streets.

Mary looked back at the spire of the centuries-old church as it reached into the brilliant blue sky. It was a sight that never failed to provide reassurance. Bernau was an old, walled city that had been chartered in the year 1232. Part of the wall was still standing.[2]

Once home, John finally raised the difficult subject, how to keep his sons out of the Prussian army. "My brother Joseph lives in a town named Dunacseb in the Banat region of southern Hungary. He and his family have been there for about five years now. I'll write and ask him what it's like living there. It's been a long time since we've heard from him."

"You mean move?" Mary's voice trailed off at the thought of leaving her beloved city.

"I've thought and thought what to do but I haven't been able to come up with a better idea," John replied morosely. "Old Heinz and I talked about it all the way back from Berlin yesterday but we couldn't think of anything. Actually, Heinz doesn't have to worry; his sons are too old for the army."

"I know nothing about that part of Europe except that the Shultzes tell of relatives who moved there many years ago. They all died of the plague. If we have to move why not to America?" Mary wondered aloud.

"That's a possibility. But it would be a long ocean voyage. And we don't know anyone there. Besides, *Herr* Mueller told us that there is a war going on in America. I don't want to raise our sons for the American army either. Do you? Besides, much of that country is wild and unexplored. But you know what? The Prussian army has sent military advisors to observe the American army's strategy and tactics.

Herr Mueller said that's a sure sign of Chancellor Bismarck's warlike intentions."

"*Herr* Mueller told you that too?" asked Mary, seeing John's increased agitation.

John nodded. "I will write to Joseph and ask him whether Dunacseb would be a good place to move."

"It seems we have little choice," Mary sighed in resignation.

Their concerns were valid. The Civil War in America eliminated it as a place for migration. On the other hand, moving to southern Hungary in the mid-nineteenth century involved considerable risk and hardships similar to those faced by Americans moving west. Emigrants to southern Hungary were, in effect, moving to Europe's *Wild East* as shown by the following excerpts from historian Sue Clarkson's article.[3]

During the eighteenth century, the Habsburg monarchy of Austria enticed Germans to immigrate to the unsettled lands in the southern regions of Hungary, which had been devastated by more than 150 years of Turkish occupation. From 1711 to 1750, approximately 800 villages were founded in Hungary by German settlers.

The city of Ulm, in the Swabian region of the German states, was a common point of departure. From there, settlers boarded boats and sailed the Danube River to Vienna, where they registered for land. Covered wagons, which also followed the Danube, were used by some for transportation. The Danube route took them through Budapest and into the Banat region.

The colonization came to be known as the "Great Swabian Trek." Most of the migration took place in three phases, which were named after their Habsburg sponsors:

1. The Caroline colonization, which occurred from 1718 to 1737.
2. The Maria Theresian colonization, which occurred from 1744-1772.

3. The Josephine colonization, which took place under Joseph II from 1782 to 1787.

Many of the 15,000 German settlers from the first colonization were killed in Turkish raids, or died of bubonic plague. Thus, the second wave of about 75,000 German colonists had to rebuild many of the settlements. They were successful in re-establishing the towns, but their life was filled with hard work. The third wave consisted of nearly 60,000 new German settlers who were able to increase the economic prosperity of the Hungarian farmland. The Banat region later came to be known as the "breadbasket of Europe." The hardship endured by the three groups of colonists is reflected in this verse:

Die Erste hat den Tod, Der Zweite hat die Not, Der Dritte erst hat Brot. Which is translated as, "The first encounters death, the second need, only the third has bread."

Once again it was spring in northern Europe. But there would be no flower garden for Mary this year. Rather, it was a time for packing up the family and its belongings for the 600-mile trek by covered wagon to southern Hungary. The journey was, essentially, from just northeast of Berlin to a point just northwest of Belgrade. A letter from John's brother Joseph had arrived shortly after the new year dawned. Joseph told them that while life in Dunacseb was hard, it was a good life, and enjoyable much of the time. Most important, he said that even though the Austrian Empire had conscription, it seemed to be far less military-minded than Prussia. A month after receiving the letter, Mary gave birth to a boy whom they named Joseph, after John's brother.

"How much is still in the house?" John asked the boys.

"You wouldn't know the place. It's so empty now," laughed Christian.

"That's good. Both of the wagons are getting full but these teams are used to pulling wagons loaded with beer. They can handle it. I just worry whether there will be enough room for all of us to ride. Guess it's time to bring the horses around and hitch them up."

John now owned two covered wagons, each with a team of strong workhorses. He had acquired them through a series of trades for some household goods and their home. *Braumeister* Heinz had made John a fair price when selling him horses from the brewery. And he still had money for the trip and making a fresh start. One of the teams was the one he had driven in so many routine trips to Berlin. Now, they were going to carry the family on a long, adventurous journey. The second team was yet another equally old, experienced set that the brewery had been nearly ready to put out to pasture. Christian and Valtina would drive that wagon. Tied onto the rear of the second wagon was old Roanie, John and Mary's aging milk cow.

Soon, the last items were in the wagons and John and Mary began "goodbyes" to the neighbors gathered to see them off. John walked back to the second wagon to see Christian holding the reins, ready to move out. Valtina was seated beside him and ten-year-old Johnny was seated on a stool behind them.

"Everyone here ready to go?" asked John.

"Yes, Father!" they exclaimed. All three were beaming with anticipation and wearing smiles that would brighten the gloomiest of days.

"Then let's go," said John, pulling himself up into the lead wagon beside Mary. Their daughter Maria was seated behind them, holding Joseph, the newest family member.

"Getup!" he shouted, slapping the reins. Slowly the wagons pulled away from their old home, heading for the road to Berlin.

Mary sat close to John, leaning on his shoulder but saying nothing. Finally she asked, "How do you know where to go?"

"We follow the road past Berlin, then take the one to Prague in the Bohemian part of Austria, and then to Olmutz. That's in Moravia, another part of Austria. Then we'll follow the road to Vienna. Just north of Vienna we reach the Danube River and we'll follow it for the rest of the trip. It goes east for a distance, south past Budapest, Hungary, then east once more. After it turns east the second time, we'll be near Dunacseb. But it's a long trip and it will be summer when we get there."

"That sounds so complicated. I don't remember all those directions being in your brother Joseph's letter."

"The ones in his letter were very general. On one of my trips to Berlin last month I asked *Herr* Mueller about making the trip. He checked with some people he knows and got better directions for us."

"I see," said Mary somewhat more cheerfully. Looking back, she waved to the boys in the second wagon, who were laughing and talking animatedly. She smiled at their enthusiasm and then caught a last glimpse of the church steeple in Bernau as it faded into the distance. After a quick silent prayer, she turned around and looked forward. Pointing toward the horses, she observed, "We are taking some of Bernau with us."

"Yes, these faithful old friends will take us to a new home but always be a reminder of our old home. And Roanie will give us milk for the trip." John was thankful the silence had been broken.

"The boys love being around horses," observed Mary.

"They really do. I've never seen anyone take to it as quickly as Christian and Val. They're naturals at handling horses. They asked me if they could have some to ride once we get settled."

The days became a jumble of repetition, stopping to rest the horses several times a day, fording small streams, crossing larger rivers on bridges or ferry boats, camping in the open at night. The little wagon train reached the Danube River near Vienna after a few weeks. "Now we'll have a ready supply of water," observed John.

"And maybe the boys can catch some fish to eat," Mary offered hopefully. "Smoked ham or sausage is good but not every day."

The weeks multiplied as they continued southward, usually keeping within view of the Danube. "Look, here comes a river boat," John shouted to the second wagon.

"We see it," Christian shouted back.

They watched as the boat drew abreast of them, waving back at the passengers on deck. "Would you boys rather travel like that?" John called to them.

"No, horses are better!" they exclaimed.

"The boys are right," said Mary. "We get to keep the horses and have them to use after we get to Dunacseb. Those people on the boat will have to buy horses when they get where they're going."

Weeks passed, each much the same as the other. But then the terrain began to look markedly different. They could see vast plains to the east as they moved south from Budapest. "I've never seen the ocean but it must look somewhat like that. Strange country," John remarked.

"You can see so far. It's like looking to the end of creation," said Mary, marveling at the sight. "What is that growing in those fields?"

"I think it's wheat. That's what we'll be raising on the land we get."

"It seems to wave, just like ripples on a lake," she commented.

"Or maybe the ocean?"

Mary agreed. The anticipation of reaching their destination was beginning to heighten their senses. Gradually, their route began turning eastward again, as the mighty Danube continued its course through Europe.

"It's been a long time since we've seen Joseph and Helena. I wonder if they're the same. She always liked to laugh and that made her such good company. I wonder how many children they have now," Mary continued.

"It's been nearly five years since they came here but they will probably be the same folks we knew, just older and with more children!" laughed John.

Mary smiled but said nothing.

In late July they arrived in a town named Palanka. "I think we must be close to Dunacseb," John announced. Stopping the wagons, he got down and walked over to a small shop. Shortly, he returned, smiling. "Dunacseb is the next town to the east. We follow this same road," he told everyone. Then to Mary, "I asked the man a question and he replied in German. That's the best sign that we're almost there."

"What did the people speak that you met farther back?"

"Well, in Hungary they speak Magyar. Luckily, most of the ones I bought eggs and bread from could speak enough German that I got by. But I think the family will need to learn Magyar."

"Won't that be difficult?"

"For you and me it may be but I think the children might find it easier to learn another language. It's the official language of the country and there will times when they need to know it. That would be a big advantage to them."

The wagons began the final leg of their journey, eastward toward Dunacseb. "How will we find your brother's home?" asked Mary.

"Just have to ask. It's a small town and it should be easy to find his place."

As they pulled up to the house, a woman came from the garden. "John? Mary? Is it really you?"

"Yes, it is, Helena," replied John, getting down from the wagon. "This is the right place, boys," he called to the second wagon.

"Helena, it's wonderful to see you!" exclaimed Mary.

"Mother, take my hand. I'll help you down," offered Christian.

Helena rushed to hug Mary. "Oh, it's so good to see you folks again. But there are more of you, aren't there?" she observed, breaking into an infectious laugh.

"Yes, a new baby every year," replied Mary, and starting introducing the family. "Christian, Valtina, Johnny, Maria, and Joseph."

"Oh, you came all this way with a new baby! How did you ever manage?" asked Helena.

"Helena, where can we put up the horses, the cow, and the wagons?" asked John.

"You can take them around back. We have plenty of room," she replied.

John and the three older boys began moving the wagons to the rear of the home. "We need to unhitch the horses and water them. We'll be in later."

"Mary, you must have a really good baby to make it all this way without any problems. Want to take him inside so you can lay him down?" asked Helena.

She ushered Mary and Maria inside to the kitchen. "Let's put little Joseph here on the cot with Adam, our little one. My! They're just about the same age, aren't they? Is he named after my Joseph? Maria, honey, I'll bet you're starving. Would you like a cookie? I made them just this morning. Mary, you still look young and pretty! How do you do it? Oh Mary, I don't mean to babble on so, but it's just so good to see family again!" she exclaimed, laughing and giving Mary and little Maria bear hugs. "Let's get that cookie for you, Maria."

Mary smiled at Helena's enthusiasm and good humor. Short and slender, her size belied the tremendous energy this dark-eyed brunette possessed. "Adam. That seems an unusual name for a baby who's not first born," commented Mary.

"We already had John, Jacob, and Michael. We thought it would be good to give him a less common name but still be one from the Holy Bible," replied Helena.

"Where are Joseph and your boys?"

"They're all in the field harvesting our wheat. It's always a busy time of year but Joe said this morning they are nearly done, may even finish today. So, they'll be ready to have company, especially family. Now, let me show you the house."

"It looks so nice. And it's so clean!"

"This way," said Helena, taking Maria by the hand and leading her and Mary out of the kitchen, through one adjoining room, then into the room that faced the street. "This is the front room. It's for guests. It even has two beds," she related, pointing to the window and the furnishings. "Now, back to the room we came through. This is where Joseph and I sleep. And see the little crib for Adam? Now we're back in the kitchen again. Still have part of your cookie, Maria, or do you want another? See the fireplace, table and chairs, cupboard, cot for the baby? Now, we go further back in the house. This is where the boys sleep. So Mary, what do you think?"

"It's very nice! And it has lots of room. Is there more to it farther back?"

"Yes, the sheds for the horses, our milk cow, a couple of pigs, and the geese are beyond this room. But you have to go outside to get to them — no doorway from there into the house! Why, you wouldn't want some old goose coming in and biting your toes in the morning, would you, Maria?" Helena hugged her again, saying, "I don't have a little girl. You'll have to come over and visit me often."

They returned to the kitchen just as John and the boys came in. "Did you find water and a place to put up the horses?" asked Helena.

John replied, "They'll be just fine out there. Say, this is quite a house. Is it made from sod?"

"Yes, but you can't tell that from the inside because the walls are plastered," said Helena. "When we first built it, with the help of many neighbors, its roof was also made from sod. But it leaked after hard rains, so after two years we put on a wooden roof. And each fall, around church festival time, everyone whitewashes the outside walls. Another good thing, notice the wooden floor?" she added, stomping her foot.

"We should have a house like this, John. Helena, is it possible?" asked Mary.

Helena burst into laughter. "For certain you will. All houses here follow this same design. You may have seen that the church is in the very center of town, which is laid out around the square. But you could make your house bigger if you wanted to. John, you and the boys follow me and I'll show you the rest of it."

When they returned Mary said, "Tell me about church, Helena."

"Well, Father Mathias is very good. He's kind, smart, and loves to laugh. Maybe that's why I like him so much. But he's getting on in years and has to walk with a cane now. He has two very young nuns, Sister Josephine and Sister Marguerite, who help him and teach at the school. There are lots of church events, too, like special dinners and dances. Sometimes we have street processions when there's a wedding or a baptism. On Sunday afternoons there are dances, which everyone attends. Once a year in the autumn there is a big feast called *Kirchweih*, the church consecration days. As Joseph will tell you, the beer and wine make these very festive at times! Oh my, it's getting dark. Time to light the lamps."

As Helena began lighting the lamps, Joseph came in with their three sons. "John, Mary!" his deep voice boomed. "So you finally made it to the Banat!"

John got to his feet, grabbed Joseph's hand, and exclaimed, "Hello, big brother!" An apt description as Joseph was burly and several inches taller than John. But the large black mustache and the sharp cheekbones presented a strong family resemblance. "How long did it take you to get here?" he asked.

"We left Bernau early in May. So about two and one half months," John replied.

"Joseph, did you finish harvesting?" asked Helena.

"No, we have to go out again tomorrow. That will be our last day. John, you and your boys might as well come with us in the morning. I have an extra scythe so you can see what it will be like for you next year. Remember what Dad always told us. *You'll never learn any younger, boys!*" Both men laughed heartily at the memory.

A few days later, Mary and Maria watched as Joseph, John, all their sons, and many other men from the town began laying out three-foot-long strips of sod for their house. Turned over by a plow, the strips were held together by the grass roots. In only a few days the industrious crew was close to finishing a home for John and Mary that was nearly identical to that of Joseph and Helena.

Mary watched, amazed, as the skilled men hewed the interior walls smooth with spades and then covered them with plaster. "John, we should have a garden, too. Helena has potatoes, turnips, carrots, melons, and tomatoes. And there are peach and apricot trees, too."

"And later, some grape vines. Grapes for eating and for making wine."

Late summer became autumn and then winter, one much milder than those to which John and Mary were accustomed in Bernau. In the spring Mary gave birth to another son. "March 12, 1864. Two weeks later and he would have been an Easter baby," chuckled John.

"What do you think we should name him?" asked Mary.

"There hasn't been a George in the family for quite awhile."

"I like that. It's a saint's name but not used quite as often as John or Joseph. Joseph and Helena did the same when they named their youngest son Adam."

"Well then, I'd better talk to Father Mathias about arranging a baptism since we have a name. We have a good life here and I'm glad we moved. Think you'll feel like dancing after the baptism?"

CHAPTER 3
CALL TO ARMS

"The mere name Benedek means that he will come quickly, dealing blows left and right."

Concerns of Helmuth von Moltke, Prussian general staff chief, regarding the skills of Austria's famous general, Ludwig Benedek[4]

John and Mary's respite from the concerns of war would last for only a few years. By early 1866 Otto von Bismarck, Prussia's iron chancellor, had maneuvered relations between Prussia and Austria to the brink of open hostility. These pretexts were efforts to remove Austria's dominating influence from the Confederation of German States, in which Prussia was only a secondary member. In addition, Bismarck had formed an alliance with Italy. Distracted by their own domestic and colonial concerns, England, France, and Russia, the Great Powers of Europe, failed to immediately recognize the significance of this shift in the balance of power. Thus, Austria was left alone against the combined armies of Prussia and Italy.[5]

Having had military observers in the United States during its Civil War, Prussia was especially well prepared for modern warfare. They had carefully noted how railroad transportation and telegraphic communications provided significant advantages to an attacking army.

One chilly, sunless day in Dunacseb a messenger delivered two letters to John and Mary's house. However, they were addressed to Christian and Valtina. "Boys, there are letters for you," John told them, apprehension showing in his voice.

"Who would send us letters?" asked Val.

John handed them over, saying nothing. Mary moved to a chair and sat down, arms wrapped tightly about her. Finally, she asked, "Well, aren't you going to open them?"

Christian ripped his open and read it quickly. "We are called into the army!" he exclaimed.

"Yes, it's true," Val echoed. Then reading from the letter, "We are to 'present ourselves in Budapest in order to be assigned for training.' We are to take a river boat at Palanka just ten days from now."

John grumbled silently to himself. At twenty-two and twenty-one, respectively, Christian and Valtina were at optimum ages for the military. Mary began dabbing her eyes with the hem of her apron. As if to add further gloom, rain slowly began spattering on the roof.

Christian and Val looked at each other, too stunned to express anything but surprise. Finally, Christian wondered aloud, "Is anyone else from Dunacseb going?" No one replied.

The ten days passed quickly. On the day of their departure, the weather brightened, providing at best small cheer for John and Mary when bidding their oldest sons goodbye. "Mary, the boys are ready to go, come outside and wish them well," called John.

But Mary remained in the house. "Better go inside boys," John told them.

Returning to the house, they found Mary sitting at the table, wracked with sobs, her face buried in her arms. "*Muter*, we have to go," said Christian, taking one of her hands.

"Yes, please get up," pleaded Val.

Slowly Mary stood, looking lovingly first at the tall, blond, blue-eyed Christian and then at Val, shorter with dark hair and eyes. In different ways each of them reminded her of John. "I don't want you to go," she murmured softly, "but I suppose you must." Then, putting an arm around each son, she hugged them with all her strength. "Go with God," she whispered.

The two-day trip to Budapest reminded Christian and Val of their trip to Dunacseb less than three years earlier. "Look. There are the church spires!" Val said excitedly. "Just as I remembered them."

"Only things are different now, much different," observed Christian.

When the riverboat docked, a burly army noncommissioned officer (NCO) approached each man of military age as he walked down the gangplank. "Reporting for army duty? Line up over there!" he barked, augmenting his verbal commands with body language. When the boat had emptied, he ordered them into wagons for the long trip to the post. Each of the three wagons carried fifteen men. "Enjoy the ride, boys. It'll be the last one for a while. You'll be walking from now on. Only we call it marching!"

As the wagons pulled out, Val nudged Christian. "From the looks of him army troops must eat pretty well, don't you think?"

A young dark-haired man sitting across from them laughed. "You're right about that. Lots of beef, pork, and bread washed down with beer or wine and sometimes schnapps."

"How do you know?" asked Christian.

"My uncle was in the army seven years ago. Fought in the war against Italy. He told me a lot about it," replied the man, still smiling. He extended his hand, saying, "My name is Karl."

Val and Christian each shook his hand, glad to meet someone smiling and friendly.

"Brothers, eh — where are you from?" asked Karl.

"We're from Dunacseb," replied Christian.

"Where is that?"

"Along the Danube, just east of Palanka," replied Val. "Where are you from?"

"I'm from Apatin," said Karl.

"It's on the river, too. I remember going through there yesterday," replied Christian.

They were silent the rest of the trip. For many of these young men from the plains and farmlands of southern Hungary, Budapest was the largest city they had ever seen. After nearly two hours the wagons pulled up to an army post east of the city. Row upon row of identical barracks buildings forming a large square seemed to fill the landscape. Larger buildings were in the middle, forming another square. A tall flagpole stood in the very center, Austrian flag waving in the chilly breeze.

And there was a welcoming committee, headed by another beefy NCO, one obviously used to being in charge. "Get down off those wagons! Line up! Line up! Stand at attention! That means head up, eyes straight ahead, shoulders back, arms at your sides! Line up!"

After forming the new recruits into a semblance of order, the NCO marched them into one of the large buildings and lined them up in widely spaced rows. "Strip down to your underwear," he ordered. "Do it now! You can't be in the army unless the doctor says you're fit for duty."

The regimental surgeon began moving down the rows. To each man he said: "Raise your arms over your head. Up like this as if you are aiming a rifle. Now move them as far back as possible. Lift your right leg as high as possible. Now the left." He spoke in German and some of the men responded immediately. Others simply looked puzzled and the NCO would repeat the surgeon's orders in a language that Val and Christian recognized as Magyar (Hungarian). For still others, it required coaching, bordering on sign language.

This rather cursory examination then took a more serious turn. The surgeon moved along the rows and once again to each man: "Open your mouth. Mmm, yes, you'll do." But to five others, including their new friend Karl, it was, "No, you won't do. How do you even eat with so few teeth? You five men move over to the corner. I'll certify on your induction notices that you aren't fit for army duty."

Karl nodded to Val and Christian as he and the other four men moved to the corner awaiting the surgeon's certification. They smiled back somewhat wistfully. Soon, the five men left the building for the long wagon ride back to Budapest. For them it was a quick return to civilian life.

The NCO addressed the remaining forty in German. "All of you are now *gemeiners* (privates) in the Fifty-first Infantry Regiment of the Army of Austria. I am *Korporal* Friedrich Szabo, in charge of your training. In what remains of the day you will be issued uniforms and located in barracks. Tomorrow we begin training in earnest." Then, he repeated his statement in Magyar for the Hungarians.

Val, Christian, and the rest of the group finally found respite in the barracks hours after sundown. Each soldier now possessed a bewildering load of uniforms and equipment. It had been a long day.

"These gray overcoats seem very warm," observed Val.

"Yes, but when you put on the white belts to hold cartridges and the field pack they form a large X," replied Christian. "It's like marking a target!"

"Well, look at these white tunics for the summer. White tunics with the tall, black *shakos* (hats) will really make good targets of us," Val added. Ever curious, he continued, "Why was the doctor was so particular about everyone's teeth?"

"Little brother, stop and think. How do you load a rifle?"

"You stand it on the ground with one hand, take a bullet from your pouch with the other hand, bite the paper off, and then pour the powder down the barrel. Yes, of course! If you didn't have enough teeth . . ."

"Exactly," replied Christian. "We better get some sleep. Tomorrow will be a hard day."

The next day began well before sunrise. After a quick breakfast of bread and bacon, Corporal Szabo lined the men up in the square. He was soon joined by another NCO, one whose slender build was in sharp contrast to the girth of the corporal. He carried a saber in his belt. That, other marks signifying rank, and the deferential manner in which Szabo treated him left no doubt who was in charge.

He addressed them in German. "Good morning, soldiers, I'm *Feldwebel* (sergeant-major) Hans Vermeich. I'm the top enlisted man in your company. Welcome to the Fifty-first Infantry Regiment. There's something we must take care of right away. It seems that within this unit and others of the rifle company we have a Tower of Babel. Some of you speak German but many speak Magyar. And there are a few who seem to be speaking Rumanian. So, our first order of business will be to knock down that tower! All who understand me take one step forward."

Christian, Val, and twenty others stepped forward. In Magyar, Corporal Szabo ordered the remaining eighteen to stand fast. Then, he began repeating the sergeant's remarks while Sergeant Vermeich moved the German-speaking soldiers several yards away.

The sergeant-major explained to his group, "In training we can take the time to interpret for those who don't speak German. That is what Corporal Szabo is doing now," he said, pointing toward Szabo and the other group. "But in battle, all commands will be in German. All of them. So, those who don't speak German have to be able to understand, at least, such words as 'March, halt, attack, or fire.' Now, we need some help doing this. How many of you can speak Magyar?"

Only Christian and Val raised their hands.

"Just two? I had hoped for more," the sergeant grumbled, shaking his head. "What about horses, can you ride? Ride well?"

"Yes, sergeant," they replied.

"Then there are two things for you. First, I want you to help Corporal Szabo in teaching key German phrases to the Hungarians during your training. I hope one or two of them can then pass that along to the Rumanians. Next, both of you will be reserve messengers since you can ride. That is something you will have to demonstrate later today. Junior officers deliver most messages during battle. But if they are lost, we need reserves."

The Austrian Empire was composed of many ethnic groups. Therefore, army training was conducted in German, Magyar, Polish, Czech, Ukrainian, Italian, Serbo-Croatian, and Rumanian. For regiments with mixed nationalities there were serious communication problems, which could result in chaos during battle.[6]

And so began Christian and Val's training. For the first few days it was close order drill, basic marching with frequent commands designed to create a cohesive unit from raw recruits. This was followed by longer marches for conditioning, and then still more close order drill, and long sessions on wearing and maintaining their uniforms and equipment.

Both brothers began to wonder whether they would do anything but the routine. "They haven't even given us rifles," Val grumbled to Christian's nodding agreement.

But their training took a more serious turn the next week when rifles were issued. In a matter-of-fact presentation, Corporal Szabo told them: "This is the Lorenz muzzle-loading rifle. After you become proficient in its use you should be able to fire, reload in one minute, and fire your next shot. It is sighted for 900 paces."

Many of the soldiers smiled. Val and Christian exchanged glances. *This was more like it!*

Corporal Szabo continued, "There is much more to this weapon." Pointing to two men in the first rank, "You there, open this box and start passing out the bayonets. As soon as you receive a bayonet, use the hooks on the scabbard to attach it to your belt. Are we ready? Everyone has a bayonet? Fine! Now, open ranks!" After a week of close order drill, the men knew how to move, providing each maximum space for maneuvering. They stood, poised for the next command.

"Attaching the bayonet securely is most important. Otherwise it falls off and then you're in the soup. Watch closely. This is how it's done. Once again, watch now! Hear the two clicks? Now here's a little something extra for you to remember. It's a saying of the Russians: 'The bullet is a fool, the bayonet a smart fellow.' From our own experience we know it's also true that many bullets miss many people in battle. But the bayonet is sure. Its twelve inches of cold steel is your best weapon. Why, Emperor Franz Joseph himself would choose the bayonet!"

Thus began days of hard training. There were long marches with rifles, bayonet practice for two hours in the morning and again in the afternoon. These practices were so strenuous the men felt as if their arms would fall off. "I'm beginning to think my name is short thrust," quipped Val one evening.

"Then I guess my name is long thrust since I'm older," replied Christian. "But you know, we still haven't even fired our rifles. Not one shot."

Weeks passed and winter became late spring. Finally, Corporal Szabo marched them to the rifle range. Hardened and wise from their training, the men responded well to the loading and reloading exercises. Each soldier fired ten rounds at his target. The training was going well.

But late one evening in May 1866 Corporal Szabo stormed into the barracks, shouting loudly, "All right, pack everything up tonight. Rifles and all your other equipment. Tomorrow the regiment is moving. There is no more time for training. War with Prussia is imminent!"

Stunned, the men were silent. Finally, one asked, "Where do we go, Corporal Szabo?"

"To the fortress at Olmutz, a long way up north in Moravia. The Fifty-first Regiment is joining up with IV Corps."

CHAPTER 4

IRONIES OF WAR

Rise from the ground
And from your rest, ye sleepers!
Our horses are already whinnying
A good morning to us.
The weapons we love are gleaming
So brightly in the red of the dawn,
And we dream of victory wreaths,
. . . we also think of death.

"Soldaten Morgenlied"
Max von Schenkendorf (1783-1817)

The next morning the entire regiment, including the regimental band, formed up for inspection. A long line of supply wagons stood loaded and ready to move, horses switching their tails and stamping their hooves as if anxious to begin the march. The troops stood at attention as Colonel Karl von Poeckh reviewed them from horseback. Then began the long trek northward as the band struck up a patriotic song.

"At least we have music for the march," whispered Val.

Christian nodded grimly. *Music yes, but not like that at the dances back home in Dunacseb.*

And they marched — long, hard days broken only by nightfall and periodic stops during the day to rest the men and horses. Finally, they arrived at the fortress at Olmutz in June.

"Val, look at the size of this place! It's almost unbelievable," exclaimed Christian.

"Yes, but as big as it is there's still not enough room for all the soldiers. Look at all the tents surrounding it," Val replied. "I wonder how long we'll remain here."

They got the answer two weeks later. "Soldiers, if you thought that little hike up here from Budapest was tough, just wait 'til you hear where we're going now," Corporal Szabo told the platoon one sunny morning. "The entire North Army is moving west to Josephstadt day after tomorrow." Seeing the puzzled looks on their faces, he added, "That's in Bohemia on the Elbe River, about 60 miles northeast of Prague. We must be there quickly so this will be a flank march."

For Christian and Val, this would once again be a familiar path. Just as the march from Budapest had been, they would be retracing the family's route three years earlier when moving from Bernau. But instead of a family of seven packed into two wagons, Val and Christian were part of an army of 240,000: infantry, artillery, and cavalry with several thousand horses, followed by 800 supply wagons. The army was divided into three columns, but their mere sizes still made getting food to all the men and fodder to the horses in the long columns a constant problem. Even Corporal Szabo grumbled, "No hot food or schnapps, two things that make soldiering tolerable. Bad luck being so near the head of the column."

But in thirteen days they arrived at Josephstadt. For Christian, Val, and the other men, flank march meant 110 steps to the minute, carrying rifles and seventy-pound field packs. There, they were to engage two Prussian armies with a combined strength totaling 255,000.[7]

In the week that followed, the Fifty-first Regiment saw no action as they were always held in reserve. Several times Val and Christian heard gunfire in the distance but never got close to the battle. However, casualties were heavy for the Austrian Army as 30,000 men and 1,000 officers were lost. General Benedek ordered the army to move south to Königgrätz, intending to move out of Bohemia and back to Olmutz.

On July 2, 1866, the Fifty-first Regiment and the other troops of IV Corps were in place west of Königgrätz near the Svib Forest. Nearby was the high ground at Masloved, high ground prized as a location for artillery and observation. At 7:00 the next morning the entire regiment formed up for a brief review by Colonel von Poeckh, who passed information and orders to the battalion commanders.

Soon the plan filtered down through the chain of command and Val, Christian, and the rest of their platoon got the word from Corporal Szabo. "You've had a vacation so far. Others have done all the fighting. Today it's our turn. But first of all we need to put some rumors to rest. You've probably heard that the Prussians outnumber us three or four to one. That's not true. Their army is the same size and it's divided. Half of it is west of us across the Bystrice River. The other half is way off to the north. We will be attacking to the west. Another thing, you've heard stories about the rifles the Prussians use. It's correct that their breech loaders can fire much faster than your Lorenz muzzle loaders. But it's not true that they can fire ten times as fast. Well, maybe ten times faster than *some* of you . . .."

He paused as the men laughed nervously, and then continued. "Their riflemen can fire four or five rounds a minute with their needle guns. They don't shoot needles. The firing mechanism just works like a needle when it strikes the cartridge. But we are also good shots and our bayonets will serve us well. And there is our cannon on the ridge east of us. They will be the equalizers in this battle. For a while we are in reserve while the Brandenstein Brigade attacks the Prussians in the Svib Forest. The Fleischacker Brigade will follow them if necessary and then us, the Fifty-first Regiment, along with an extra battalion of riflemen. Colonel von Poeckh expects our best effort."

Svib Forest was an area 1.2 miles long and 0.7 of a mile wide. The trees were firs mingled with oak, densely planted many years earlier. Less than half a mile to the east was the Masloved height, occupied by other elements of the Austrian IV Corps and its headquarters.

By 8 a.m. the Fifty-first Regiment was at the edge of the forest, along with the Brandenstein and Fleischacker Brigades. "It's already getting noisy," observed Christian, "and no one's even firing yet except the bands." It was true; the bands of the Fifty-first Regiment and the Fleischacker Brigade seemed to be dueling as to which most could inspire their soldiers. Val gave Christian a grim look and shook his head, saying nothing. Christian was equally glum. They and the other new soldiers were about to face the first real test of their courage. *How will I handle the test? Will I stand and fight or run away?*

At 8:30 a.m. Austrian cannons began a barrage on the Prussian locations in the woods. After a few minutes the Brandenstein Brigade marched into the forest.

"All right boys, the dance has started," shouted Corporal Szabo, as rifle fire erupted in the woods. "Here come the quartermaster's wagons. We won't have to stand here much longer if they're already serving schnapps," he added.

One of the wagons stopped near the corporal. Four grizzled men jumped down from the wagon and two started passing out battered drinking cups. The other two moved along the ranks, pouring out liberal servings of schnapps. "Drink up quickly and pass the cups back to us," said one. "Yes, drink up. The Prussians will have it out of you soon enough with their bullets or bayonets. Or maybe it will just come out with your breakfast when you get so scared you throw up!" mocked another.

"Get on with you! These men of mine can whip you old has-beens any time!" snarled Corporal Szabo. Intimidated by both his tone and bulk, they stopped their taunting and moved along the line, handing cups to Val and Christian. They quickly downed their large rations of schnapps. Its burning sensation was intensified by the dread of what was to come as well as the early hour for imbibing. But a numbing effect soon began and the dread became less onerous.

Rifle fire from the Svib Forest and the Austrian cannon fire were now constant, macabre special effects for the patriotic marches the bands were playing. A gray, cloudy day threatening rain added to the ominous setting.

By 9 a.m., what remained of the Brandenstein Brigade began retreating from the forest, badly mauled by the Prussian riflemen. Val and Christian watched as a messenger, mounted on a fast horse, galloped by for General Festetics's IV Corps Headquarters to the east on Masloved height. "Do you think we will be messengers today?" asked Val, his anxiety showing.

"If we do, it will mean that things are going as badly for our regiment as it did for the brigade that went into the forest less than an hour ago," predicted Christian.

Shortly, the messenger galloped back from IV Corps Headquarters, handed a note to the commander of the Fleischacker Brigade and then trotted over to the Fifty-first Regiment's formation. Val and Christian watched him closely. Following a renewed artillery barrage from the Austrian guns, the Fleischacker Brigade marched into the forest at 9:30 a.m., its horns and drummers beating out a fast marching song.

Perhaps portending disaster, this Austrian barrage was answered by Prussian guns, which had been moved across the Bystrice River in order to get in range of the Austrian positions at Masloved. Once again, the men of the Fifty-first Regiment heard the loud crackle of rifle fire. "It sounds as if the Prussians have been reinforced. We'll go for sure now," cautioned Corporal Szabo. "Check your equipment. Make certain your rifles are loaded and your bayonets securely attached."

The corporal's words were prophetic. Shortly, elements of the Fleischacker Brigade began retreating in disarray from Svib Forest.

At 10 a.m. Colonel von Poeckh called the Fifty-first Regiment to attention. He rode up and down their ranks, staring intently at the men as if trying to memorize each face. Val and Christian's battalion was in the center, giving them a close view of the colonel and the staff officers who flanked him. He finally gave the command, "Port, arms!" In unison the men brought their rifles up from the order arms position and held them at the ready. Giving a slight nod, Colonel von Poeckh slowly turned his gray stallion toward Svib Forest, raised his right arm and brought it forward, the signal to march. The band played a stirring number but remained in place. They would not be going into the forest.

Val and Christian exchanged looks of relief as they began marching. Finally, the waiting was over. Even Corporal Szabo gave a slight nod of satisfaction. *The men in this platoon are good soldiers. They will do well this day.*

The regiment halted at the very edge of the woods and the men wondered: *Why? What are we waiting for?* The band finished its marching song. But Austrian cannons were still firing into the forest. When the firing stopped after a few more minutes, Colonel von Poeckh once again signaled the regiment to advance.

It was now eerily quiet as the regiment's 4,000 men entered the forest. The only sound was the crunch of their boots on leaves, twigs, and chunks of wood. After a hundred paces they began to see a few bodies, then heaps of both Austrian and Prussian dead. The bloodstained white tunics of the Austrians made them easy to identify. Some had been impaled by huge splinters of wood or struck by shell fragments flying around as the Austrian cannon fire exploded in the treetops, not differentiating between friend and foe.

The density of the forest made it impossible for the regiment's battalions to maintain contact and it was gradually lost as they marched deeper into the woods. But the battalion Corporal Szabo and his platoon were in had Colonel von Poeckh and his officers' horses to follow. They stayed with him as the pace quickened.

Rifle fire erupted to their left and the men instinctively ducked but kept the pace. "Corporal, look!" exclaimed Val. Several Prussian riflemen had moved into a small clearing seventy-five yards ahead. They fired, moved back among the trees, reappeared, and fired but missed again. Bullets passing overhead thudded against tree trunks, some ricocheting off sounded like angry bees. "Maintain formation. Keep up the pace," warned Corporal Szabo. "Remember what I always say? Many bullets miss many people in battle."

Deeper and deeper into the forest marched the Fifty-first, not as a regiment but as separated battalions left to their own devices except for Val and Christian's. Colonel von Poeckh pressed forward and the Prussians seemed to be in retreat, their resistance light and sporadic. Soon, they entered the northwest quadrant of the forest where the main Prussian forces were thought to be.

Val and Christian again exchanged looks of relief. So far this hadn't been too bad. The battalion entered a small glade. Suddenly on a ridge to their right, masses of Prussians appeared and opened a murderous fire. "Return fire!" ordered the Colonel. "Return fire!" echoed the officers. "Now, let's give it back to them!" shouted Corporal Szabo. The noise was horrendous as continuous rifle fire clashed with the screams of the wounded.

An officer leading a horse ran over to Corporal Szabo. "Do you still have reserve messengers in your platoon?" he asked.

Szabo called "Welli! Christian Welli, over here!" Christian ran to them. "Welli, this is Captain von Klobus. He has an urgent message to be delivered."

Christian replied "Yes, Corporal. *Herr Hauptmann,* what are your orders?"

"Deliver this message to General Festetics. We have been ambushed and need reinforcements immediately. We are near the western edge of the forest," said the captain, handing Christian a note to confirm the request. Then, giving him the horse's reins, von Klobus added, "Sheath your bayonet. Go quickly and stay low. A man on horseback is a tempting target."

Christian mounted the horse, flashed a quick smile and wave to Val, and then thundered off on the spirited bay. A hail of bullets whistled by as he rode out of the glade and back into the deep woods. Clutching the reins and his rifle, he leaned low over the mount's neck until out of the Prussians' field of fire. He was now in the quieter area but the battle noise behind him seemed to increase in intensity. *Faster, must get there quickly. The regiment's in trouble. Val is in trouble!* He nudged the horse with his heels, urging him on.

Soon, he was out of the woods and on open ground for the half-mile dash to the IV Corps Headquarters of General Festetics. Met by a sentry, he reined in the gallant bay. "A message from Colonel von Poeckh for General Festetics!" he shouted. The sentry called an officer over and Christian handed him the written message. "I'm to wait for a reply," Christian told him.

"General Festetics has been wounded, General Mollinary is in command now," advised the officer. "Wait here." He walked toward a tent shelter a few yards away.

Christian dismounted and started walking the horse to cool him down. "How was the general wounded?" he asked the sentry.

"Prussian cannon fire reached our position. During the barrage, the general had part of his left foot blown off. He's handling it rather well. I heard him tell the other officers that now he will have to polish only one boot!"

The battalion was in danger of being annihilated. Seeing Christian ride off with a message so soon after the Prussians' attack worried Val; now his fears were being confirmed. Men were falling all around him as the Prussians continued their rapid fire. Amazingly, they were shooting from the prone position and reloading without having to stand! By contrast, the Austrians' rifle fire was sporadic and ineffective. Men were killed while standing to reload their outdated muzzle loaders. It was turning into a slaughter.

"Stand up and fight, you cowards!" screamed Corporal Szabo at the distant Prussian riflemen. He fired and began to reload. Just as he started pouring powder down the muzzle, he stood straight up, looked at Val, and then crashed to the ground. He didn't move. As if in the fog of a bad dream, Val saw an ugly round, black hole in the corporal's right temple.

Now the Prussians were advancing on the ever-diminishing ranks of the Austrians. An officer leading a horse headed Val's way, the same one who had sent Christian out as a messenger. No other officers were in sight. Their horses were milling about, riderless.

At IV Corps Headquarters, Christian was becoming impatient; it seemed he had been there all morning. *Have they forgotten I'm here?*

Finally the same officer came out of the tent, walking briskly toward Christian. Handing him a note, he said, "You can tell Colonel von Poeckh that General Mollinary has ordered two more regiments into the battle."

Giving the officer a quick salute, Christian wheeled his horse around and charged back toward the forest. Over the open ground they sped, then plunged once again into the deep woods. It was quieter now as only sporadic rifle fire punctured the silence. But then there was a shot not more than fifty paces ahead. Christian reined in his mount and proceeded at a cautious walk, rifle at the ready. Finally, he saw an Austrian officer standing over a dead horse — Captain von Klobus! "*Herr Hauptmann*, may I help?"

The captain turned quickly but upon recognizing Christian simply shook his head. "I was going to IV Corps Headquarters myself as we thought you had been killed. I got this far when a stray shot hit my horse. I just ended the poor brute's suffering."

"How is the battle going?" Christian asked anxiously, as he quickly dismounted.

The captain grimaced. "It's over. The Prussians surrounded us and the fighting became hand to hand. We lost many men."

"My brother Val?"

"Your brother fought bravely. He tried to rally the platoon as the Prussians closed in. I wanted to send him out as a messenger but it was too late," related the captain.

"Too late?" Christian echoed.

Von Klobus paused, looking closely at Christian. Finally, in a lowered voice, he said, "Your brother fought and died bravely. He was a good soldier of whom you can be very proud."

Christian's worst fears were realized. He simply nodded at the captain's words, saying nothing.

"What is your message from corps headquarters?"

Handing him the message, Christian reported, "*Herr Hauptmann*, they are sending two more regiments into the battle, hoping to save the day."

"Colonel von Poeckh and all the other officers were killed, as well as your NCO, Corporal Szabo. I'm afraid we've lost well over half the regiment. It's too late to save the Fifty-first," von Klobus remarked sadly. He began scribbling out a lengthy note, which he finally handed to Christian. "This will report the extent of our losses. Secondly, it will place you at corps headquarters' disposition. You're a good rider and can serve much better as a messenger than as an ordinary rifleman."

Christian thanked von Klobus, and then mounted the bay for the return to IV Corps Headquarters. Soon, he had to slow the horse, blinded by tears at the loss of Val and so many others. *This won't do. Must compose myself before reporting.* As Christian rode at a slower pace to his new assignment, Austrian cannons opened another barrage on the Svib Forest. It was 11 a.m. Only an hour earlier the Fifty-first Regiment had marched into that wooded death trap.

It was a perfect late summer day in Dunacseb. Early September had become Mary's favorite time of year when Sunday afternoons became even more enjoyable. At mass that morning she again prayed fervently to St. George and St. Michael for the safe return of Val and Christian. Now, with the younger children napping, the afternoon was hers to enjoy.

She admired the garden, which had taken so much of her time since spring. *Perhaps we should plant some more grapevines*, she mused. She surveyed the garden area, making mental notes of where they could go. Engrossed in her thoughts but still observant, she noticed a man walking down their street. He was still too far away to be recognized but there was something about the way he was dressed. As he drew closer, Mary could see that he wore a tall military hat, a *shako*. The hat, the white tunic and crossed white belts across his chest, and his stride marked him as a soldier. There was something familiar about his walk. *Is it Christian? Yes!*

She ran to him as he approached their gate. "Christian, is it really you?"

"Yes, Mother, I'm home!" he shouted, putting his arms around her when they met.

"Valtina, he's coming later?" Without waiting for a reply Mary ran into the house shouting, "John, Christian is home!"

Inside the house, John grabbed Christian's hand and hugged him closely. "But where is Val?" he asked anxiously.

Christian lowered his eyes and paused. When he looked up, they were full of tears. "Val didn't make it. He died in a huge battle early in July."

"No! Did you see it happen?" asked John.

"No, not possible," echoed Mary, shaking her head. "No!"

"I was delivering a message to headquarters when it happened. Captain von Klobus told me about it. He, he said that Val was a good soldier, one who died bravely."

Mary burst into loud sobs. "Our beautiful son Val. It's just too much!"

John stood up, shook his head, and began pacing. "I'm such a fool! We moved here to get away from the Prussian military. Now, my son is killed by soldiers from the very army I wanted to keep him out of. Such a fool!" He continued pacing, muttering under his breath.

Mary sobbed quietly, saying nothing. Standing up, she said, "I'd better check on Joseph and George."

"I'm sorry to bring such terrible news, Father," offered Christian.

After further pacing, John finally sat down. "Tell me, Christian, how is it you were spared?"

"Because we were good riders and spoke Magyar as well as German, they made both of us messengers. The regiment was ambushed in a place called the Svib Forest and the captain had me take a message to headquarters asking for reinforcements."

"I'm glad you made it back. Losing one son is bad but losing two? It's impossible to even think about."

Continuing, Christian told John, "I learned later on that we lost over half the regiment Val and I were in. Of 4,000 men who charged into the forest, only 1,800 came back. The Austrian Army lost many more that day. But they were able to save many others because their cannons held off the Prussians until the army crossed back over the Elbe River."

Mary finally reappeared, hers eyes red from weeping. She brought Joseph and George, now aged three and two, with her. "Look, your big brother has returned from the war," she told them. "You remember him, don't you? He's your oldest brother." Then, "I pray that you boys will have a better life and not have to go through what he did."

EPILOGUE

According to the Austrian General Staff's account of the Austro-Prussian War, Austrian casualties at the battle of Königgrätz amounted to 1,313 officers, 41,499 men, and 6,010 horses. Of these, 330 officers and 5,328 men were dead, 431 officers and 7,143 men wounded, 43 officers and 7,367 men missing, and 509 officers and 21,661 men captured.

Prussian losses were markedly lower. Total casualties for the day (July 3, 1866) came to 359 officers, 8,794, men and 909 horses. Of these, 99 officers and 1,830 men were killed, 260 officers and 6,688 men wounded, and 276 men missing.[8]

Shortly after the armistice with Prussia, Hungary demanded and received home rule for Budapest as well as Magyar domination of the so-called subject peoples of eastern Austria: the Rumanians, the Croats, and the Slovaks. By the constitutional *Ausgleich* (compromise) of 1867, Austria was renamed Austria-Hungary.

Prussia, on the other hand, became France's equal in population, national income, armed forces, and the capital and energy reserves vital for industrialization. Furthermore, their quick victory negated objections by the Great Powers, England, France, and Russia, to Prussia's expansion.

CHAPTER 5
THE NEXT GENERATIONS

Herr Welsch, this Sunday is the Kirchweih feast and I would like permission to ask your daughter Anna to the big street dance.

George Welli, October 1888

The fire was out of control. Fueled by the building's decaying, dried-out wood along with explosive grain dust, the blaze at the Welsch flour mill had quickly turned into an inferno. Flames now engulfed the entire structure, with sparks leaping high into the nighttime sky. The clanging of the church bell in the village square added to the turmoil of this brisk autumn evening. Here at the edge of town, the flames gave off so much light it was like an early dawn.

"Back, folks! Keep back!" ordered the young policeman. "Let the firefighters do their work!" John Welli's youngest son George was now age twenty-four. Only recently appointed by the area's chief of police, this was a major incident at which he must keep order.

Reluctantly the crowd moved back at the sight of a uniformed policeman, but only a few steps. "Move back! Farther!" shouted George, motioning them with his arms. But the fire was an irresistible sight, providing high drama, unusual for a village as small as Dunacseb. And second only to the church, the mill was the tallest structure in town.

The firefighters were now limiting their efforts to making certain the fire didn't spread to nearby buildings.

"Got things under control, George?"

George turned to see his cousin, Adam Welli. "What are you doing up? You have to take over for me at 7 a.m."

"How can anyone sleep with that bell ringing?" Adam motioned toward the church steeple. "Why are they still ringing it? The whole town is awake by now."

"I know, but I've been too busy to go tell them to quit."

"How did the fire start?"

"Haven't had chances to talk to the firefighters. They've been too busy and so have I."

"I'll go stop that bell ringing and come back and help." Adam headed toward the church at a trot.

"Thanks. I have the crowd under control now, but you're welcome to join me." George watched as Adam moved quickly toward the church. He would be glad for Adam's help. A year older, he had been a policeman for more than two years. Although only first cousins, many people assumed they were brothers, so close were their family resemblances. Each was lean, nearly six feet tall, with dark hair, blue eyes, and distinctive high cheekbones. Both wore luxurious full mustaches.

George continued to watch the crowd, which now included most of the village residents. They stood in awe as the old flour mill succumbed to the ravaging flames. As the fire continued to roar, the roof caved in, sending up a huge shower of sparks. "Ohhhhh!" they marveled.

"What's that smell?" one man asked to no one in particular.

"That's what grain smells like when it burns," answered another.

"Like when your wife leaves bread in the oven too long," cracked yet another.

Finally, the church bell stopped its clamor. George relaxed somewhat for the first time in more than two hours.

Shortly Adam returned, smiling broadly. "George, I wondered how anyone could ring that bell for so long without wearing themselves out. Well, Sister Josephine and Sister Marguerite were taking turns pulling the rope. I told them the alarm had been properly sounded and they could rest now."

"They must have felt they were really doing the Lord's work this night," George chuckled. "You know, I don't think this fire was an accident. It may have been set."

"Think so? Well then, you have a lot of work to do."

For a few more hours they monitored the crowd, keeping it away from the fire scene and watching for signs of unusual behavior. By now it was well after midnight. Gradually, the people wearied of the diminishing drama and began returning to their homes.

"Where's George Welsch?" asked Adam.

"One of his neighbors told me that he and his wife went to Palanka for a wedding," replied George. "They won't be back until Monday."

"He and Katherine are really in for a shock. Their flour mill burning down is a big loss. I'm glad you'll be the one who has to talk to him about this. Now, I have to go try and get some more sleep. Oh — this Sunday, why don't you come to our place after mass? Eva will have a great dinner for us."

George smiled. "I'll be there. Always like to eat with the 'first family.' Is she going to offer us apples with the meal?"

Adam laughed at the Biblical reference to his and his wife's names, a standing joke between him and George. "Apple pie, maybe. I'll see you later."

Monday afternoon George began his shift early by calling on George Welsch, owner of the mill. "*Herr* Welsch, I'm George Welli, Bács-Bodrog County Police. May I talk with you?"

"Yes, come right in," Welsch replied, swinging the door open. "Let's sit over here at the table. I suppose you want to know about the fire, right?"

"Yes, I was wondering whether you can help me figure out what may have caused it."

"It's a mystery to me. On Friday we operated as usual, milling about two hundred bushels of wheat. It was past sundown when we closed, but I made certain all the lanterns were out before we locked up. The next morning my wife Katherine, my daughter Anna, and I went to Palanka for a wedding. When we got back late yesterday, a neighbor told me about the fire."

George continued, "Do you store anything in the mill that's explosive?"

"Some extra kerosene for the lamps, but it's in a metal can. Nothing else. However, if grain dust builds up it can sometimes be explosive."

"Do you think this was a grain dust explosion?"

"Not on its own. The mill was very clean. It's close to the end of the milling season and my helpers and I had just cleaned the place thoroughly a week ago."

George sat back in his chair, mulling over the information. Then, leaning forward, he asked, "Would someone else want to start a fire at your mill?"

Welsch thought for a moment, frowned, and replied, "I hope not. But in this business you sometimes have unhappy customers. Some want their grain milled immediately, ahead of others who have asked first. And then there are some who grumble that the amount of flour produced seems small, considering the amount of grain they brought in to be milled. However, that's something that can vary according the grain's quality. Yes, there's opportunity for disagreements with customers."

"Have you had problems with any customers this year?"

"This season was a good one and went smoothly. Everyone was satisfied."

"Can you remember or have any records about customers with whom you've had disagreements in the past?"

"I would have to go through all my journals but I think I could come up with their names. Would you like to come back tomorrow and go over them?"

George nodded and sat back. "Certainly. That would be good."

"I've almost forgotten my manners. Would you like a drink of water or something to eat?"

"Just a drink of water."

"Katherine, would you bring a cup of water for Officer Welli? Katherine?"

A young woman appeared from the bedroom. "She's at the Hohensteins, Father. Their baby is almost due. I'll get the water for you."

"Oh yes, I forgot." Turning to George, he said, "My Katherine is a midwife and she gets called away very suddenly sometimes."

The young woman brought two cups of water to the table. "Anna, this is Officer George Welli."

George stood up. "I'm pleased to meet you." He couldn't help but notice her height, a good five feet, seven or eight inches. Her dark brown eyes could almost look directly into his.

Anna smiled and nodded to George. "Likewise." Then, she glided away from the table toward another room, pausing to quickly look back, a move not lost on him.

"So, are you Joseph Welli's or John Welli's son?" asked Welsch.

"John was my father."

"I knew him. He was a good man. He's been gone for over a year now, right?"

"Yes, he passed away a year ago last April, my mother just six months later."

Welsch finished his drink. "The other officer named Welli, he's your cousin?"

"Yes, Adam is my first cousin. Joseph Welli was his father. I must be going now. I'll see you about the same time tomorrow."

Once outside, he paused to put on his cap. From the corner of his eye he saw a curtain move in one of the other rooms. *Well, she wants another look, eh? Very interesting woman. Not too shy but not too bold. And the long dark hair and brown eyes, very attractive. I've seen her at church but always from a distance.* Setting his cap at an angle and squaring his shoulders, he walked away with a spring in his step.

The next day, George went back to the Welsch home, not without pleasant anticipation. *Will she be there? I should say something to her, but what?*

Once seated at the table with Welsch, he asked, "How many names did you find in your journals?"

"I was able to go back twelve years and came up with twenty-one names. Here's the list I made."

George perused the list, noting that it provided both names and years. "What can you tell me about them?"

"With most of them, the disagreements were minor and we handled them in a friendly manner. Now, there are five I put checkmarks by where we had bitter arguments. But two of those men died in the past few years and two have moved to America. This last one, Heinrich, I haven't seen for several years."

George made a note of the name. "Not much to go on, but I'll see what I can learn about him. What do you think may have happened?"

"Yes, I agree there isn't a lot to go on. The thing that disturbs me is that the fire started after the mill had been shut down for two days. If it had started Friday night instead of Sunday night, I would think that maybe one of my helpers or I caused it accidentally. Maybe we lit our pipes too quickly when leaving or maybe one of the lanterns wasn't completely out. I just don't know."

"Will you rebuild?"

"No, I don't want to have to do that. If Dunacseb still needs a mill let someone else build it. They can put in one of those new roller types instead of a grist mill. I'm getting up in years and it's not a good time to start over. I've saved enough for my old age and I have a young wife to look after me," he added with a smile.

"I see." George stood up to take his leave. "Thank you for the information *Herr* Welsch. When I learn something about this man Heinrich, I may be back to talk with you some more."

Once outside, he stopped to put on his cap. *There, the curtain moved in that other room again. Interesting, she stayed out of sight this time but still spies on me!* With a wry smile he squared his shoulders and walked away.

For the next week George was preoccupied with other business, both police and personal. The house he had bought from a family who immigrated to America was suitable but needed work before he could call it home. But he still pondered the fire. *Was it an accident or deliberately set? And where was Walter Heinrich, the only possible suspect? And the tall, elegant Anna Welsch, was she really interested in him or just curious? Got to find that out!*

A few days later, he set off for the Welsch home, confident and resolute on both issues. An older woman answered his knock. "You must be Officer Welli. Come in," she invited. "I'm Katherine Welsch. George, Officer Welli is here."

Seated once again at the now familiar table, George made his report. "Adam and I both made some inquiries about Walter Heinrich. As it turns out, he was badly injured about a year ago. His horses bolted while he was adjusting the wagon hitch and the fully loaded wagon ran over him. His legs are paralyzed and he now lives in Palanka with one of his daughters. The accident happened there, so not many people in Dunacseb heard about it. It seems also that he wasn't that well-known in Dunacseb."

Welsch frowned. "That's tragic. He and I had a bitter disagreement but I wouldn't wish that on him. I guess this pretty much leaves us in the dark regarding the fire, doesn't it?"

"It certainly does. I won't be doing any more work on the case unless I receive new information. For now we have to consider it as unsolved." Then, with a wry smile, George continued in a lower voice. "There is another matter I wanted to ask you about. It's something more of a personal nature. Could we speak privately, perhaps outside?"

"Certainly," Welsch replied in an equally low voice. Then, more loudly, "If you have time, Officer Welli, I'd like you to see our garden, especially the grapevines."

Once outside, Welsch, curiosity aroused, turned to George. "What did you want to talk about?"

"I would like to begin seeing your daughter at the weekend dances. This Sunday is the *Kirchweih* (church consecration day) feast and I would like to ask her to the big street dance."

Smiling, Welsch replied, "You certainly may ask her. I like a man who's direct. Let's go back inside."

Returning to the house, Welsch said, "Katherine, please come out to the garden with me. Anna, I need you in the kitchen."

Anna appeared, a slight flush coloring her cheeks. "Your mother and I are going out to the garden. Officer Welli wants to speak with you."

"Good afternoon, Officer Welli," said Anna, nodding to George. Her voice was so soft it was almost inaudible.

"George, my first name is George," he replied amiably. "Anna, I would like to see you at the *Kirchweih* street dance this Sunday. Would, would you like to dance with me there?"

As Anna's cheeks flushed even more, she stammered out a reply, "Why yes, George. I would like that very much." Then, she broke into a dazzling smile that matched George's smile at her reply.

"That is very good!" George exclaimed. He was a bit shocked at his effusiveness. But such positive replies generate gratitude that is difficult to restrain. Furthermore, positive replies generate confidence. "Well then, I will truly look forward to Sunday. However, I must be going now. It's nearly time to relieve my cousin Adam."

"All right," Anna replied. "Thank you for asking me to the dance. Will you be at the dinner too?"

"Yes, I will be with my brother Joseph, my cousin Adam, and their wives. I'll see you there."

Sunday came and George, eager to see Anna, was at church much earlier than usual. His mind wandered during the lengthy special high mass as he could see Anna and her parents several rows in front of him. Finally, the priest gave his benediction and the congregation began filing outside to the nearby hall for the festival dinner.

To George's discomfort, most of the dinner conversation dwelled on his commitment for the dance. Augusta and Eva, Joseph's and Adam's wives bombarded him with good-natured comments and questions. "You met her while investigating the fire? Isn't that an interesting sign?" teased Augusta. "Yes, and she's so tall. But she's still shorter than you and that's important," laughed Eva. Joseph and Adam talked about other things the few times they spoke. They had made their "points" the day before while helping George repaint his house.

The dinner over, George walked over to the Welsch family. "Good afternoon, *Herr* Welsch, *Frau* Welsch. Good afternoon, Anna!"

Anna stood, a warm welcoming smile setting off the visual impact. She wore a long, full, pale blue dress with a decorative apron and shawl. A matching scarf was braided into her long, done-up hair. She looked like a princess who had just stepped out of a fairy tale. "Good afternoon, George."

"The dance procession is about to start. We should line up," said George.

"First, here's the processional hat I made for you," she replied, handing it to him.

"Why, thank you! It's very nicely decorated." George placed it on his head. Looking around, he could see that his hat was far more decorative than the ones the other women had made for the men with whom they were attending this special dance.

Spotting her friend Helga, Anna asked who would lead the procession. "The Schwab's, they are the couple most recently married," was her reply.

And so, George and Anna were off on their first dance. The festivities continued until well past sundown, when the lanterns brought by many revelers provided a softer, more romantic light. The music was sprightly, slowing only occasionally for a waltz. Older couples then joined the young dancers. Mostly, however, the older wives watched the dancers, taking note of who was dancing with whom, thereby serving as chaperones. The older men continued quaffing beer and sampling the many homemade wines proudly served. It was a grand time! This *Kirchweih* was better than last year's, which was better than the one the year before . . . better than any wedding dance . . . better than any baptismal dance . . . The accordion player, the violinist, the harmonica player, and the pianist were never better, their playing inspired by the night's festivity.

When the long evening ended, George and Anna smiled knowingly at each other. "I would like to see you at next Sunday's dance," George told her.

"I'd like that very much." This was a reply that would be repeated every Sunday night for more than a year.

And now it was November 12, 1889. The just-married George and Anna led the wedding dance procession in the hall adjoining the church. Surrounded by well-wishers, they beamed with joy. "You know, George, it's just over a year since our first dance," said Anna. "Did you think it would lead to this?"

"Well, you just never know where things will lead," said George, a broad smile betraying the noncommittal nature of his reply. In 1891 the first member of the next generation was born.

"Mother! Mother! Am I going to be all right?" cried Anna.

"Yes, Anna, dear. You're just fine and you have a beautiful, healthy baby boy," replied Katherine Welsch.

"Are you certain?"

"Yes, Anna! I've delivered nearly two hundred babies. He's normal in all respects. Now, it's time to bring George in to see his first-born son." Katherine opened the door and called to him.

"Are you all right, Anna?" George asked.

"Yes, Mother says I'm doing well. We have a son, now."

George smiled but said nothing. His gaze was fixed on Anna and the baby.

Katherine returned with the family Bible. "We should record this right away. It will be needed when he's baptized. The date is April 12 . . ."

Pulling out his watch, George replied, "It's more than two hours past midnight. So April 13, 1891, is the proper date."

"What will you name him?" asked Katherine.

"I was thinking of Mathias for a boy," George replied.

"I like that," said Anna. "If we have another boy, we should name him after you."

Smiling, George replied, "And the first daughter should be named after you."

CHAPTER 6
APPEAL TO THE ALMIGHTY

"You will have three minutes to make peace with your God."
Police chief, Bács Bodrog County, to condemned prisoners,
1888-1901

As the twentieth century approached, George and Anna lived a comfortable life, surrounded by friends and relatives in this small town on the Hungarian Plains near the Danube River. They were now a family of five. Two years after Mat's arrival, Anna gave birth to a son they named George. Sadly, he died of diphtheria when only a few months old. In 1897 Anna, their first daughter was born. In 1898 they had another daughter, naming her Katherine, after Anna's mother.

Life, including the social side, continued to revolve around church events. Weekends were spent with George's brother Joseph and wife Augusta, his cousin and co-worker Adam and wife Eva. In late 1899 they had lively discussions whether the next century began January 1, 1900 or a year later.

George and Anna had a discussion with young Mat that was even livelier. "Mat, come here. Your mother and I have something to tell you," said George.

"Yes, Father?"

"We met with Father Michael today. He needs a new altar boy and thinks you would be a good one. So, next April when you turn nine you will start training."

"But Father, regular school ends in May. That means I will have to go to school during the summer."

"It will be good experience and you learn much. But best of all, you will be doing the Lord's work," said Anna, with an encouraging smile.

"But I'll have to learn Latin," Mat protested.

"You'll also learn much more history than you are getting in primary school," added George.

"But Sister Josephine and Sister Marguerite are old and cranky . . .."

"Enough! As your mother said, it will be good experience as well as educational. It's done. I don't want to hear any more about it," said George, looking at Mat intently.

"All right," conceded Mat. He knew from the look in George's eyes that the "discussion" was over. Nineteen-hundred was going to be quite a year.

In late April, Adam went to Palanka to testify at the trial of a man he'd arrested for arson. He returned to the combination office-prisoner lockup in Dunacseb late in the day and anxiously waited for George to come on duty.

As George walked in, Adam exclaimed, "George, you've got to hear this!" his face ashen.

"What is it?" Adam was usually the calm, easy-going type. George had never before seen his cousin this distressed.

"The trial in Palanka, they're going to execute the prisoner!" Adam blurted out, jumping to his feet.

"What! Why?"

"It's true. The prisoner made no defense and the judge sentenced him to death."

George was incredulous. "But you arrested him for simple arson, burning a man's barn. No one was killed. He endangered livestock, not human beings!"

"That's true and that's how I testified. But the judge didn't even hesitate. He sentenced him to death without giving any reasons other than the man had admitted the crime."

"Well, what did Chief Kleinschmidt say about it?" George continued to probe, trying to find some logic for such a drastic sentence.

"I waited around trying to see him but he was with others, including the judge. Finally, I decided it might be better to talk to him later and came home."

"We'd better talk to him soon. Will he be in Palanka tomorrow?" George's mind was spinning, full of questions that needed to be asked.

By 8:00 the next morning Adam and George's buggy pulled up in front of the county police office. They walked in quickly to find Gustav Kleinschmidt seated at a battered desk, littered with papers of varying importance.

"Good morning, men," he greeted them. Not knowing the purpose of their visit, both his tone and his demeanor were cautious. He remained seated. "What's so important it brings both of you to Palanka?" His voice was raspy and his hand had a slight tremor. That and his snow-white hair and mustache betrayed his age. The mustache was beginning to yellow from years of heavy smoking.

George and Adam returned his greeting and sat down. "It's about the sentencing of the prisoner who was tried yesterday," said Adam.

"Mmm, yes. That," mumbled the chief.

"Why was he sentenced to death? He never killed or even injured anyone. I'm certain it was revenge. But he set fire to a barn, not a house," said Adam.

"Well, times are changing," replied the chief.

"The 'times are changing'? What does that mean?" queried George in astonishment.

"Did the judge give any explanation for such a drastic sentence?" asked Adam.

Kleinschmidt sighed, as he began filling his pipe. He meticulously tamped the tobacco into it and lit up before replying. After a few long pulls he leaned forward and told them, "He said the prisons are overcrowded and that there would have to be more executions. He also said that for some time now there has been a feeling that time in prison doesn't help the prisoners. It just makes them worse. I think the word the judge used was recidivism."

"But we haven't heard any of that," replied Adam.

"Could there be something else? Was this prisoner a Serb or a Rumanian?" probed George, looking for another possible reason.

"That's getting into political considerations. I'm not prepared to do that," replied Chief Kleinschmidt. "But you should remember that since Austria lost the war with Prussia in 1866 the Magyars control Hungary much more than before. The Compromise of 1867 made Hungary an equal partner with Austria instead of just being one of Austria's provinces. The Emperor in Vienna is mostly a figurehead and the real power is now in Budapest. That power has been growing. Neither of you would have your jobs unless you spoke Magyar as well as German."

"I know," replied Adam but persisted with another question. "Were there indications he was a terrorist, a member of the Black Hand?"

Kleinschmidt shook his head, saying tersely, "I don't know. But he is to be beheaded next Wednesday at noon. Both of you are to be here for the execution."

"Will the judge be there?" asked George.

"No, he's already left for Neusatz to hold another trial. The Bács Bodrog County Advocate will preside over the execution."

Kleinschmidt began rifling through papers on his desk. Sensing correctly that he had nothing more to say, Adam and George took their leave. "Goodbye," he said without looking up.

Initially, the officers were too dumbfounded to talk during the trip back to Dunacseb. Then incredulity mixed with a sense of outrage hit them. "I can't believe he said that: 'Those are political considerations. I'm not prepared to go into them!'" Adam exclaimed.

"There has to be more to this than just prison overcrowding," added George. "Executing the prisoner just on one arson charge is wrong. It's not an eye for an eye. It's an eye for a bruised knee or a skinned elbow."

"Do you think there was something the chief wasn't telling us?"

"Well, you could suspect that. Remember him saying 'times are changing'? That was really puzzling."

"Yes, he told us about changes that took place thirty years ago but didn't explain what's changing *now*."

The following Wednesday George and Adam went back to Palanka to witness the execution. They returned grim-faced. In a brief conversation with Chief Kleinschmidt they learned nothing more about the reasons for such a harsh sentence.

"Are you going to tell Eva about this?" asked George.

"This case may be an isolated event. Maybe it won't happen again. No, I won't tell Eva. She shouldn't have to worry about our work."

"Then I won't tell Anna either. I hope you're right about this being an isolated case."

The summer passed uneventfully and all seemed serene. But one night in mid-October as George was making his rounds, he happened upon a young man hitching a team of horses to a wagon loaded with ridge poles and other lumber for the annual homes repair work in Dunacseb. He watched in the moonlight as the stranger then began pulling away with the wagon. George followed him to the outskirts of town, then ran to the horses and grabbed their reins.

"Halt! Where are you going with this wagon?"

The man jumped down from the wagon seat to make his escape but stumbled and fell face down. George pounced on him, subdued him, and then tied him up with leather straps. He loaded the man onto the wagon and drove it back to the lockup. Despite George's questions, the suspect refused to say anything about the attempted theft.

When Adam came on duty at 7 a.m., he made a gloomy assessment: "Now we may find out if that execution last spring was just an isolated case."

"I've spent the past several hours thinking the same thing."

After testifying at the trial in Palanka two weeks later, George got his answer. Not only was the prisoner condemned to death but the execution was to take place in Dunacseb in just a week! Both officers agreed they now had to tell their wives about the perversions of justice in which they were reluctant participants.

Anna seemed to take the news calmly and George was relieved. "I agree, execution seems very drastic just for attempted thievery," she observed.

"It's uncalled for and the execution is gruesome," George continued. "The prisoner is to be executed at the town square here in Dunacseb at noon, a week from Friday. You could watch it if you like."

"I'll go."

"Are you certain?" asked George, taking her hand.

"Well, yes. How bad could it be?"

On the scheduled day, Anna had Mat, Annie, and Katherine put on their coats for the walk to Adam and Eva's house. Mat protested, "My friends and some other boys are going to the execution. Why can't I go, too?"

"Just because other boys get to go doesn't mean that you do. You'll all stay with Eva. Only your father, Adam, and I are going," replied Anna.

"But Father Michael will be there," Mat persisted.

"He won't need an altar boy for what he has to do," George replied curtly.

After leaving the children, George, Anna, and Adam began the walk to the town square. The bright early November sun belied the grim occasion. "Who will do the execution?" asked Anna.

"Heinrich Schultz," replied George.

"Him? The man who comes around to pick up dead animals?" Anna was incredulous.

"The same man," said George.

"I don't like being around him. He always smells bad and he seems half-drunk most of the time." She shook her head at the thought.

"Well, he looked a lot cleaner when he did that execution in Palanka last April. He even had an assistant. But he still smelled of schnapps," said Adam. "However, if I had his job, I would drink a lot too."

Upon arriving in the square, Adam went directly to the lockup. The prisoner had been placed in it after being brought to Dunacseb by Chief Kleinschmidt and another officer.

"Anna, since I was the arresting officer you get to be in front where you can sit down. Come with me," offered George. He took her arm and escorted her to the single row of chairs placed just a few feet from a scaffold that had been erected by the executioner and his assistant. George then went to the lockup. Anna was seated next to a man she didn't know. However, the two men to his right were Father Michael and the mayor of Dunacseb.

The wooden scaffold was about five feet high and had a stairway. The only item on its platform was a wooden stool, about two feet tall. Although it was still nearly an hour before noon, the scheduled execution time, a huge, noisy crowd had gathered. Many were in a festive mood, laughing and talking animatedly. Several men in back were downing large mugs of beer. Others were holding their young sons on their shoulders to afford them a better view. Only low murmurs from a few ran counter to the theatrical atmosphere.

Shortly before noon, George and Adam brought the prisoner to the scaffold. He shuffled along as they held his arms to prevent him from stumbling. The shackles he was wearing added an eerie, metallic rattling sound to an already grim scene as he slowly climbed the stairs. Once on the platform they had him sit on the stool. Chief Kleinschmidt, the executioner, and his assistant went up onto the platform, followed by Father Michael and the man who had been sitting next to Anna. The executioner's assistant blindfolded the prisoner.

The unknown man called for silence and then introduced himself as Erich Gabor, the Bács Bodrog County Advocate. He opened the proceeding by reading a statement to the prisoner: "George Welli, a duly appointed officer of the law, arrested you in the act of stealing a wagon load of ridgepoles and other lumber here in Dunacseb. At the hearing you gave no defense for your actions. Therefore, the judge sentenced you to death. We are here to carry out the sentence." He left the platform and returned to the seat beside Anna.

Then Chief Kleinschmidt stepped forward and addressed the prisoner: "Do you have any last words at this time?"

The prisoner shook his head, his shackles again rattling.

"Do you wish to make a confession? Father Michael will hear it," asked the chief.

Again the prisoner shook his head, to which the chief responded: "Then you will have three minutes to make peace with your God." Chief Kleinschmidt and Father Michael left the platform and took seats near Anna. Only George, Adam, and the executioners remained with the prisoner.

The prisoner bowed his head and began mumbling in a language that George couldn't understand. "That isn't Rumanian or Serbian. What is it?" he whispered to Adam.

"I don't know. I've never heard it before," Adam said out of the corner of his mouth.

George looked down at Anna and saw that she was gripping the arms of the chair tightly. Maybe bringing her was a mistake, but it was too late now. It seemed she wanted to look away, but couldn't. The macabre scene had totally captured her attention and she couldn't break its hold.

The three minutes were up. Heinrich Schultz, the swarthy, powerfully built executioner, stepped forward to the stool where the prisoner was seated and withdrew a heavy sword nearly four feet long from its scabbard. A hush fell over the crowd. He positioned himself behind the prisoner, awaiting the order from the chief. His assistant stood to the prisoner's right, holding a wicker basket.

At his seat Chief Kleinschmidt looked up at the executioner, nodded, and said: "Now!"

The blade swung around in a horizontal stroke from left to right with tremendous force, severing the prisoner's head instantly. "Ohhhhh!"

exclaimed the crowd, some quickly turning away from the grisly scene. Many women screamed, clutching the arms of the men they were with for support.

The head hit the edge of the basket, rolled off the scaffold onto the ground, and then toward Anna. She stared, transfixed, as the head with its tongue moving in and out, making grotesque, animal-like noises rolled to her. It stopped; face up, at her feet with the blindfold still in place. In one lightning-like move Adam seized the basket, leaped off the scaffold, grabbed the head by its hair, dropped it in the basket, and handed it back to the executioner's assistant.

George was at her side almost as quickly. "Anna, are you all right?" She said nothing. "Do you want to go home?" She nodded.

Once they were home she finally spoke. "George, that was like a trip to the place of the Evil One. What should we do?"

"Adam and I can't continue being police officers, not with this kind of justice. There is a man who comes here about every month to recruit men for work in America. The next time he's in Dunacseb we are going to meet with him."

EPILOGUE

Adam and George's outrage was justified. At the turn of the twentieth century things were chaotic in the Habsburg Empire, more commonly known as Austria-Hungary and, at times, referred to as the Dual Monarchy. Historians have been extremely critical of the Empire, especially Hungary.

Oscar Jászi pointed out that until its demise in 1918, the empire remained feudal, in that the land was controlled by the aristocracy and high-ranking ecclesiastics. This was a system that had been abolished in Western Europe by the eighteenth-century French Revolution. He observed that in most of the counties, three or four leading families filled most offices with family and friends — a classic recipe for corruption.[9]

Edward Crankshaw, another historian, described the Magyars' extreme contempt for minorities in the Habsburg Empire.[10] In the nineteenth century, Hungary, Italy, and Greece were cited as three countries where it was claimed that the death penalty could not be abolished as the state needed to defend itself.[11] From 1880 to 1914, imprisonment lost its place as the preferred sanction in Europe. The public became increasingly aware of the prison system's failure to rehabilitate wrongdoers and its success in fostering a culture of recidivism. Some prisoners were considered incurable.[12]

Chapter 7
Over the Waves — Verse One

Your name? "Welli"
How do you spell? "W-E-L-L-I"
You are now listed as passengers on the ship manifest. When you reach New York you will be given numbered tags that correspond to this manifest. Attach them securely to your coats and don't lose them. They are important for processing you through Ellis Island.

Passenger boarding procedures
Port of Antwerp, Belgium, 1901

Between 1876 and 1910 more than 3,500,000 people emigrated from the Habsburg Monarchy, 2 million of them to the United States. The economic and cultural backwardness was especially severe in the Hungarian part of the monarchy; thus, from 1890 to 1908 it lost 1,500,000 emigrants.[13] American industry needed workers and many recruiters combed European countries urging them to move to the United States.

Similarly, agents for steamship lines traveled to Europe eager to sell tickets. At the turn of the twentieth century, steerage class transatlantic tickets cost about $25. However, the *annual* wages of a Hungarian worker ranged from $60 to $100. The average for women laborers was even lower, $45. To these huddled masses, the American worker's $9.60

average *weekly* salary seemed a golden dream. Thus, the opportunity was well worth the cost of a ticket.

In January 1901 George and Adam met with an industrial recruiter from America who plied southern Hungary. "It's all set, Anna. We're going to America in May," announced George.

"All of us or just you and Adam?" Anna asked.

"We believe it's best if Adam and I go first and get established in the new country. Then we would have you and Eva and the children move later on after we are certain we want to stay. The man from America told us that many people from Europe do it like that. But it won't be easy for us or you and Eva being apart."

"Being apart will be all right for a while. How long would it be before we could come there?" Anna looked at George intently.

"He told us that many men wait a year before bringing the rest of the family over. It gives them a chance to save up some money. American is a big country. Adam and I will be going by train from New York to a city in New Jersey named Trenton. We will stay with the Piller family for a day or two. They moved to America from Palanka several years ago. From there, a large group of us will be going farther west to work in a steel mill, either in Pittsburgh, that's in a state called Pennsylvania, or in Youngstown. That's in Ohio." George took her hand, adding, "But I will miss you terribly."

"And I will miss you, too, but it's probably the best way to do it. Oh, and I have something to tell you . . .."

"We're having another baby?" George asked with a broad smile.

"No, nothing like that," Anna laughed. "Mother told me she would pay our steamship fares if we take her with us. What with Father dying last year and my brother Mat moving to America, she would have no family left here when we move. She still has money that Father left her and she is renting out half of that double-size house now that she's all alone."

"That would be very helpful, especially since we have to purchase round-trip tickets. That's a requirement in case the immigration office in America turns you away."

"Turn you away?" she echoed.

"Sometimes people are found to have diseases that keep them from being accepted in the new country. We have enough now for my passage to America but it might shorten the time we are separated if your mother is willing to help. Yes, it's a good idea. We should take her with us. And if we have another baby, it would be good having a midwife in the house!"

Anna laughed long and hard. "I'll tell her she's welcome to come with us."

The remaining months rolled by quickly. Adam and George were relieved that there were no cases where they had to arrest anyone. In April they went to Palanka and told Chief Kleinschmidt they were resigning from the county police force and moving to America. "Good luck," he told them and, surprisingly, shook their hands. "I had a chance to go there twenty years ago but didn't take it," he added with remorse.

On a bright, early May morning Joseph Welli pulled his buggy up to George and Anna's house. It was time to take his brother George and his cousin Adam to Palanka, the first leg of their trip to America. During the ride it was the usual happy, carefree banter among this close trio. Then, melancholy descended as they drove into town.

Their mood shifted again as the sight of the county police office reminded them why they were making the trip. Adam glared at it and nudged George. "Do you think old Kleinschmidt has hired replacements for us yet?"

"He probably has. I'm glad we're getting one last look at that office. It makes me just that much more certain we're doing the right thing. I haven't forgotten the day he wouldn't give us straight answers when we asked about executing that young prisoner."

Joseph pulled the buggy up at the town square, where they saw the recruiter from America. "Good morning, men," he greeted them, stepping forward to shake hands. "Put your bags in that wagon over there and climb aboard. You have a nice long ride to Agram (Zagreb), where you will catch the train to Trieste. There you board a small ship that will take you to Antwerp. That's in Belgium. In Antwerp you board the Red Star liner *Kensington* for the transatlantic crossing. Got your tickets with you?"

They nodded and walked over to the covered wagon, where Joseph helped them load their bags. "Good luck," he told them as he shook hands. "Augusta and I will look out for Anna, Eva, and the children in case they need help with anything."

George and Adam climbed aboard, taking seats at the front just behind the driver, a portly German with a weathered, reddish face from long days driving his wagon in hot sun and cold winds. "You must be going to America," he chuckled. "Since you're sitting in the front, you're looking forward to it. Otherwise, you would be sitting in the rear looking back."

They laughed with him as they waited for the remaining passengers. Soon, the wagon and its seven passengers pulled away, drawn by four sturdy horses. After several days they arrived in Agram, where the driver deposited them at the train station and told them where to catch the train for Trieste.

Despite the aging railroad cars and rough track, the ride to Trieste seemed a luxury after days in the covered wagon. The old train made the trip in just over a day. "Just follow the crowd. Most of them are going to the docks," the conductor told them. There, they boarded a small, nondescript steamship for the voyage to Antwerp. "Look at the rust on this thing! It's even older than the train," observed Adam. But the little ship moved briskly away from the dock and sailed around the toe of Italy, past the island of Sicily to Naples, Italy, where more immigrants boarded. From Naples they sailed past the island of Sardinia, through the Straits of Gibraltar, and into the Atlantic Ocean. The final leg of the voyage was up the Atlantic coastline, through the English Channel, then docking at Antwerp, where the passengers got their first look at the Red Star liner S.S. *Kensington*.

George and Adam stared at the huge ship. It was 8,669 gross tons, some 480 feet in length, with a fifty-seven-foot beam. It had one stack and four masts. The vessel still looked new, having been launched just more than seven years earlier in October1893. "I think this one should get us to America, Adam!"

"Right, it looks much better than the boat we came here on. This is more like it for crossing the ocean," Adam laughed.

Once again it was simply a matter of following the crowd as it obeyed signs, hand signals, and verbal commands in several languages for getting their names on the passenger list and boarding the ship. "Here's a line where the man is speaking German," said Adam. He and George queued up.

Then they reached the front of the line. "Name? How do you spell?" asked the man after inspecting their tickets.

"Welli, W-E-L-L-I," each replied.

"Nationality and extraction?" he asked.

"Hungarian, German extraction," they replied.

"What's the address of your contact in the United States?"

"212 Genesee Street, Trenton, New Jersey."

"Your occupations?"

"Policeman," each replied.

"Do you speak English?"

Since both answered "No," he wrote "Laborer" as occupation. "You are now listed as passengers on the ship manifest. When you reach New York you will be given numbered tags that correspond to this manifest. Attach them securely to your coat and don't lose them. They are important for processing you through Ellis Island."

Soon, they were boarding the ship, where a crew officer motioned single men toward the bow and men with families aft. They descended down into the "tween decks" area known as steerage. Each took a straw-filled mattress and placed it on a bunk, their home for the next several days. Adam and George looked around in the dimly lit area. "That smell, it reminds me of when one of the children gets sick," commented George.

"Better pray for good weather," laughed Adam. "I've heard that seasickness is terrible."

Perhaps a combination of chance, timing, George's prayer, and those of the other 900 steerage class passengers blessed their voyage. The sturdy *Kensington* crossed the Atlantic in just less than ten days, staying close to its fourteen-knot top cruising speed. There was very little fog and, more important, no icebergs. On the morning of May 23 the two cousins went up on deck with the other passengers to witness their arrival in the new world.

"Huge city!" exclaimed Adam.

"And look at that tall statue in the harbor. It must be the one we've been hearing about," added George.

Once the ship docked, the steerage class passengers were loaded onto a ferry boat that would take them to Ellis Island. Being crowded amidst the excited babble of different languages was in itself an experience.

"I hear German, Magyar, and Rumanian," George remarked.

"There are others. One of them has to be Italian, since we stopped in Naples. But there's another that I don't recognize, Greek perhaps," replied Adam.

After the ferry docked, the first stop was a huge baggage room where all passengers checked their bags. Traveling relatively light and without families, George and Adam quickly checked theirs and briskly climbed the stairs to the main hall. They spotted a sign indicating where the interpreters who spoke German were working.

"Your name is spelled W-E-L-L-I on the ship manifest. Is that correct?" asked the inspector.

"Yes," they replied.

"Why are you going to 212 Genesee Street in Trenton?"

"We will stay briefly with a family from the old country then join a group of workers that is going to Pittsburgh, Pennsylvania and Youngstown, Ohio," replied George.

The inspector smiled, saying, "They need healthy young men out there in the steel mills," and passed them on.

Then it was back to the baggage room to collect their luggage and onto another ferry boat to New Jersey, where they caught a train for Trenton.

"Well, the man at Ellis Island seemed satisfied that we weren't anarchists, didn't have any serious diseases, and would be able to support ourselves," remarked George.

Adam nodded, replying, "Yes, we made it through the process easily. But I saw an older man and his wife who might not. When they got to the top of the stairs, a man made large chalk marks on their clothing. One of the ship stewards told me a few days ago that if that happened, it meant you would be held for further examination."

"I saw how difficult it was for them getting up those stairs. It was sad to see. If they don't make it they will have to use the return trip parts of their steamship tickets and go back to the old country. I hope they got through the inspection."

When the train arrived in Trenton, they followed the directions they had been given and spent the night with Jacob Piller and his family, folks from Palanka they knew casually. Late the next day, Piller escorted them to the train station, where they saw a man holding a sign with the name of the company that had recruited them, an event that now seemed so long ago to both Adam and George. "This is the train that will take you out to Pittsburgh and Youngstown," he told them.

Once on the train the babble of different languages was again almost dizzying. They didn't hear any others speaking German but heard several conversations in Magyar.

The next morning George awoke with his back stiff from the hard, straight seat of the railway car. The sun was coming up and he had a view of steep, tree-covered rolling hills. Some of them were nearly mountains. "Adam, wake up. Look outside," he said.

Yawning, Adam stretched his back then looked out the window. "It doesn't look anything like Dunacseb or Palanka."

"It certainly doesn't. Such strange country," George observed.

Soon, the train pulled into a large city, stopping at the railway station. "This must be Pittsburgh. That's the first place we stop," said Adam.

They saw men getting off the car behind them and start walking into the station. But the doors to their car remained closed and soon the train was moving again. "Well, this must mean we're going to Youngstown," said George.

About two hours later, the train pulled into another city situated along a river and stopped at the station. The conductor came into the car and called "Youngstown, everybody off for Youngstown," motioning all the men in the car to the front doorway. George and Adam didn't understand anything but "Youngstown" but that was good enough for them. They had reached their destination.

They followed the group of men into the station, where they paused, not knowing what to do. There was no one to meet them so they sat down in the waiting room, confused and talking animatedly. Twenty minutes later, a man about the same age as George and Adam walked into the room and called out, "*Sprechen sie Deutsche?*"

George and Adam raised their hands, shouting, "*Ja! Ja!*" and quickly got up from their seats. No one else responded so it seemed they were the only German-speaking men in the group.

The man told them, "My name is Walter Keilman. Are you looking for work?"

"Yes, we are," replied Adam.

"Well, I'm not from a steel company. I'm a foreman at the Smith Brewery and I need a couple of strong, young men to help me keep the fires going there. We will pay you twelve dollars a week. Are you interested?"

Adam and George looked at each other and quickly said, "Yes." Meeting a personable man their age who also spoke their language was a good thing. And twelve dollars a week sounded like a fine wage to men who had been living on far less in the old country.

"Great," replied Walter then asked, "You probably don't have a place to stay, do you?"

"No."

"Then pick up your bags and come with me. I'll take you first to see the brewery, where you start work Monday morning. Then, I'll take you to a rooming house just a few blocks from there that's run by a nice German woman named Aggie Schmidt. She's also a very good cook and makes breakfast and supper for her boarders. She even packs a lunch for the midday meal and does laundry. How does all this sound?" asked Walter.

"Wonderful!" they exclaimed.

After loading their luggage into his buggy, Walter drove away from the station, then west on Federal Street. To George and Adam the sight was awesome. Three-story brick buildings housing all types of businesses flanked the street. But the line of poles was most curious. "All those poles with wires strung between them, are they for the telegraph?" they asked.

"Some are for the telegraph but most are for the *telephone*," Walter replied. "You can talk over the wire. Many people in town have them."

"That must cost a lot of money. Such a luxury," said George, shaking his head.

"It's two dollars a month," replied Walter.

"How many people live in Youngstown?" asked Adam.

"About 45,000 right now, I think. More people are moving here all the time and going to work in the steel plants."

By now their gaze had shifted downward. "Those tracks, do trains run down the middle of the street here?" asked Adam.

"It's a lot like a train only it's called a trolley. That's what many people ride to get around the city. But the trolley cars don't burn coal. They run on electricity," Walter replied.

"We've heard of electric lights. But electricity can provide power? How?" George was incredulous.

"Look straight overhead. See those wires? The trolley is attached to them and that provides power to run the car's motor," explained Walter. "Just a few more blocks and we'll be at the brewery."

Shortly they reached a large brick building and turned in. "This is the main building where the brewing process goes on. It used to be a tannery but John Smith converted it to a brewery when he moved here from England more than fifty years ago."

The building was an imposing three stories high, 136 feet wide and 40 feet deep. The arched windows and doors lent a fine architectural touch.[14] "This is where the malt rooms, malt kilns, barley and malt storerooms, brewing room, and barreling rooms are located. Underneath the building are the vaults for stocking ale. The ceilings of two are arched in order to help maintain an even temperature, winter or summer. You'll be working in the smaller building around back," Walter told them as he guided the buggy to the rear of the main building.

He continued, "Tomorrow is Sunday, which is a day off. You can get settled and then come here Monday at 7 a.m. to start work. Now it's off to see Aggie Schmidt."

Four blocks from the brewery, Walter stopped in front of a huge, white three-story house that would be George and Adam's home for the next year. Their long odyssey, which started with a buggy ride, had finally ended with a buggy ride. Sandwiched in between were rides in a covered wagon, two ferry boats, and three trains, and the centerpieces of their travels, two ocean voyages. It had been quite a journey.

CHAPTER 8
BEAUTIFUL OHIO

Everybody breathing dirt, eating dirt — they call it "pay dirt," for Youngstown clean would be Youngstown out of work.

Frank Bohn, economist and author, 1915[15]

Walter Keilman led George and Adam to the rooming house and knocked. Shortly the door opened and a woman stood, framed by the doorway. "Walter, it's been a long time since I've seen you!" she exclaimed.

"Aggie, I heard you have some vacancies so I brought you a couple of men who will be going to work at the brewery on Monday. This is Adam Welli and George Welli. They are Germans who just moved here from Hungary."

"Why, thank you for thinking of me, Walter," she replied. "My goodness, they look like they're fresh from the old country, nothing but skin and bones. I'll have to fatten them up with extra food for a while," she added, then broke into a hearty laugh, which complemented her full face and buxom figure. There were ample touches of gray in her dark brown hair, that of someone in her early fifties. But her demeanor was that of a younger woman.

"Come in George, Adam. I'll show you around. Goodbye Walter, thank you again," she said as he took his leave. "Here's the parlor off to the right. It doesn't get used much. To the left is my nice big dining room. See, there's room at the table for twelve. What type of work will you be doing at the brewery?"

"We will be firing the furnace in the boiler room," Adam replied.

"Oh my! That's hard work and very dirty. I have a room back of the kitchen that I call my cleanup room. For men who have really dirty jobs there is a back door they can enter when they come home in the evening. I keep soap and tubs of water there for washing up. Now, let's go up to the second floor. I have a large room with two beds on the east side of the house that will be a good place for you. There are two other rooms like it on the second floor. On the third floor it's one big long room with six beds."

She showed them to their room. And it was as she said, large with two single beds and two chests of drawers, one of them with a mirror.

"Do you still have families in Europe?" Aggie asked.

"Yes, we plan on having them come to America a year from now," replied George.

"That's good. A man shouldn't be without family for too long. When you write home you can give me the letters and I'll put them out for the postal carrier. You must be starving by now. Unpack your things and come downstairs. We'll have something to eat," she said, closing the door as she left.

Finally, Adam and George would be able to unpack their belongings. For someone from the old country, this seemed like upscale living. Room, board including a lunch to take to work, and laundry for three dollars a week, very fair.

The next day George and Adam used the afternoon to get acquainted with their new hometown. They walked east past the brewery at 507-

533 Federal Street, fascinated by all the homes and businesses. This area of Youngstown, shortly after the turn of the twentieth century, has been described as both a charming and interesting place, one midway between the "good old days" and modern times.[16]

At 7:00 Monday morning George and Adam reported to the brewery, ready to begin their new jobs in a new country. Walter Keilman gave them the basic instructions: Keep the fire even and don't let it get too high by shoveling in too much coal. But don't let it get too low either. Take turns on the shoveling. Bank the fire at night (except Saturday) so you won't have to build a new fire the next morning. Haul out the ashes in the morning before stoking the furnace. Clean the soot from the furnace and flue on Monday mornings before starting a new fire.

"It's hard but good, honest work, George," Adam commented at noon as they ate the generous meals Aggie had provided.

"Yes, and it pays pretty well. I hope to start sending some money home to Anna."

By Saturday the newness of the job was gone. "Adam, tell me something funny," said George as he shoveled coal into the furnace's insatiable maw when it was Adam's turn to rest.

"Hmm, I guess this reminds me of that time when the grist mill burned down. Sister Josephine and Sister Marguerite were taking turns pulling the church bell rope to sound the alarm. Now we're the ones who are taking turns." Both laughed at the old memory.

"That reminds me. We'd better write letters home tonight," said George.

June 14, 1901

My darling Anna,

Adam and I are settled in America now. We are in Youngstown, Ohio where we work at a brewery. It's called the Smith Brewing Company.

"Smith" is an English name but our foreman is a German named Walter Keilman. He is about the same age as me and Adam.

When our ship docked in New York, we went through immigrant processing at a place called Ellis Island. Then we caught a train to Trenton, New Jersey and spent a day with the Piller family, who used to live in Palanka. The next day we caught another train that took us out to Pittsburgh, Pennsylvania but it didn't let us off so we had to go on to Youngstown. We thought we would be working at a steel mill but we met *Herr* Keilman at the train depot and he offered us jobs at the brewery. It pays $12 a week which seems like a good wage. It's strange, I come to America and end up working at a brewery just as my father did in Bernau.

We are living in a boarding house just a short walk from the brewery. Aggie Schmidt, the landlady, is very kind. She treats me and Adam like her sons. We have two hot meals a day and she packs dinner pails for us to take to the brewery. She also does our laundry. We are being well-taken care of and so are the other ten men who live there. Aggie has two women who help her make the meals and do the laundry.

There are modern things here that you won't believe until you see them. They have devices you can talk over called telephones. You can call someone many miles away or they can call you and talk over a wire. And they have trains that run down the streets on tracks that people can ride to go to a place that's too far away to walk. But these trains aren't pulled by horses and don't run on steam. They run on electricity.

They also have electric street lights instead of gas lights, although the electric company doesn't turn them on if the almanac says that the moon is supposed to shine. But when there are clouds, you can't see the moon and the streets are very dark on those nights. Walter Keilman said many people are unhappy about that.

There will be much to get used to living here but I believe it's good that we came.

Give my love to Mat, Katherine and Annie, also to your Mother. I think of you all the time and will be so happy when you can come to America.

All my love,

George

The next day being Sunday, George and Adam again planned to explore Youngstown. As they were about to leave Aggie asked them, "How do you like America by now?"

"It is much different from the old country but I like it very much. The work is hard but the pay is good and you are taking very good care of us," replied Adam.

"Why, thank you!" she exclaimed.

"Your food is delicious. And I really like the big meals you make for us to take to work," added George.

"Well, thank you again. But you know what I'm doing with those dinner pails you take to the brewery?" she asked.

Both men shook their heads and Aggie went on. "I'm just doing what President McKinley promised when he was running for re-election last year. His slogan was 'Four years more of the full dinner pail.' Well, if the president says to feed our workers properly that's what I'll do," she said, breaking into a hearty laugh. She paused upon seeing their puzzled expressions, and then explained. "In this country there is a presidential election every four years. There are two parties, the Republicans and the Democrats. Even the president who's in office has to run for re-election when his term is up. President McKinley is a Republican and he's also from Ohio. He defeated the Democrat William Jennings Bryan in the last election by promising full dinner pails if re-elected."

"I see now," said Adam, breaking into a chuckle. "That's much different from what we have been used to. In Austria-Hungary, Franz Joseph was the emperor before I was born and he's still the emperor."

"And when he dies his son will take his place," added George.

And so the two cousins settled into a routine, feeding coal to the furnace six days a week, church on Sunday and letters home. Months passed. One Saturday in late December, Walter Keilman came into the furnace room. In addition to the daily banter and news about the brewery he extended an invitation.

"Next week is Christmas and we should do a little celebrating. Tonight after you've cleaned up, I'll come by Aggie's. You've been really good employees and I want to buy you a couple of beers at Scotty's Bar on Phelps Street. There's only one condition: It has to be Tip Top beer. We only drink what we brew ourselves!"

Adam and George laughed, agreeing that a couple of schooners of Tip Top would taste mighty good. Scotty's was legendary as a place that also served great food, some of it free, along with its five-cent schooners of beer.

Several weeks after Christmas, George received a letter from Anna.

February 10, 1902

My dearest George,

I must start this letter with very sad news. Our beautiful daughter Katherine died of diphtheria last week. Mother and I tried our best but there was nothing we could do to save her. Many other children in Dunacseb have died of it this winter. It will be so sad leaving part of our family behind when we come to America.

The blessing is that Mat and Annie haven't caught the disease. They are very healthy and send their love. They are doing well in school and Mat is doing a good job as an altar boy. He has mastered Latin and that was very difficult. But he enjoys learning so much history.

I am glad you sent those directions and instructions for our trip to America in May. Eva and I and the children are all looking forward to it. We also look forward to seeing you and Adam once again. Our separation seems to have been forever. But it will soon end.

Your brother Joseph has been very helpful to me and Eva. So has Augusta. They send their love and regards.

Your loving wife,

Anna

Walter Keilman walked briskly into the furnace room. "George, here's a telegram for you," he said.

George tore it open and read it aloud: "May 13, 1902. Our train arrives Youngstown tomorrow at 4:00 p.m. (signed) Anna and Eva."

"Great news!" exclaimed Adam.

"Is it ever. They made it!" George added.

"Good for you both!" said Walter. "I'll get someone to come in and spell you at noon so that you can leave work early. You need to move your belongings out of Aggie's place into the apartments you've rented, right?"

"Yes, thank you. That will be very helpful," said George.

The next day Adam and George watched as the train pulled into the station. As passengers got off, the cacophony of different languages reminded them of their own arrival nearly a year earlier. "There they are!" exclaimed Adam.

Anna, Mat, Annie, and Anna's mother, Katherine Welsch, stepped off the train. Right behind them was Eva along with her daughters Anne and Elizabeth. George and Adam ran to greet them. After hugging Anna, George turned to Mat and Annie. Annie gave him a hug but

Mat extended his hand. "It's good to see you, Father," he said in a surprisingly adult manner.

George smiled and shook Mat's hand. "You've grown taller in the past year."

Finally, the greetings had been extended all around in both families. "Where do we go now?" asked Eva.

"We have an upstairs apartment in a house. George and Anna have one in a house just two blocks from us," replied Adam.

"The brewery lent us a team and wagon to haul the trunks and suitcases to our new homes," added George. "We should start loading up."

The two families adjusted to life in Youngstown. The summer seemed to pass far too quickly and soon it was time for Mat and Annie to start school.

"You have both been through primary school once but you will have to do it again in order to learn English," George told them.

"Since I learned Latin maybe learning English will be easier," Mat replied hopefully.

The family grew in size. In February 1903 Anna gave birth to a boy, whom they named Michael. In April 1905, she gave birth to a daughter and they decided to name her Mary. Anna's mother, Katherine Welsch, ever the competent midwife, handled both deliveries.

Mat and Annie now spoke English fluently and read voraciously. "Mat, these books you bring home, they all seem to have cattle, horses, and men with guns on the covers. Are they for school?" asked George.

"No, Father. They are what many of the boys like to read for fun. They're about the Wild West. My friend Billy Craig's father buys them often and then they lend them to me. The books are very interesting and exciting. This one is about Bat Masterson."

"Who is he?"

"A famous marshal out in Dodge City, Kansas with another marshal named Wyatt Earp."

"I see. Well, I guess stories about lawmen are probably very interesting," smiled George, recalling the days when he and Adam were policemen.

Life for the family continued to be simple but pleasant in 1905. Late in the year, however, George developed a persistent cough. It was especially bad on Mondays, the day when he and Adam had to clean the furnace at the brewery before building a new fire. At night, he began sleeping propped up with two pillows.

"George, your cough just won't seem to go away. Even sleeping sitting up doesn't seem to help you," said Anna, deeply concerned.

"I know. I've been taking Dr. James Cherry Tar Cough Syrup, almost a bottle every week. It helped at first but now it doesn't seem to do much good, except to make me drowsy."

"Maybe you should go to a doctor," Anna advised, now even more concerned.

"I'll ask Walter Keilman if he knows a good one."

The next Thursday George visited a doctor who practiced from his home nearby. After listening to George's labored breathing and to his heart he asked, "Where do you work?"

"At the Smith Brewery."

"Doing what?" asked the doctor, seeming quite puzzled.

"My cousin and I work in the boiler room firing the furnace."

"How long have you worked there?"

"Since May 1901."

"And when did your cough begin?"

"About four months ago."

The doctor frowned. "You seem to have developed a very bad case of asthma. I usually see this in men who work at the steel mills."

"What can I do about it?" Concern began to flood George's thinking.

"You need to get away from Youngstown. In addition to all the smoke, soot, and ashes you have at work there's lots of smoke from the trains that run all over the city. I'm talking about real coal-burning railroad engines, not the trolleys. And the steel mills are also adding smoke and dirt to the air — more every month it seems," replied the doctor sympathetically.

"But I have a family. Where could we go?"

"You need to move to a higher, dryer climate. Go out west."

"What would happen if I stay here?"

The doctor looked at him intently and put a hand on his shoulder. "You need to move to a higher, dryer climate that doesn't have all this smoke around. Otherwise it's likely you'll be dead in six months. That's how bad your asthma seems to be. One more question, do you smoke?"

"Yes, I smoke a pipe but not cigars."

"Well then, there's one more thing. Throw that pipe away. Stay just as far away from tobacco as possible."

"Anna, the doctor had very bad news," George said upon returning home. Then he told her the diagnosis and recommendation.

"That's terrible. I was afraid you had a very serious problem. But where could we move?"

"I've heard there is free land available in some parts of the west. Perhaps someone at work will know something about that. I'll ask Walter Keilman. I hate the thought of having to move again, especially to such remote country. But if I die here, what would happen to you and the children? It's better to keep trying than just give up. If we have to move again in order to survive, that's what we'll do."

Walter Keilman listened intently as George told him of the doctor's diagnosis and recommendation. "We had a similar problem a few years ago. I'll speak to the owners," he said. "I'm really sorry this has happened. Both you and Adam have been such good employees."

The next day Keilman came into the furnace room shortly after the workday began. "Come outside with me, George," he invited.

As they walked around the building area, Keilman told him, "There was a man who worked here for several years who developed the same problem you have. His name is Joseph Udry and he moved out to the Oklahoma Territory, a place in the far western part, where there was homestead land available."

"What does 'homestead' mean? Is that the same as free land?"

"There's a law in this country that permits a man to claim vacant land as his own by just living on it. We suggest you write to Joe Udry and see if land is still available there. If you decide to move, the brewery will pay you $600 to help make a new start. What do you think?" asked Keilman.

"Thank you very much!" For the first time in several months George felt relieved and his hopes renewed. "The $600 sounds quite fair. That's about a year's wages. I think we could make it with that financial help. I'll write to Mr. Udry and find out what it's like out there now."

"The owners reminded me that this is a family-owned business. We try to help our employees when we can," said Keilman, extending his hand.

On a warm Sunday afternoon in late April 1906, there was an atmosphere of excitement at George and Anna's apartment. Adam and Eva and their children were there as George shared what he had learned from Joseph Udry. "He says 'Come on out. Free land is still available.' That's really good news!" exclaimed George.

"How would you get there? Will all of you move at the same time?" asked Adam.

"He says that he moved out on the train to a town called Goodwell in Oklahoma Territory. His wife came out later with their furniture and other belongings," George replied.

"How did she move with all their belongings?"

"Hmm, his letter doesn't say. We'll have to ask about that at the railroad station, I think," George replied, then continued, "What about you and Eva? Do you want to come too?"

Adam shifted in his chair and glanced at Eva. "We've spoken about that, George. While we hate the thought of being separated after so many years of being together, we've decided it would be better for us to stay here. I can't stand the thought of farming again. Remember how hard your dad and my dad had to work in the old country? And we just don't want to live in such remote country. Coming to America and a town like Youngstown was real progress for us and it would be a shame to give it up."

There was a melancholy silence that Anna finally broke. "It will be sad being apart but I can understand, truly I can. Why go back to living in an area that may be more primitive than Dunacseb when you don't have to?" Then, in tears, she hugged Eva, saying, "But we will miss you so much. You've always been such good friends as well as family." After Adam and Eva left, Mat asked, "Father, does this really mean we're moving out west?"

"Yes, it does. And I think that since you speak English it will be good to have you go with me. Your mother and grandmother and the other children will come out later. They have Annie to speak English for them."

Mat was beaming. "Moving out west! Wait 'til I see Billy Craig! All right to tell him?"

George nodded, smiling at Mat's enthusiasm. After Mat ran out Anna said, "George, there's something I must tell you."

Still smiling about Mat he jested, "We're going to have another baby?"

"Yes, I think so."

"Really? Really! When?"

"Sometime in November I think."

"Oh, that means we'd better have you and the children and your mother move out there just as soon as we can get settled. Mat and I will go to the train station tomorrow and make arrangements."

George and Mat went to the Baltimore and Ohio train station the following afternoon. Except for the agent the place was deserted. "Good afternoon, gentlemen. May I help you with something?" he asked.

"Yes sir, we're moving out to the Oklahoma Territory and need tickets," said Mat.

"What part?" asked the agent.

"Goodwell. It's very far west, I think."

The agent squinted at a large map on the wall. "Well, it certainly is! It's almost as far west as you can get and still be in the territory. Much farther west and you'd be in New Mexico Territory. How many tickets will you need?"

"Two tickets for my father and me. We want to leave in two weeks. Then my mother and the rest of the family would move out there in two or three months. They will be bringing our furniture and other belongings. Is there some way they could come out there on the train?"

"There sure is. Here son, take this paper and pencil. You'll want to write some of this down. Now, the tickets for you and your dad will be very easy to take care of. They will be twenty dollars each. That's all the way from Youngstown to Goodwell," he said after consulting his fare book.

"Now for the rest of your family there's what we call immigrant cars. They have plain seats or benches but you can rent straw-filled mattresses for sleeping on. You can put them on the seat or on the floor between the seats. There's a stove at one end of the car that they can fire up if it's cold and they can cook meals on it. And there's a toilet at the other end of the car. How many people will there be?"

"My mother, grandmother, two sisters, and little brother."

"All right, let's just see here. Five people, five mattresses, and all your household goods. Is that right?" asked the agent.

"Yes sir."

The agent did several calculations as Mat and George watched intently. "We can send your family and their goods all the way to Goodwell for $150. Their car will be switched to the Rock Island in Chicago and they won't even have to get off. How does that sound?"

Mat translated the information into German for George. George thought for a bit and smiled. "*Ja!*" he exclaimed. Then he took $190 from his money belt and handed it to Mat, who paid the agent.

"Very good. Here are the tickets for you and your dad and the reservation for the immigrant car. Tell your mother that we will need ten days notice when she wants to leave. That way we can have the car here and ready for them the day of their departure."

Mat was busy making notes as the agent told him, "There's one more thing. You and your dad will have to change trains in Chicago. Ever been there?"

"No, we never have."

"Well, the B&O that you catch here in Youngstown goes into Grand Central Station in Chicago. Then, you have to catch a Rock

Island train for the rest of the trip out to Oklahoma. The 'Rock' leaves from the La Salle Street Station. That means you'll have to get from Grand Central to La Salle. Here's the best way to do it." He paused to let Mat catch up with his note-taking and then continued, "When you get off the train, go out the main entrance and look for a large coach with a Parmelee sign on it. They are owned by the Parmelee Transfer Company, which has contracts with the railroads to move passengers among all the train stations in Chicago. You can trust them with your luggage and to take you to the right place. Don't talk to anyone else or give your bags to anyone else outside the station. Big cities are full of thieves and renegades who may try to steal your money and luggage. Part of the Parmelee Company's job is to protect travelers from such people. Got all this down?" he asked, smiling at Mat.

Two weeks later George and Mat were at the B&O Station waiting for the early morning train. Anna and the other children and Adam and Eva were there to see them off.

"Anna, I hope this is the last time we have to be separated," said George, hugging her and then the younger children.

"Be careful," she cautioned.

Then it was a sad "goodbye" to Adam and Eva. "I hope we get to see you again sometime. We've been through some tough times together but we've had some good times, too," George told them.

"I do too, dear cousin, dear friend," said Adam as he gripped George's hand tightly. "We will look out for Anna and the children and help them get to the train when it's time to move."

Soon the train pulled away from the station. George and Mat waved to the family until they could no longer see them. They looked out the window as the train reached the outskirts of Youngstown, then open country.

After several hours they arrived in Chicago, pulling into Grand Central Station. Mat took a quick look at his notes from their meeting with the station agent in Youngstown. "Father, we go out the main entrance and look for a large coach that says 'Parmelee' on it," said Mat as they descended from the train.

Once outside, they quickly spotted a large Parmelee coach hitched to a team of huge white horses. "Where are you going?" asked the driver.

"We have to go to the La Salle Street Station to catch the Rock Island," said Mat.

"Climb aboard. That's our first stop."

They sat in the Rock Island car for nearly an hour before the train left the station. George relaxed, happy that they had made their connection without a hitch. "Well done, Mat!" he said, clapping him on the shoulder.

Mat was impatient, anxious to get moving. Finally the train departed and eventually reached the outskirts of Chicago. Now they were truly headed for the west.

"What did your friend Billy Craig think about us moving?"

"He said he wished he could go with us. He even gave me a book that I could keep. His father said it was all right."

"What is this one about?"

Mat opened his valise and took out the book. "This one is about Buffalo Bill."

PART TWO:

HOME IN OKLAHOMA, 1906-1920

INTRODUCTION

In the Compromise of 1850, the state of Texas ceded to the U.S. government a vast region claimed by Texas since its days as a Republic. By 1854 the land was apportioned among the new territories of New Mexico and Kansas. An early proposal for Kansas Territory's southern boundary was to have it run along the northernmost Texas state line, continuing eastward along the same line of latitude (36° 30'N) to join the Arkansas-Missouri boundary (the 1820 Missouri Compromise Line). Under objections that much Cherokee land would thus be swallowed, the Kansas boundary instead was moved northward in 1854 to 37°N. This left, between 36° 30'N and 37°N, a rectangle of federal public land west of the Cherokee Outlet, north of the Texas Panhandle, east of New Mexico Territory, and south of Kansas and, after 1861, Colorado territories.

This 34.5-mile-by-167-mile rectangle was unattached to any state or territorial government from 1850 to 1890. It was identified on most government maps as "Public Land" or "Public Land Strip." After a federal judge ruled that no one could own land in the strip, it became popularly known as "No Man's Land." In 1890 Oklahoma Territory was organized and the strip was added to it. Oklahoma became the forty-sixth state in 1907; thereafter, the strip was known as the Oklahoma Panhandle.

Dr. Kenneth R. Turner, Custodian of Collections
No Man's Land Historical Society

* * *

Notwithstanding the Oklahoma Panhandle's unique history, its residents shared a need common to citizens everywhere in the United States, the desire for a social life. However, schooling for young people usually ended at the eighth grade, shortly before most became interested in the opposite sex. Further, because of the isolation, they couldn't count only on chance meetings at the water well or some cattle chute. Country dances every Saturday night held at various homesteads or ranches, sometimes in a house but often in a barn, provided the best pairing opportunities. These and most other dances in the area lasted all night long, not ending until sunrise.

Folks often traveled twenty miles for a Saturday-night dance — fifty miles for a special holiday dance. Here, travel could be hazardous even during daylight hours over roads that often were mere trails with deep, bone-jarring ruts. The romantic notion that "the horse knows the way home" may have been valid in towns and cities back East with their gaslight-enhanced streets. However, in an area with prairie dog holes, wolves, coyotes, and rattlesnakes, all the romance went out of "a moonlight ride home."

In the West as well as other parts of the country, Saturday dances were also held in the towns, many lasting through the night. These were in halls, often owned by a local government unit, civic group, or veterans' organization. The dance hall described in Chapter 14 is a composite of such facilities.

The "all-night dances," whether in the country or in town, were major social events. For many people, they were the most significant social events of their lives. "Why, that's where I met your grandfather (or grandmother)" would become increasingly fond reminiscences as the decades passed.

In these days before television and radio, newspapers were the primary source of information, keeping readers informed of world, national, and local news. There were a few dailies but many, especially in the smaller towns, were published weekly. An issue might contain articles on subjects ranging from the Great War raging in Europe and the revolution in Mexico to small local items reporting how well the Saturday dance was attended. Some papers also included serialized adventure stories or, during the Great War, propaganda pieces. Panhandle residents often passed newspapers along to friends and neighbors to read and many a conversation began with "I see in the papers where . . .."

Stan Welli, author

CHAPTER 9
ON THE BRINK

Chapter LXXV. – An Act to secure Homestead to actual Settlers on Public Domain.

Be it enacted by the Senate and House of Representatives of the United States of America in assembled, That any person who is the head of a family, or who has arrived at the age of twenty-one years, and is a citizen of the United States, or who shall have filed his declaration intention to become such, as required by the naturalization laws of the United States, and who has never borne arms against the United States Government or given aid and comfort to its enemies, shall, from and after the first of January, eighteen hundred and sixty-three, be entitled to enter one quarter section (160 acres) or less quantity of unappropriated public lands . . .

Homestead Act of 1862

When the Rock Island train pulled into Liberal, Kansas, all the passengers except George and Mat got off. The conductor helped the three well-dressed women down the steps of the passengers' car, saying, "Ladies, enjoy your stay in Liberal."

"Why, thank you! We're going to a friend's wedding," one of them replied.

Shortly, the final leg of their journey began with the familiar lurch as the train left the depot. George was now as intrigued as Mat in seeing the country through which they were traveling. After a few minutes the conductor stopped by Mat's seat. "Right now we're crossing into Oklahoma Territory. If you look out the window on the left, you'll soon be seeing Tyrone. That was the final destination for many cattle drives. Off to the south of Tyrone is a big well — Shade's Well is how it's known. The cattlemen watered their herds there while waiting for them to be shipped out on the Rock Island."

Mat looked out, trying to visualize the scene. "You said earlier that those drives stopped in 1901. That's only five years ago!"

"That's right. Five years ago this was the end of the line for the Rock Island. A lot has changed since then."

Soon the train pulled into what seemed a relatively large town for the area. "Guymon!" called the conductor even though there were no passengers getting off.

To Mat it looked like a town out of a novel: dusty streets, buildings with false fronts, saddle horses and wagon teams standing in front of them. One large sign read "El Paso Saloon" and another, "Star Mercantile." There were also signs for a hardware store, a barbershop, a restaurant, and another saloon. Mat took a deep breath. *We really are in the West.*

"Goodwell is the next stop," announced the conductor with a broad smile. "If you thought Guymon looked western, just wait 'til you see Goodwell."

"How will we know Mr. Udry when we get there?" asked Mat.

"He said in his letter that he'd have a sign with his name on it," George replied.

The train quickly made the last ten miles to Goodwell. "Here you are. Good luck son," said the conductor, extending his hand as they left the train. "Say, what's your name?"

"Mat Welli. My father's name is George."

"Good luck, George. I hope you do well out here."

George smiled and shook hands, replying, *Danke*, after hearing Mat's quick translation.

"My name is Emil Hatchett. That's with a 'T' in the middle and two at the end," said the conductor. "We'll be taking on water here. Your first look at Goodwell will tell you why it has that name. The Rock Island put in the well but lots of folks here who don't have windmills can use it too. It's been a pleasure visiting with you, Mat. So long now!"

As George and Mat walked toward the depot entrance they saw a tall man holding a sign that read "Udry." "You must be George Welli. I'm Joe Udry."

"We're very happy to meet you. This is my son Mat. Don't know what we would have done if you hadn't been here for us," replied George.

"My wagon is over there near those waiting in line for water. Let's put your bags in it and then we'll go out to my place. But before we leave town you should get regular hats for yourself and the boy. They don't have to be fancy, just something like mine with a broad brim that keeps off the sun. It burns bright and hot out here." Joe took off his hat, offering it to George to inspect. His dark brown, curly hair seemed a contradiction to his sharp features, which were set off with a large, dagger-like nose. He appeared to be about the same age as George, perhaps a few years older.

The visit to a store afforded George and Mat a good look at their new hometown. In only its third year of existence, Goodwell was a collection of business buildings on its main street. The street itself was little more than a trail that was alternately dusty or muddy and rutted, depending upon the season. There were boardwalks instead of brick sidewalks and there were wooden benches in front of the stores for customers who wanted to take their ease. Mat was fascinated by the array of merchandise in the store. It had everything from tools and farm implements to clothing, groceries, patent medicines, dishware, and firearms. Even the customers were interesting. They dressed to cope with the sun and other hostile elements of the territory. All the men wore hats and boots, while the women wore deep, shade-producing bonnets and long dresses.

After George and Mat selected hats, Joe pointed to a used double-barrel shotgun on display. "That's another necessity out here. I know the man who used to own that one. He took good care of all his guns and equipment. For ten dollars you'll have a gun that's as good as new."

Shortly they were loaded into Joe's wagon, George and Mat sporting new hats and carrying a shotgun. As the wagon moved southward out of town, they could see that much of Goodwell was still a collection of shacks, dugouts, and tents.

"How far is it to your homestead, Mr. Udry?" asked Mat.

"It's a little over three miles southwest," Joe replied.

"You said a shotgun is a necessity out here. Why is that?" asked George.

"This is still a tough place to live. If you look under that blanket in back of the wagon, you'll see my shotgun, which I always take with me. First of all there's lots of wolves and rattlesnakes around. And this is open range, which means that cattle can go anywhere. Once you get settled and have some hay or fodder stacked up for your own horses and cows, you got to keep the range cattle away or they will truly eat you out of house and home, meaning that your own horses and cattle will starve. And if they starve, you starve! Most of the time you don't have to kill them, just pepper them with a little rock salt or birdshot. There's also several herds of wild horses living around here. Some of the old-timers say, 'Those wild ponies are sometimes real partial to fodder and hay.' So, you have to keep them away too," he said, shaking a finger for emphasis.

Joe continued, "There's one more thing. I have a second shotgun that I leave at the house for Rosina, my wife. There's still some bad types around and sometimes their intentions aren't the best. So, I taught her how to shoot just in case she has to protect herself when I'm gone to town or out in the field."

"Has she ever had to use it?" George asked, thinking ahead to when Anna and the children would arrive.

"Only on rattlesnakes so far. They like to come up around the house and the garden for shade in the summer. She's killed three of them in the time we've been here."

About two miles south of town they left the high plain that surrounded Goodwell and began a gradual but noticeable descent. Occasionally Udry applied the wagon's brake to keep from pushing the horses.

"Mr. Udry, is this a valley?" asked Mat.

"Around here they call them breaks. They're too gradual and not deep enough to be valleys. Look off a couple of miles ahead and you'll see that it gets flat again when we climb out of the break. The land down here isn't much good for farming. It's a lot better for grazing cattle."

George looked around at the grassland through which they were traveling. It was dotted with occasional clumps of sagebrush and soapweed. "Strange country," he mumbled. Continuing, he told Joe, "You speak German the same way we do. Where are you from?"

"Austria-Hungary, a town on the Danube named Apatin," replied Udry.

"That's not far from where we used to live, Dunacseb, just east of Palanka on the Danube," said George, continuing with, "As I said in my letter, I had to come out here because of asthma. You came for the same reason, right?"

"Yes, and it was a good move. It took close to a year but the coughing finally stopped and I was able to breathe easily again," replied Joe.

George smiled broadly. "That's good to know, really good!"

After traveling up out of the break they were once again on the high plain. Soon, they reached a small frame house, where Udry lived. There was a sizeable barn and there were several smaller buildings for pigs and chickens. George and Mat could see that Joe had prospered in the three years since moving here. He had four wagons of varying size, age, and condition as well as farm implements. The pasture adjoining the barn held more cattle and horses than they could count. And there was the all-important windmill, the source that supplied one of the most critical needs of homesteaders and ranchers as well as their livestock. Two large shepherd dogs ran out to greet them, sniffing at George and Mat but wagging their tails.

"Looks like you've done pretty well out here," George observed. For George, who had spent twelve years working as a policeman and five as a brewery fireman, the number of buildings, wagons, implements, and livestock required for successful homesteading, the sheer size of the operation was reason to marvel.

"Thank you. But it was pretty tough the first couple of years. Rosina and I weren't sure we could make it. We were right on the brink of failure and starvation. Once we got the windmill put in things got better. Having to haul water is a real nuisance. It takes so much time and it limits the number of horses and cattle you can own. I sure wouldn't want to go back to those days. Now, come on inside and meet Rosina."

They walked into the house and were struck by the fact that it was all one very large room. One corner served as a kitchen area with a stove for cooking and heating, a freestanding cabinet, table, and four chairs. Grouped around the cabinet were milk pails and a butter churn. Two other corners served as bedroom areas. Assorted chairs and kerosene lamps were strategically placed. In the remaining corner there was a large, heavy table piled with newspapers, bridle and harness parts, a few odd-looking rocks, and some items unrecognizable to Mat and George. Another shotgun was on a rack above the table. With the windows open a breeze blew in freely, providing comfort despite the hot sun that was beaming down.

"I'm really happy to meet you, George. You too, Mat," said Rosina after Joe made the introductions. "We're here all by ourselves so it gets lonely at times."

"You have no children?" asked George.

"Yes, we have three boys but they are all grown. Joe lives in southern Missouri. John and Frank are a little closer. They live in Kansas in a town named Iuka," she replied.

"Frank was an officer in the Hungarian army, stationed in Budapest. He moved to America just a few years ago," added Joe.

"Let's sit down and eat," invited Rosina.

Placing their hats on the worktable, George and Mat quickly sat down at the dinner table. It had been nearly four days since their last hot meal and they were on second helpings of ham, potatoes and gravy, beets, greens, and radishes before they felt like having dinner conversation. Hot baked bread thickly spread with fresh butter set off the meal and Mat was on his third slice.

Rosina was pleased. "I like to see men with good appetites," she laughed.

"This is all so good, Mrs. Udry!" exclaimed Mat.

George nodded his agreement, smiling inwardly. *She's like a young Aggie Schmidt back in Youngstown!*

"I'm sorry that these are last year's beets and potatoes," she apologized. "It will be a few more weeks before this year's crops are ready. Mmmm, there's nothing tastes as good as new potatoes. Now, save room for apple pie."

Once the dinner was finished, it was time for more serious talk. "What land is available for homesteading?" asked George.

"There are several quarters nearby that are vacant. And there's a place about two miles east where the owner is getting ready to give up. His wife died so he's moving back East," advised Joe.

"You mean it already has a house on it?" asked George.

"Yes, and it looks to be about the same size as this one. Also, the land there is good since it's up on the plain, not down in the breaks where some of the other unclaimed quarters are. I'll take you there in the morning if you want to see it."

"That sounds good. I want the rest of the family to come out as soon as possible. My Anna is expecting another baby sometime next fall. In addition, her mother lives with us and there are three other children. So, land with a house already on it would be a big advantage," said George. "Tell me, Joe, how is it you know so much about what's going on around here?"

"When I used to haul water from town, I got used to meeting people, learning what's going on from notices put up in the stores, and from reading the newspapers. The papers report almost everything that's even close to being news, and sometimes people have a public sale of their livestock and implements when they decide to give up their claims. Would you hand me that stack of newspapers, son?"

Mat took the papers off the table and handed them to Joe. "These are in English," he observed.

"Yes, I learned it when we lived in Ohio. Now, let me read you some items," he said, translating them into German.

Early the next morning Joe, George, and Mat drove two miles east to the land Joe told them about, where the homesteader was giving up his claim and moving away. It was the beginning of a perfect day as the sunrise was unimpeded by clouds. A few jackrabbits scurried about in grass that was still wet with dew. Occasionally a meadowlark burst into song. "Mr. Udry, what are those strange looking plants growing in that field?" asked Mat.

"That's broomcorn. It's an important crop around here. You plant it in rows and when it matures, you go along with a knife and cut off the stalks. Then you have to bale the stalks and take them to Guymon. One problem with broomcorn is that the market price goes up and down so much. You never know for sure what it will bring. Some people are also raising wheat since it does very well here."

"Wheat? That's what my father and his brother raised in Austria-Hungary," commented George. "It was a lot of hard work, broadcasting the seed by hand, covering it with a harrow, and then finally cutting it with a scythe."

"They've developed machinery pulled by horses that do that here," replied Joe. "That makes wheat a very good cash crop, as long as a man has the machinery."

"There's another thing. I was wondering what you use for fuel around here. There's no wood or coal nearby."

"Oh yes. Well, we burn cow chips. They're all over the place what with all the ranches around and this being open range," Joe chuckled, anticipating their reaction.

"Does that mean what I think it means?" was George's quick rejoinder.

"It sure does. I collect them from a ranch a couple of miles west of my place. Mat, do you think you'll be any good at picking up cow chips?" asked Joe.

"I suppose so. I've read in books where they used buffalo chips for fuel many years ago."

Joe and George laughed heartily at Mat's grit. "Well, let them get good and dry and cow chips burn just the same as buffalo chips did in the old days. You need to stack them in a rick as long as possible before you use them. That way they get real dry. If they ain't real dry, you'll notice some awful smells coming from your stove! And you need to be careful when you pick them up. If the grass is a little long, be sure to check for rattlesnakes. Then watch out for centipedes on the bottom of the chip. They bite too," Joe added.

Shortly they pulled up to a frame house. George and Mat noted that there were also a barn, a chicken house, and a small pig shelter. However, two wooden barrels standing next to the house brought home an important point. There was no windmill!

"Hello! Anyone home?" shouted Joe.

After a minute or two a rather disheveled man who looked to be in his fifties appeared. "What do you want?" he asked.

"I've brought some folks who may be interested in picking up your claim on this place," Joe replied in English. "Would you show it to them?"

"I guess so. Nothing to lose by doing that," the man replied. He invited them into the house.

George and Mat saw that it was indeed about the same size at Joe's house and was all one large room. While the place was messy, they could see it was similarly arranged. After a quick look at the barn and other buildings they returned to where the wagon was parked. "Ask him if he's going to take the stove, barrels, and those tools out in the barn with him. We might be interested in them," said George.

The man replied, "If I leave everything I think I ought to have $200."

George shook his head upon hearing the man's offer and pointed to the barrels. "There's no windmill. He can go back home with $100 or with empty pockets."

The man smiled wryly upon hearing Joe's translation. "All right. I'm leaving tomorrow so if you're here $100 will be the price."

The next morning they returned in two wagons. Joe had lent one to George until he had a chance to buy horses and a wagon. In addition to their bags there were several jars of canned beets, some potatoes, part of a smoked ham, and two loaves of bread that Rosina had thoughtfully packed for them. "If you get hungry for hot food come over any time," she invited.

When they arrived, a neighbor was helping the former owner load what few belongings he was taking with him. "You can send the boy down to the barn to see that all the tools are still there," he told Joe and George. "One of these water barrels is full but the other is nearly empty. There's also about a week's worth of cow chips stacked up behind the house."

"Where do you go for water and cow chips?" asked Joe.

"I always hauled water from town. I didn't have any special place to get cow chips, just wherever I could find them," he replied.

Mat returned from the barn and told George, "Everything is still there."

George took $100 from his money belt and gave it to the man. His eyes brightened upon seeing hard cash, which he carefully folded and put in his pocket. Then he pulled himself up into the wagon. As it drove away, he turned to take a final look at his former home. He waved, saying, "Good luck to you."

After helping move their belongings into the house, Joe took his leave. "Come over any time if you need anything. And we'll help out when your wife and the rest of your family get here. Or, just come over to visit. Rosina and I enjoy your company."

"We better put up the horses, look around a little more, and see what it's going to be like living here," said George. "Tomorrow we should go to town and get some supplies. We'll take that one water barrel too. And now that we've got a place to live, I should write your mother."

May 10, 1906

My darling Anna,

There is very wonderful news. We now have a place to live, which is about three miles from Goodwell. We met Mr. Udry at the station and he knew about this land where the owner was giving up his claim and going back East. It already has a frame house on it so we won't have to build one out of sod. But it doesn't have a windmill, so we will have to haul water from town. If things go well, we can have one drilled later on. We will also need to dig a cellar so that we have a shelter from tornadoes and a place to store root vegetables. It would also be a place for Mat to sleep now that he is older. The sod dugouts here are much like those in Dunacseb.

You can get ready to move out here now. Be sure to tell the man at the B&O station ten days in advance so they can have the immigrant car ready. Send us a telegram the day you leave Youngstown and we will meet you at the train depot in Goodwell. Joe Udry and his wife Rosina will help us move our things out to the house. She is a very fine woman and I think you will enjoy knowing her.

I will arrange credit at a store here but you should bring some extra groceries when you come, things like flour, sugar, dried beans, and coffee. And buy a hat for Michael that has a broad brim. Also, see if the store has bonnets for you, your mother, and the girls to wear. You will need them for the bright sun out here.

Give my love to Annie, Michael, Mary, and also to your mother. I will be so happy when you all get here.

All my love,

George

CHAPTER 10
HOME NEAR FRISCO CREEK

"Can a farmer make a living as far west as this?"
"Yes," came the answer of the cowman. "But he can't make money. He may, by hard work, do better in some seasons than (just) a living, but he can't get rich. The only way a farmer can do well here is to combine stock-raising with farming."

Charles Goodnight, High Plains pioneer, cowman, and blazer of the Goodnight Cattle Trail, to a reporter of the *St. Louis Globe-Democrat* **in 1892.**[17]

George and Mat spent the next week getting familiar with what was to be the new family home. This included cleaning up the house as best they could, making small repairs to the barn and other buildings, and staking out a place for the dugout, which would adjoin the house. On trips to Goodwell, George established credit at a general store and bought supplies and groceries. They also bought two mattress ticks and stuffed them to capacity with clean straw found in the barn. Lacking bedframes, they placed them on the floor.

Meals eaten at the battered wooden table left by the previous owner were repetitive, heavy on bacon, beans, and crackers in order to ration some of the tastier food Rosina had given them. Another cooking limitation was the one frying pan, one pair of tin plates, two sets of flatware, and two porcelain cups that comprised their kitchen utensils.

Nights were spectacular, so beautiful as to be almost breathtaking. It seemed there was more intense light from both the moon and stars. They marveled at how many more stars were visible in the dry, clear air and at the Milky Way's long, wide streak of light across the nighttime sky. It was incredibly quiet except for the occasional howl of a wolf or coyote. There was no trolley car rumble or any of the other sounds to which they had become accustomed in Youngstown.

On one exploratory outing they found a small creek. "This must be Frisco Creek, the one Joe Udry told us about," said George. "The shame of it is that you can't drink that water anymore. The rivers and creeks have been fouled by too many people and their cattle."

Early one morning as Mat was about to leave the outhouse, he heard something stirring outside. There were snorting sounds and footsteps, many of them. Still adjusting his clothing, he threw open the door to find himself face to face with a large steer. Looking around, he saw at least a dozen more nosing about. "Hey ah! Hey ah! Get on out of here," he shouted, waving his arms and looking for small rocks or clods of dirt to throw. "Move out! Moooove out!"

George came out of the house to see what was causing the commotion. Alarmed at first, he quickly saw that Mat had things in hand. "Good for you, Mat! Get them out of here!" He watched as the steers trotted away then broke into a gallop as Mat pursued, firing away with his small store of rocks. George put his hands on his hips and began to laugh, a hearty belly laugh. "Keep going, Mat! That'll teach 'em to interrupt you on the toilet!" Tears streamed down his cheeks and he began holding his sides.

Finally, Mat walked back to the house, winded, with sweat running down his temples. "I don't think they'll come back, at least not today," he told George between gulps for air.

Still smiling, George asked, "Which way were they headed?"

"Straight south. And I noticed something interesting about several of them when they were up close. They had dried mud on their lower legs."

"From the creek?"

"I don't think so. The color wasn't right."

George paused for a moment. "Straight south, eh? We haven't explored very far in that direction yet. Let's hitch up the wagon and take a ride down that way."

Finally, after riding over more of the seemingly endless high plain, they saw a windmill off in the distance. They were now in grazing land and began seeing more and more cattle. "We'll keep on going. Might as well take a look at that windmill," said George.

Soon, they were close enough to see a large stock tank surrounded by cattle. Despite their steady drinking, the tank was overflowing as the windmill continued pumping at a steady pace, propelled by a south wind that seemed to blow perpetually in the High Plains. The area around the tank was a small sea of muck continually churned up by thirsty cattle coming and going. And it was noisy as the bawling, jostling herd milled about. Small calves, temporarily separated from their mothers, bawled and their mothers obligingly bawled in return to signal their whereabouts.

Still in a jovial mood, George said, "I think we know where the mud came from that was on those steers that paid you a visit. Does this look and sound like the West, Mat?"

Mat laughed. "It sure does."

George looked around. "You know, there's a lot of water going to waste with that tank running over. This windmill is just as close to our place as Goodwell. If the owner would let us get water here, it would be real helpful and we could also get all the cow chips we needed at the same time. There has to be a ranch house somewhere nearby. Let's get a bucket of water for the horses then ride on a little farther."

A *little farther* turned out to be nearly an hour before they saw a ranch. Their arrival was announced by two large dogs, who charged the wagon, snapping at its wheels. They were quickly silenced by a command from the rancher coming out of the large, sprawling house. "Good morning! Go ahead and get down from the wagon. They don't bite," he greeted them. "What can I do for you?"

"Good morning. My father and I saw a windmill about an hour's ride north of here. We were wondering if it belonged to you," Mat told the rancher.

"Why, yes. Is it working all right?"

"Yes sir, it is. In fact the tank is running over."

"Glad to hear there isn't a problem. It's a long ride up there so we just let it run and maybe check on it every week or so. Where are you from?"

"North. It was pretty long ride before we came to the windmill," Mat replied. Then he translated the rancher's comments to George.

"Oh, then you live up in the Neutral Strip."

"Yes, we just claimed a homestead there. My father wants to know if it would be all right to get water from that windmill since the tank runs over all the time."

"Why, sure," smiled the rancher, taking off his tall, wide-brimmed hat to mop his brow.

"Thank you. And would it be all right to pick up cow chips there too?"

"Take all you want. There's an endless supply of that stuff," said the rancher. "Why, you and your pa can get real high tone with your neighbors up there in the Strip."

"High tone?"

"Sure! You just tell 'em that your water and cow chips are imported from Texas!" he exclaimed, laughing and slapping his knee.

"Texas? Really?"

The rancher nodded. "Yep, you crossed over into Texas a little while before you got to that windmill."

George laughed upon hearing Mat's translation. "We thank you very much," Mat told the rancher.

"There is one thing you could do. If you ever find that the windmill has quit running 'cause it's broke down or been hit by a twister, would you come tell me?" asked the rancher, extending his hand, first to George, then to Mat.

"Certainly," replied Mat.

As they began the long ride back to their place, Mat asked, "Should we start getting water from this windmill right away?"

"Yes, I want to get a good store of cow chips so we'll have them for fuel when your mother gets here and begins cooking meals. But we might as well keep getting some of our water in town. Your mother will be sending us a telegram when they leave Youngstown to let us know when they arrive in Goodwell. We need to check for a telegram every day or so until it gets here."

George received his telegram the last week of May. "Our train arrives Goodwell noon, June 1, 1906. Anna."

Nearly an hour early, George and Mat waited at the Rock Island depot in Goodwell. Soon they were joined by Joe and Rosina Udry, who were helping with the move. Joe had his largest wagon hitched to a four-horse team. At noon they heard the whistle of an incoming train and broke into smiles. "They're here!" exclaimed Mat.

"Let's make sure the car they're in is part of this train," said George.

Mat counted off the cars as the train neared the depot: "Engine, coal tender, passenger car, baggage car, box car, another box car, one that looks like a box car with windows, caboose. That must be them right in front of the caboose."

"It sure is. They're waving to us!" exclaimed George.

"Wonderful!" exclaimed Joe and Rosina.

The train stopped at the depot and disconnected the caboose. Then, it began backing up onto a track spur. After the brakeman unhitched the immigrant car, the train moved back to the depot to unload passengers and baggage after reconnecting the caboose. A young conductor stepped down from the train. To Mat's disappointment it wasn't Emil Hatchett. But now it was time to greet family. George and Joe moved their wagons to the platform where the immigrant car was positioned. The brakeman was opening its door for unloading.

Just as the family's arrival had been in Youngstown four years earlier, the greetings were warm and high-spirited. George hugged Anna, Annie, Michael, and Katherine Welsch and kissed little Mary, who was now just over a year old. Michael, aged three, ran to Mat and hugged him. "Where have you been, Mat?" he asked to their amusement, clutching Mat's hand.

George introduced the family to Joe and Rosina Udry. "Welcome to Oklahoma Territory," Joe told them.

Soon the wagons were loaded and made the three-mile journey to the new family home. "How was your trip on the train?" asked George.

"It was all right, rather comfortable. It was much better than that ship we came to America on. What was its name, Mother?"

"The *Vaderland*," replied Grandma Welsch. "I agree. This railroad car was much easier on us passengers. None of us got seasick and we didn't have to share it with hundreds of other people!"

Anna was dismayed upon seeing the house. "George, it's all one room! It will take a long time to decide where to put things and figure out where we will all sleep. And what kind of stove is that?" she asked.

"It's what they call a 'topsy stove.' See, the oven is up above the burners. It gets heat from the stovepipe that runs through it. Rosina Udry bakes very good bread in hers," George replied as Mat smiled in agreement.

The following day they finished unpacking and organizing the living arrangements. George and Anna's bed was in one corner. It was high enough that a large box with a feather mattress and lots of blankets would fit underneath during the day. At night it would be pulled out and Annie, Michael, and Mary would sleep in it. Grandma Welsch had a cot in the kitchen area near the stove. Mat would continue sleeping on his straw mattress in another corner.

Then it was time to address the need for an income, another priority. George told them, "It's already the first week of June. We have to get some broomcorn planted while the soil is moist. If we have good luck, we might get two cuttings of it. And I'll have to buy some horses so we can give this team back to Joe Udry. He told me I could keep the old wagon as long as I want. We also have to plant some sorghum, so we will have fodder for the horses and a couple of milk cows when winter comes. As soon as we get the crops planted, I'll borrow Joe's scraper and make us a dugout."

"And we should plant a garden, too," added Anna. "Do we have a big enough family to do all this work?" she laughed.

"There's another due in November or December," was George's quick rejoinder. "First of all we need to get the broomcorn planted. That will be mostly hand work and I think Mat and Annie can help me with that."

"I'll help on that and the garden too," offered Grandma Welsch. "I did a lot of gardening in the old country and still know how to make things grow. Besides, I should do something besides delivering babies to help earn my keep. Let Annie help her mother around the house."

"But Mother, you're almost sixty. Are you sure?" asked Anna.

"I feel fine. I can do it."

A few days later they began planting. George made rows in the soil about three feet apart. Mat deposited the seeds, allowing nine inches between what would become tall stalks of broomcorn. Grandma Welsch followed along, covering them up and tamping the earth. They used a similar procedure for the sorghum to be raised for their livestock. Now it was up to nature.

Working hours were sunrise to sunset, even longer at times. And there was still the need for water. Every other day George and Mat or Mat and Annie would ride south to the windmill in Texas to fill the two water barrels. The trips for water gave Mat time to practice his harmonica. Soon, he had "Buffalo Gals" mastered and was working on other songs. "I've got it now. I'm beginning to see that if I can hum the tune I can also play it. That's really great!" he beamed. "Your harmonica makes these trips fun," Annie would tell him.

Then it was time for adding a dugout onto the house. "We want to have it for a storm shelter, a place to store vegetables, and a place for Mat to sleep," George reiterated for Anna. "I think we should make it large enough to put in another topsy stove, too. That way you could do your baking down there in the summertime and not have to heat up the house."

Anna smiled in agreement. "It will be like the early homes in Dunacseb."

Fortunately the soil was easy to dig and the horses made fast work, pulling a scraper through it for the excavation nearly eight feet deep. With lumber obtained in Goodwell, George constructed a roof with tarpaper nailed over the boards for waterproofing. Then, the family cut slabs of pasture sod to place on the roof for further sealing and insulation. The finishing touches included a wooden floor, store-bought plaster for the walls, and a stairway. The entrance, with a door tight enough to keep out rodents and snakes, was only a few steps from the back door of the house. The only thing it lacked was another topsy stove to attach to the stovepipe, which was now in place.

Another stove would come later when there was more money available, as would other needs such as wire and posts to fence off a pasture for the cows. For the time being any cows acquired would stay in the barn at night, then be staked out in the pasture in the mornings where they could graze but not wander off. Their care and milking would be Annie's responsibility.

One cool day in late November 1906, George told Mat, "You and Annie take Michael and Mary to the dugout for a while. Play some tunes on your harmonica, sing, or tell stories. I'll let you know when to come back in." Needing no explanation, they took the younger children to the dugout. Anna was in bed and Grandma Welsch was sitting beside her. After nearly two hours George came to the door of the dugout and announced, "You can come back in the house now. You have a new baby sister."

Once inside, they marveled at the new family member. "What's her name?" asked Annie.

"We'll name her Katherine," Anna replied.

"After Grandma or the sister we lost?" Mat asked.

"Both," replied George. "If the weather is good the next time the priest is in Guymon, we'll take her there for baptism." The Catholic parish in that part of the Oklahoma Territory was small. Thus, a circuit-riding priest held services in Guymon only one Sunday a month.

Winter closed in on the family home late in December. For Anna the work routine was essentially the same except there was no garden to tend. The harvest of potatoes, beets, and other root vegetables was stored on shelves in the dugout.

For George there would be no work in the fields until broomcorn planting in May. But his work became similar to that of a night watchman or a policeman back in Dunacseb, especially when snow covered the ground. While horses knew they could find grass by digging down through the snow with their front hooves, cattle were not similarly blessed with such wisdom. They drifted about seeking food that wasn't snow-covered. Thus, they were drawn to homesteaders' haystacks and other unprotected feed supplies. Loss of these precious supplies meant their own horses and the two cows they had acquired would starve. "If they starve, we starve," George reminded Anna. He maintained nightly vigils with his double-barrel shotgun loaded with birdshot. Several times a month he charged outside with the gun and a lantern to chase away range cattle. By February his store of shells loaded with birdshot was nearly exhausted.

During these nights he kept the fire going in the topsy stove, else the indoor temperatures drop below freezing. It was one thing to have to break ice on the water barrels outside but having to break ice on the water bucket in the kitchen before one could get a morning drink was intolerable!

One evening before going to bed Anna observed, "George, you don't cough much anymore. Are you feeling better?"

"Yes! This climate must be helping me. I don't even think about the asthma any longer."

In late summer 1907 George followed Joe Udry's advice and planted winter wheat on some of his land that wasn't devoted to broomcorn. Still lacking machinery, he had to walk about broadcasting the seed, a technique from Biblical times still followed by farmers in Austria-Hungary. However, he used a horse-drawn harrow to run over the acreage, working the seed into the soil. To his satisfaction the wheat sprouted, stooled out, and grew to a height of five inches, turning the field into a luxuriant green carpet before winter set in. "This will be winter pasture for our cows, unless it's covered with snow," he told Anna.

In early November Joe and Rosina Udry came to visit, bringing the customary Goodwell and Guymon newspapers to pass along. Later, Mat or Annie would read them to the family in German. "There's interesting news. Oklahoma's going to become a state on November 16," Joe told them.

"What will that mean to us?" asked George.

"Well, for one thing they say we will have better representation in Washington. We'll have to see about that. We will also have more local government. Instead of the Panhandle being one big county — Beaver County — there will be three: Beaver, Texas, and Cimarron. We'll be in Texas County. Any time you got business at the county seat you'll go to Guymon."

"Bah!" exclaimed George. "I remember government in the old country. Tell me something that will have some effect on us."

Everyone chuckled at George's reaction. "There's one thing that's going to change, even way out here in the Panhandle. Oklahoma's gonna' be a 'dry' state. That means no more beer or whiskey and no more saloons," Joe continued.

"That's one thing I don't understand about America, people saying that alcohol is bad. In Europe we never had such thinking. Where will we get our medicinal whiskey?" asked George.

"For you and me it won't be a problem. Texhoma is almost as close as any other town in the Panhandle and the state line runs through it. Just go across the street and you'll be in Texas, where you can buy whiskey. I'll bet there's going to be some big parties at the saloons in Guymon the night before we become a state," said Joe.

George laughed, observing, "We already get water and cow chips from Texas. May as well get our whiskey there too!"

On November 16, 1907, Oklahoma became the forty-sixth state in the union. The evening before statehood went into effect the saloons in Guymon served free drinks to all. A few days later, the Senate Saloon on Main Street changed its name to the Senate Smokehouse so its doors could remain open.

For George, Anna, Grandma Welsch, Mat, Annie, and the younger children, statehood meant little change in their lives. George still worked dawn to dusk in spring, summer, and fall. In winter he still maintained nightly vigils to protect their livestock feed supplies. For Anna, even though having help from her mother and an older daughter, life was still just as strenuous. As with most pioneer women, her days and nights were filled with constant work: baking and cooking; making, mending, and washing clothes; tending a garden; nursing sick children; and helping take care of farm animals. In effect, the family was still living on the brink.

Regarding the role of women on homesteads, Oklahoma historian George Rainey observed that much had been written of the brave men who heroically defended their families. However, too little was said about the devoted wife and mother who, in such soul-testing years as faced the settlers in No Man's Land, bravely and uncomplainingly held the home together.

Chapter 11
Music and Dancing

All night long, listen to the fiddle,
Music's going strong.
Heart's are light, it's Saturday night,
Gonna have a party all night long!

Chorus from "All Night Long,"
Johnny Gimble and Bob Wills, 1949. By Permission.[18]

On a Saturday in late May 1908, George, Anna, Mat, and Annie loaded up the wagon and drove to the Udry homestead. "We're hosting a dance in our barn. Come over about sundown. There will be lots of music and food and you can dance 'til sunrise the next morning if you want to. Better bring a couple of chairs, too," Joe told them.

They were surprised at the number of teams and wagons already there. Fiddle music was coming from the barn. Rosina came out of the house with a large platter of cookies as George secured his team to a nearby post. "I'm so glad you came! Come out to the barn with me. There are two other families here who speak German and I want you to meet them. Anna, your mother didn't make it?"

"She said she would stay with the younger children and tell them stories."

The barn had been transformed into a place of festivity. A long table laden with food was in a corner. Chairs circled the dancing area, which was lit by strategically placed lanterns that provided just enough light for the dancers, but not too much. At the far end of the circle an accordion player and a fiddler were just beginning a stately *schottische*. "George that sounds like some of the music they played in Dunacseb" said Anna with a smile.

"Yes, I remember," he replied.

"You two go dance to that old song. I'll introduce you to those folks later," said Rosina as she took the platter over to the food table, which was already groaning with its load of victuals brought by the partygoers.

As they moved among the dancers, Anna told George, "This song is like the slow polkas we used to dance."

George smiled. "It seems so long ago. In fact it's been nearly twenty years since our first dance."

When the song ended the accordion player began another number. A few bars later, the fiddler joined in. Mat nodded and told Annie, "He must play the fiddle the way I play the harmonica. After he hears part of the song, he joins in. If he can hum it, he can play it."

A shy-looking boy approached Annie. "Would you like to dance?" he asked her, and then looked at Mat.

"It's OK, she's just my sister," Mat told him.

After the number, Annie returned to Mat's side. "Where did you learn to dance like that?" he asked her.

"Mother and Grandma have been teaching me."

"I'd better watch more closely. I don't want to be the only one in the family who can't dance!"

"Maybe you can learn some new songs to play on your harmonica, too."

As the evening wore on, those with young children took them into the house where they could sleep. The older couples began to sit out more dances, leaving the faster numbers to the young folks. They talked about weather, crops, and stories from the newspapers. On some news events they pondered why one paper would carry a story while another wouldn't. Some of the women exchanged recipes. The dance continued for hours, interrupted only by short breaks for the musicians.

Mat watched, wishing he had his harmonica so he could try some of the new songs he was hearing. When they played "Buffalo Gals" he knew he could play along with them. He also recognized the slower Stephen Foster songs they occasionally did. But when they broke into a fast number called "Sally Gooden" and followed it with the equally catchy "Cotton-Eyed Joe," he told Annie, "I'll have to hear those songs a few more times. They're great!"

Finally it was daybreak and the fiddler called "Last dance!" The dancing area filled up for a slow song to end the night.

"Next Saturday at our place!" a man called out when the song ended and everyone applauded. A few dancers asked directions to his homestead.

George and his family were the last to leave. "This was a fine evening. Thanks for inviting us," he told Joe and Rosina as Anna smiled her agreement.

"These dances are open to anyone who wants to come. The one next week is at the Thomas place. They live only two miles east of you," Joe replied. "People who have the room either in their house or barn take turns having them. It's a good way for everyone to get acquainted, especially the young folks. Why, some of these families live twenty miles away."

Joe handed George a stack of newspapers. "George, there's a long story about Goodwell on the front page of the April 8 *Goodwell News.*

It says Goodwell is in the best broomcorn and wheat country in all of Oklahoma. Be sure to have Mat read it to you."

"If my crops are good, 1908 may be the year we are able to get out of debt and put in a windmill," replied George. "It will really be great to have the storekeepers in Goodwell paid off," he added.

Joe continued, "Mat, there's a story you'll like in the May 7 paper. It says that Hans Wagner, the Pittsburgh ballplayer, will be paid $10,000 for playing this summer."

George and Mat were incredulous. "That much money? Just for playing baseball?"

On Monday, Mat and Annie drove down to the Texas windmill with the once-again-empty water barrels. Mat played some of the songs he had heard Saturday night, working most on "Sally Gooden." Along for the ride, Michael exclaimed, "I really like that song. It's a good one!"

Mat and Annie began attending dances every Saturday night. Occasionally George and Anna joined them, especially if the dance was at the Udry homestead. By late autumn Mat had become an excellent dancer, thus avoiding any "stigma" of being the only family member who couldn't dance. He continued to add to his repertoire of music and began taking his harmonica to the dances so he could practice new songs on the ride home.

One Saturday in mid-November 1908 he and Annie arrived at the Thomas place. All the furniture had been moved back against the walls or taken outside in order to allow room for dancing. The small children were already in the bedrooms. Large groups of people were standing around talking instead of dancing. "Mat, did you bring your harmonica?" asked Frank Thomas.

Mat nodded. "Yes, I always bring it so I can practice new songs on the way home."

"Good! The Harmon brothers gave up their homestead and moved back East, so we don't have any musicians for tonight. Would you play for us?"

"I know only fifteen or twenty songs."

"That's all right, son. When you run through your list, just start over. It might be good if you would mix up slow ones and fast ones."

Mat moved to the head of the circular dancing area and took a deep breath. Then, after taking a quick look around, he began with "Golden Slippers." Couples quickly moved onto the dance floor, Mat saw to his satisfaction. He switched to a stately waltz for the next number and then did "Buffalo Gals." The dancers stayed with him and he began to relax, even enjoying this opportunity to play.

When the dance ended, three attractive young women came up to him. "Mat, are you playing next Saturday?" asked one, her eyes boldly meeting his.

"Well, I guess so. I'm the only musician around here now."

"Good!" they chorused, then hurried away. Mat could hear suppressed giggles. Feeling his face redden, he smiled to himself. This was heady stuff for a youth just turned seventeen the previous spring.

One sunny morning in late March 1909 George told Mat and Annie, "Take Mike, Mary, and Katie down to the dugout and play some music for them." They knew what that meant as Grandma Welsch was once again seated at Anna's bedside. After nearly three hours George called, "You can come back upstairs now."

Relieved to be out of the dugout, they bolted up the stairs and into the bright sunlight once again. "Come on, let's see if we have a new baby sister or brother!" exclaimed Annie, still shielding her eyes from the brilliant sunshine. They ran into the house and saw Anna and her mother each holding a baby. George was looking first at one and then the other, chuckling and shaking his head.

"*Two* babies?" asked Annie in amazement.

Still smiling, George turned and said, "Yes, two little boys."

Mat, Annie, and the younger children moved closer to Anna's bedside. Anna and Grandma Welsch held up the new arrivals to afford a better look. For an instant there was silence, then a torrent of questions. "What will you name them?" Mat and Annie chorused, following with "They look just alike — how will you tell them apart?"

Anna laughed at their excitement. "We couldn't decide whether to name a boy John, after your grandfather, or George, after your father. Now it's easy: John and George. As for telling them apart, your grandmother says it's possible, even with identical twins."

Mat reread the mesmerizing ad in the February 10, 1910 *Goodwell News,* then read it aloud to George and Anna: "Wild West Show — Coming to Goodwell, Sat. Feb. 19th. Bring in your broncos and have them rode. — ADMISSION FREE — To all who furnish horses to be ridden. You will not be disappointed. We have some of the best riders in the world. — Frank Still."

"Who is Frank Still?" was George's noncommittal reply.

"I don't know. But take a look at this ad. There's three pictures of bucking horses," Mat persisted in an effort to pique George's interest.

"We don't have any bucking broncos. What will it cost us to get in?" asked George, winking at Anna.

"It doesn't say, but it shouldn't be much."

"We have to go to town this Saturday anyway. I suppose it won't hurt to look."

The festive show exceeded Mat's expectations. Many local ranchers and a few homesteaders had entered mounts they felt couldn't be ridden. Before each ride an announcer with a megaphone gave the name of the rider and the name of the horse's owner. When the show ended, about half the horses still hadn't been ridden, at least for a period exceeding a few seconds. The announcer told the crowd, "We'd like to have those horses back at our next bronco ride. There may be someone who can ride them."

"How did you like the rodeo?" asked Mat as he and George walked back to their wagon.

"It was fun to watch. I guess it was worth the ten cents apiece," smiled George. "Look over there," he continued, pointing to a spring wagon across the street.

The wagon was hitched to two horses. But tied on behind with tethers of varying length were three columns of horses, three to a column. A man leaning against one of the wagon wheels straightened up when he saw George and Mat approaching. "Looking for some horses, men?"

"Tell him we might be," George said after hearing Mat's interpretation.

"I have workhorses and a couple that are broken to the saddle as well as being good carriage horses," said the trader.

"Which ones are they?"

"The middle horses in the first and second rows."

"That's interesting. I wonder if there's a reason those are the most difficult to take a close look at without taking them completely out of the lines," George told Mat. "Ask him to spread out the rows." Then, he mumbled a few calming words to the horses and worked his way in between them. George inspected each of the two horses in the middle column. He continued speaking soothingly as he ran his hands over their sides, legs, and necks. Then, he looked into their ears and inspected their mouths closely. Without a word he came away from the horses and stared at the trader.

"Ask him how well the first horse in the middle row eats," he told Mat. Mat quickly translated the question.

"Oh, you'd be surprised at how he eats," said the trader.

George grimaced upon hearing the trader's evasive reply. "Well, I think that horse likes to chew and suck on wood. There are small wedges of wood driven between some of his biting teeth to make his gums sore. That's so he won't chew for a while. He's what they call a stump sucker. Bringing him home would be the worst thing we could ever do. The other horse has wool cloth stuffed way down in her ears so she can't hear very well. That, with the scars on her legs, tells me she's too excitable to have around."

"What should I say to the man?" Mat was shocked by the trader's deceit.

"Tell him we don't want any stump suckers or horses that spook easily. Tell him to come around to our place when he's got some good stock." George started back across the street to the wagon.

"I didn't know you knew so much about horses," said Mat on the trip home.

"We had lots of them in Dunacseb, remember? But I also know people and that man looked at us as if we were fools. That's why I checked those two so closely."

"Do you think he will come around with horses again?"

"I doubt it, not unless he changes his ways."

Horses or mules that had the annoying habit of chewing on fenceposts, cribs, or stall edges were called stump suckers in the High Plains. In the East they were called cribbers. Some horse traders masked this by making small cuts on the animal's gums or placing wedges between their teeth. This temporarily stopped the habit until the horse's gums healed or the wedges fell out. Stump-sucking horses or mules make unearthly noises, always appear bloated, and may even get very sick. For horses easily spooked by noise, unscrupulous traders would place wool or cotton in their ears to impair hearing. To someone who professed being very knowledgeable of horse trading, it was considered a major disgrace to get slickered into taking such an animal.

Mat had been playing harmonica at the dances for well over a year. In early May 1910 he arrived at Joe and Rosina Udry's place for a Saturday dance. As usual, Mat was there well ahead of the other guests. "Good news tonight, Mat. There's a young guy about your age whose folks moved into the place just west of us last week. He plays the fiddle and he's very good at it."

"That's great. Will he be here tonight?"

"Yes, and I expect his folks to come too. They just moved here from a farm near Kansas City."

About thirty minutes later the dance area in Joe's barn was filling up with people. All were in a festive mood. The weather had been glorious with bright, sunny days and cool evenings. It was the much-savored period between the cold, dark days of winter and the scorching hot days of summer.

Mat watched as Joe Udry welcomed three new arrivals. The man and his wife were about the same age as Mat's parents. The young man with them was carrying a fiddle case. "Mat, come over here and meet the Fishers," called Joe.

Mat walked over to the group. "Good evening, folks."

"This is Arnold and Mary Fisher and their son Ray. He should be able to give you some help with the music. I've told them you've been playing harmonica alone at these dances for well over a year. A fiddle player will kinda' round things out, music-wise."

Mat shook hands with the new arrivals. "I'm really happy to meet you."

"Arnold, Mary, let me introduce you to some of the other folks here while these musicians figure out how they will entertain us," offered Joe.

He led them away slowly, to accommodate Arnold Fisher's noticeable limp.

"I always like to lead off with 'Golden Slippers,' then a slow waltz, then 'Buffalo Gals,' and follow with 'Sally Gooden' and 'Cotton-Eyed Joe.' Then I play some slower Stephen Foster songs," Mat informed the new arrival.

Ray smiled. "I know all those except 'Cotton-Eyed Joe.' But just take off with it and I'll catch up. Usually I can play a tune after hearing a few bars."

"Where did you learn to play the fiddle?"

"From my dad. He's always been real good with the fiddle. And my mother used to play piano at the church we went to in Missouri."

"Can you sing?"

"A few songs. What about you? How's your voice?"

"I've been told it's very good. But since I've been the only musician there just hasn't been a chance to sing. It's time to start the dance so let's move up to the head of the circle."

Mat began with "Golden Slippers," his trademark opening number. After a couple of bars Ray joined in with the fiddle. The dancers enjoyed the new, fuller sound. They applauded loudly when the song ended. *So far, so good,* Mat thought to himself, showing his appreciation with a quick wave to the crowd.

The new routine worked well. By daybreak it was as if Mat and Ray had been playing together for years. And they were appreciated for more than their music. Many young women approached them after the dance ended, complimenting them profusely. "Will you be able to sing some numbers now, Mat?" asked one, beaming a warm smile. "How long have you been playing the fiddle, Ray?" asked another. "You'll both be playing at the dances from now on, won't you?" asked yet another, her eyes moving from Mat to Ray and back again.

146

Clearly this new team of musicians was appreciated, for both their talent and their appeal. Mat, the taller with dark hair and blue eyes, was complemented by Ray, somewhat shorter and stockier with blond hair and blue eyes. Eventually, the group went their own way, giggling and chattering.

Ray looked at Mat. "It's nice to be well thought of."

"Better get used to it," Mat laughed. "They may be dancing with others but they don't seem to miss anything a musician says or does."

"You know, there are a couple of songs you might like to add to our play list."

"Certainly! I'm always glad to learn some new ones. Next Saturday the dance will be at the Browder's place just south of here. We could get there early and try them out."

"This first one can be played really fast or at a medium pace," said Ray the following Saturday. "It's called 'Hot Time in the Old Town Tonight.'" He started slowly and finished at a blazing speed, his bow hand almost a blur. "Well, what do you think?"

"I remember that song! They used to play it at parades in Youngstown on Decoration Day and the Fourth of July. But it sounded like a march then," Mat replied. "How did you learn to fiddle it?"

"The song is one of my dad's favorites. He learned it when he was in the army, went to Cuba with Teddy Roosevelt's Rough Riders."

"That's interesting. I didn't know your dad had been in the war."

"He sure was. You probably noticed how he limps. He has a bullet in his right leg from a battle. Anyway, the Rough Riders adopted 'Hot Time in the Old Town' as their very own song. Dad still loves to hear it."

"That's great! Got any others?"

"Here's one that must be kinda' new. We just started hearing it in Missouri a couple of years ago. It's called 'Red Wing' and it's another toe-tapper," said Ray, placing his bow on the strings.

Mat listened closely and began smiling as the number progressed. "Do it one more time. I want to see if I can follow along." By the time they finished the number he was swaying and tapping his foot to the infectious tune.

"You must like that one a lot!"

"I really do. We'll give the folks a change of pace tonight. Instead of starting the night with 'Golden Slippers' we'll do 'Hot Time in the Old Town.' Then, we'll play 'Red Wing' for them a few times," Mat replied with a broad grin.

Written in 1907 by Kerry Mills, "Red Wing" quickly became a family favorite. The chorus follows:

Now the moon shines tonight on
Pretty Red Wing. The breeze is sighing,
The night bird's crying. For afar 'neath
His star her brave is sleeping, while
Red Wing's weeping, her heart away.

CHAPTER 12
PRINCE

WHEREAS, A certificate of the Register of the Land office at Guthrie, Oklahoma has been deposited in the General Land Office, whereby it appears that pursuant to the Act of Congress May 20, 1862, "To Secure Homesteads to Actual Settlers on the Public Domain," and acts supplemental thereto, the claim of George Welli has been established and duly consummated, in conformity to law, for the Southeast quarter of Section Six in Township One North of Range Fourteen East of the Cimarron Meridian, containing one hundred sixty acres.

IN TESTIMONY WHEREOF, I William Howard Taft, President of the United States of America, have caused these letters to be made Patent and the Seal of the General Land Office to be hereunto affixed. GIVEN UNDER MY HAND, At the City of Washington, the twenty-third day of May in the year of our Lord one thousand nine hundred and twelve.

Homestead Patent, Texas County, Oklahoma

On a blistering hot afternoon in the summer of 1911 Mat and George were repairing the pasture fence, repositioning some of the posts and re-stretching the three strands of sharp barbed wire. Mike, now age eight, watched them at their work. "Look, someone's coming," he said. They were glad for a pause, no matter how brief. Fixing fences was work much despised.

Peering through the shimmering heat waves, George looked in the direction Mike pointed. "That's right and raising a lot of dust. Must be several horses," he observed.

The three watched as the travelers moved closer. "Well, look at that. Two horses in front of the spring wagon and several tied on behind. It must be a horse trader. I wonder if it's the same one we met in town a year ago last winter," said Mat with a chuckle.

"I'll be really surprised if it is," laughed George.

The wagon pulled up and the driver, a burly, mustachioed man who looked about the same age as George, stepped down. "Good afternoon!" his voice boomed. This was followed by a broad smile. "I saw your windmill. Could I water my horses here?" Upon hearing Mat relay the question to George in German, the newcomer repeated it in German.

"Certainly," replied George, then to the dogs: "Bruno! Towser! Quiet down!" Ever curious about horses, he looked over the ten that were tied to the back of the wagon while Mat helped carry buckets of water to them.

Upon hearing the dogs, Annie came out of the house followed by Mary and little Katie. They stopped near the front door and marveled at what seemed an entire herd of horses. Drawn by curiosity, they gradually moved closer in order to hear the conversations. The dogs came over and sat at their feet, mostly quiet but still voicing low growls.

After the horses had been watered, the trader soaked a large rag and applied it to the left front leg of a tall, black gelding. "Pardon my question but why are you doing that?" asked Mat. Equally curious, George moved closer, holding onto Michael's hand to keep him from getting too close.

"I'm trying to give him some relief from a sore shin. See the swelling? Here, put your hand on it. You can feel how hot it is."

"I see what you mean," replied Mat as he touched the swollen shin. "How did it happen?"

"The people who used to own him were using him to help pull a heavy wagon. That's work he's just too young for. So, the shin on his left leg is very sore. The right one isn't swelled up quite as badly but it needs rest too. Besides being too young, a horse this tall should be a saddle or carriage horse. Nature didn't intend for him to pull a heavily loaded wagon. I'm beginning to wonder if he can make it all the way to Fort Sill." He patted the horse sympathetically.

"Why Fort Sill?" asked Mat.

"The army needs more horses. Maybe you folks heard about the revolution that broke out in Mexico last year. President Taft sent a whole army to guard the border. Horses collected at Fort Sill will be sent on down to Fort Bliss, Texas and points west of El Paso."

Then he told George, "This is a fine, young horse. I hate to take him all the way to Fort Sill and turn him over to the army. He needs some time to recover and finish maturing. He won't get that there. Do you have a horse you'd like to trade for him? This would be a good one for your son, especially when he starts courting some young lady," he laughed.

George smiled and then thoroughly inspected the horse. "What do you think, Mat? You meet all those young women at the dances. Find one for courting?"

"Well, since I'm always playing music I haven't gotten to know anyone that well, leastways not yet." He glared at Annie, giggling at his discomfort. "But I really like this horse. Is he saddle-broke?"

"Yes, he is."

"What's his name?"

"They called him Prince, although they sure didn't treat him like a prince."

"We do have an odd workhorse. Otto's teammate died last winter and we haven't matched him up with another because we just haven't needed to. He's a good workhorse and he's only six years old. Want to look at him?" George asked.

Anna and Grandma Welsch came out of the house with the twins George and Johnny. Just more than two years of age, they had to be watched closely around horses. After listening for a while Anna went back inside.

"You have a fine-looking family," said the trader.

"Thank you. It takes a large family to keep a homestead going. Mat and Annie are old enough to help and my wife and her mother are also a big help."

After taking a close look at Otto, the trader agreed to an even trade for the black gelding. "Well son, just let time and nature heal Prince's sore shins. Help out by putting cold compresses on them each day for a couple of months. You should be able to ride him and have him pull a buggy or spring wagon in three or four months. The two of you will be really good friends by then. Now, I'd better be getting on my way."

Anna came out of the house and hurried over before he got into the spring wagon. "Here's a little something for your trip, some cookies and a piece of rhubarb pie," she said, handing him a cloth-wrapped package.

"Well, thank you very much," he said. Then, turning to George and Mat, "Thanks for helping me water the horses. Good luck with Prince," he called back as the little caravan moved away from the homestead.

Bruno and Towser continued growling at the stranger and his horses, then renewed their barking as he left. However, a look and a sharp command from George quickly silenced them.

The family watched until the trader and his string of horses faded away in the distance. "He seemed like an awfully good man," said Grandma Welsch. The others quickly voiced their agreement.

"And it surely was nice meeting someone new," added Anna.

Mat's daily chores now included a new task. Each day he rubbed Prince down and applied cold compresses to his shins, speaking to the horse almost constantly as George had taught him. The routine included giving the horse half a turnip before treating his shins, the other half afterwards. At first he used carrots as treats, but Anna objected. "Save the carrots for us, the family. Turnips are a lot easier to grow so that's what you'll give to that horse!"

As the hot summer faded away into the brisk but sunny days of autumn, George announced, "I think his shins are healed now. This would be a good day to see how he takes to the saddle."

Mat gave Prince half a turnip and then put a bridle and saddle on him. So far so good. As Mat climbed into the saddle George told him, "Start slowly, and let him get used to you. Keep talking to him. Work up gradually from a walk to a trot, canter, and gallop."

Mat started toward the end of the pasture a quarter of a mile away, first a slow walk and then a trot to the fence line, where he turned around. "All right, go!" he said, digging his heels into Prince's flanks. The horse took off as if propelled from a catapult, with Mat nearly losing his hat. It seemed there was no limit to Prince's speed. In short order he pulled up beside George near the barn.

"Good ride," said George. "Looks like he loves to run!"

"He sure does. That's the fastest ride I've ever had. And he gets up to top speed in just a few strides, too."

"Ride around some more then put him up. This is a truly fine horse. We'll try him with the buggy tomorrow and just hope he doesn't want to run as fast with it," George added wryly.

Autumn days were short-lived in 1911. In mid-October the family woke up to a heavy snowfall totaling eight or nine inches. "That's not a good sign," George observed. "After it melts we'd better go after some extra cow chips. It could be a long, cold winter."

Mat and Annie groaned inwardly. They knew it would be their job to visit the windmill area across the line in Texas. It was a rather pleasant trip in good weather. But in bad weather it could be an ordeal. Always the optimist, Mike urged, "Bring your harmonica, Mat!" However, nearly a week would pass before the snow had sufficiently melted off.

Ever unpredictable, the weather was moderate until just a week before Christmas, when the Panhandle was hit with another blizzard, this one dumping eighteen inches of snow. "If the wind comes up and blows all this snow around we'll have problems just getting the chores done," said George. "The next time we go to town we'd better buy some extra rope."

"Rope? Why rope?" asked Anna.

"We need to tie lines from the door of the house to the barn, the toilet, the cow chip rick, and the chicken house. By holding onto the ropes we can make our way back to the house after doing chores. I'm glad we've already butchered those three hogs. That's one less line to run, and we have a good supply of hams and sausage."

"We sure do. Mat always smells like smoked hams now!" Mike exclaimed to everyone's merriment. It was true. Barrels packed full of smoked ham, bacon, and sausages were down in the dugout where Mat slept.

On their trip to Goodwell a few days later, Mat learned from the storekeeper that the pre-Christmas snow was widespread. Guymon had large drifts as did Beaver City to the east. "Never seen anything like it since I been here," said the man.

There were occasional snows in January and early February 1912, but none matching the ones in October and December. Mat continued working with Prince, the two becoming fast friends as the horse trader had predicted. In a few weeks it would be spring. George began to wonder if it was time to take down his rope lines.

But on February 24 a mist began falling, driven by a southeast breeze. By late afternoon it was snowing hard. "We'd better move the horses and cows into the barn," George told Mat. The animals needed little urging to move into a dry shelter out of the wind. By the time they were fed, the snowfall had become a blinding blizzard. "Good thing we didn't take those ropes down," George said.

Then began hours of waiting out the blizzard with only a few necessary trips outdoors. Grandma Welsch and Anna retold all their stories to the younger children. George sat in his chair, alternately gazing out at the blinding snow, then getting up and walking to different windows to see if there was any change in the storm.

Finally the stories ran out. "Mat, get your harmonica," urged Anna.

"Yes, let's have something to brighten things up," added Grandma Welsch.

Mat began with "Golden Slippers," Anna's favorite, following it with "Buffalo Gals" and "Old Folks at Home."

"Don't make us wait, Mat!" laughed Grandma Welsch. "Play 'Red Wing'!"

Mat gladly obliged and everyone, even George, listened intently to what had become the family favorite.

The blizzard raged on through the night, the next day, and well into the next before blowing itself out. Immense snowdrifts changed the landscape to an eerie collection of strange, wind-blown shapes that defied description. Even though the storm had finally passed, the routine was the same. George and Mat shoveled paths to the barn and other outbuildings. But the snow would have to melt before the family could do much more than exist. Trips to town, to a neighbor's place, or to gather cow chips were out of the question. They were truly snowbound.

George and Mat began sitting up at night to listen for stray cattle, taking turns napping. "With this much snow on the ground there's going to be herds of starving cattle roaming about," he told Anna. "Our livestock have enough feed to get through the winter but if range cattle get to our haystacks our cattle and horses will starve. And if they starve, we starve!"

Anna smiled grimly. She had heard this often during the nearly six years on the homestead. "Survival" and "success" had nearly the same meaning.

The family's isolation continued for several more days. It seemed they would never see bare ground again. The snow was melting but ever so slowly. One morning just before sunup, George shook Mat. "Get up, Mat. I hear cattle and they aren't ours."

"Are they range cattle from down south?"

"I can't tell for certain but the noise seems to be coming from the direction of the Stonebreaker Ranch."

"But that place is fenced."

"If the poor devils are starving and desperate, they can break through almost any fence, even three-strand barbed wire. Or, there could be some big drifts packed up against a section of the fence. That might give them a way of getting over it. When they get wind of our haystacks, they'll head this way. Get dressed and we'll take a look outside." George walked over to the workbench, took the double-barreled shotgun off the rack, and then started filling his coat pockets with shells. "Grab the single-barrel gun and plenty of shells, buckshot, not birdshot!" he urged.

Mat struggled into his boots, hat, and coat, then grabbed the remaining shotgun and plenty of shells. Once outside it was a pleasant day, with the sun nearly up and unusual warmth in the air. "The wind is from the south, Dad. Maybe we'll soon be rid of all this snow. It's not nearly as deep as it was a few days ago."

George held up his hand for silence. "Listen," he said, pointing to the west. "Let's set up over by the haystacks. We've got to keep that herd away from them."

"If we don't, they won't leave any feed for our livestock. And if they starve, we starve!"

George smiled at Mat's reflection of his bywords. "How many years have I been saying that? About five?"

From a distance they could hear cattle bawling. And the noise was getting ever closer. Finally, in the light of early dawn George and Mat could see a large herd of white-faced cattle headed their way. They picked up speed as they neared the haystacks, sunlight reflecting off their horns. Eventually, they broke into a trot and then an all-out stampede. George fired a shot over their heads but to no avail. The herd continued its charge.

"Shoot to kill!" exclaimed George, firing the other barrel at the lead steer, which wavered only a bit and continued. He reloaded and fired simultaneously with Mat. "Don't wait for me. Just keep shooting!"

As the herd got closer, George and Mat's shots began to take a toll on its leaders. One by one they dropped, some not moving, others writhing in agony.

"Keep shooting!" ordered George. Each man fired many more shots before the herd turned away and back toward their snow-covered grassland.

Eventually it was quiet except for the bawling of wounded steers as they writhed on the ground. "Come on, Mat. Let's put those poor brutes out of their misery." George began walking toward the grisly scene.

"We hit a lot of them," Mat observed.

"Gunfire didn't bring all of them down. Some of them stumbled, and then got trampled by the rest of the herd."

After a few minutes it was quiet, except for George's outrage. "Those idiots! Those fools! When are they ever going to learn that you can't put cattle out on the range and just forget about them, especially during winter? Even those poor devils still alive will end up as food for the wolves and coyotes if this winter lasts much longer!"

Mat nodded grimly. Their feed supply had been saved and their own horses and cattle wouldn't starve. Then he recalled the old but fallacious conventional wisdom of the High Plains: *Get yourself some good grassland, just put cattle on it, and the dollars will jump right into your jeans pockets.*

CHAPTER 13
NEW FRIENDS

All I have left is ham and beans this time of day.

Gus Schubert, Guymon restaurant owner

Spring 1912 finally arrived. Gone were the deep drifts of snow, melted away by a sun that climbed higher in the brilliant blue sky. The south wind bathed the High Plains in soothing warmth that embraced all it passed, as if apologizing for the cruel wrath of its northerly brother. Grasslands, fields of winter wheat, and all other plant life welcomed this harbinger of new growth. Even the gray-green clumps of sagebrush took on a brighter hue. Newborn colts frisked beside their mothers as the herd of wild mustangs returned to graze near the homestead at Frisco Creek.

For Mat as well, this was the beginning of a new season. April 13 was his birthday. Now twenty-one, he was a man full grown. Six feet tall with blue eyes and dark brown hair, he was considered handsome. "Mat always looks well-dressed, even in work clothes," said his friends. Somehow he felt different today. Perhaps this came from seeing the glow in his mother's eyes when she wished him Happy Birthday. Or was it the smile and firm handshake of his father? Never mind. There were still the morning chores to be done, even for a new adult.

Midway through breakfast of sausage and eggs, the talk turned serious. "Mat, you're old enough to do business now. I think they call it legal age here," said George. "There's a piece of land just north of us that we can claim for you."

"That quarter down in the breaks, the one where the people gave up and moved away?"

George nodded. "A lot of it isn't good farm land, but it has fine grass. And it has a house. All we would have to do is pay any taxes owed on the property. If we file a homestead claim on it you'll have a place to live and we'd have a place to raise cattle. What do you think?"

"Well, I guess it sounds good," Mat said somewhat haltingly. "And, uhhh, I mean, yes, it's a really good plan," he added much more emphatically.

"Fine, then on Monday we'll go to the courthouse in Guymon and file a claim."

"My son is going to own land. I'm proud of you, Mat," said Anna, squeezing his arm.

"Mother, can I go live with Mat?"

"Michael, you're only nine years old." *This one always knows what he wants and isn't shy about asking for it,* she mused, exchanging looks with George and Grandma Welsch.

"Please?"

"Maybe Mat will let you visit him."

"Would you, Mat?"

"Sure," said Mat.

But Anna had a point to make and continued. "Mat is a full-grown man and needs his own place. Before long he's going to meet a nice woman, marry her, and start his own family."

"I'd better get the rest of the chores done," said the new adult. Once outside, the impact of the news hit him. He would have a place of his own. It would end sharing a one-room house and its adjoining dugout with his parents, grandmother, and six young brothers and sisters. Well, Annie was only a few years younger than he. But the rest of them were small children. It was a house full; especially since the twins George and John came along three years ago.

At the dance in Schultz's barn that night he played his harmonica with noticeable fervor. Ray Fisher picked up on it and his fiddle licks were just as hot. Even the dancers seemed to relish the lively music more than ever before. *A place of my own.* The thought kept his spirits high.

Monday dawned bright and sunny. Going to the pasture, Mat called the handsome black gelding. Prince trotted over quickly and began nuzzling his hand. "I didn't forget, old fellow. Here's half a turnip. You get the rest after you're harnessed and hitched." He led the horse into the barn and quickly had him ready to begin the trip. Prince whickered and swung his head toward Mat. "Here you are," laughed Mat, giving him the rest of the turnip. This routine seldom varied.

George came out of the house carrying the single-barrel shotgun and climbed into the waiting buggy. "Do you think we'll need this to get our claim filed?"

"I hope not," Mat replied in an equally light-hearted tone.

"But you never know, and I always like to be prepared. We could spot a wolf or a rattlesnake on the way to Guymon."

"Giddap," said Mat, shaking the reins. Prince moved out at a fast, easy gait that would soon have them at the courthouse.

Once again, George had played the patriarch, keeping his cards close to the vest. About a mile from the house Mat could no longer contain his curiosity. "We hadn't talked about getting more land for so long I'd totally forgotten about it. How long have you been planning this?"

After lighting his pipe, George looked at Mat through the first cloud of smoke and smiled. "About six years. A 160-acre homestead provides, at best, a modest living for a family. But if a man can pick up additional land, his chances of succeeding in this country are much better. The extra land gives him a chance to diversify his crops and begin raising cattle."

The rest of the trip was uneventful. Mat made certain the buggy avoided the deep ruts left in the trail by heavily loaded wagons. Shortly, they rode into Guymon, stopping at the courthouse.

"Yes," said the man at the register of deeds office, "that land is available. But there's thirty-six dollars in delinquent taxes that would have to be paid first. You can pay at the treasurer's office across the hall. Bring the receipt back here and I'll record your claim."

Mat quickly translated this for his father. While grumbling at the "bother" of having to go to another office, George quickly headed toward the door, reaching for his money belt. "We'll be right back," Mat told the man.

The rest of the week flew by as Mat moved into the new place. A small frame building, it wasn't much to look at but it was divided into a kitchen, living room, and two bedrooms. There were also a small barn and other outbuildings. When a brief thunderstorm blew up, he found the house had good windows and a roof that didn't leak. The days became a blur of cleaning, moving his things and those few items of furniture his mother could spare from the family home. Then there was a trip to town to buy more household goods and grocery staples. By Saturday it finally looked like a home. It was sparse, but at least he had a topsy stove for cooking and heating, a table and chair, and a new straw-filled mattress.

Tonight there would be a dance at the Thomas place. Only Mat wasn't going. It was time to visit some other Saturday dances, like the ones in Guymon. These were held in a hall, rather than a neighbor's house or barn. He gave Prince a vigorous combing and rubdown until highlights of the gelding's coat reflected the sun like a mirror. Same for the buggy. Mat washed the wheels and wiped away the dust that had settled on the carriage and its awning. The only thing left was to get him cleaned up. In an hour he had shaved, bathed, and combed his hair. He brushed his teeth with a liberal spoonful of salt. It left a brackish taste in his mouth but still didn't taste as bad as baking soda. Then, he put on his best shirt and trousers, dancing shoes, and a hat. He carefully checked the hat's angle in the mirror to make sure it was just right. A man had to look his best, especially the first time at a dance in town. People there were bound to be fussier than those at the country dances.

After hitching Prince to the buggy, he started for the trail to Guymon. *No, better go by the folks' place first.* He reined the horse and trotted him to the family home, pulling up to the house just as Annie was returning from the barn.

"Well, Big Brother, you sure are early for the dance. And all dressed up too. Are you going to meet someone special tonight?"

"I'm not going to the dance at the Thomases. I'm going to the one in Guymon."

"No! Are you really?" Annie seemed both excited and disturbed by the news. "Who will play the harmonica for us?"

"There are two others who play pretty well, now that some new families have moved into the area. Let one of them fill in for me. And there's still Ray to play the fiddle. I told him last week that I would be going to Guymon pretty soon."

Annie nodded. "I'll tell Ray you won't be there tonight. Going all the way to Guymon for some dance sounds exciting. Think you'll meet some interesting ladies?"

"Maybe. I'd better be going. I won't be back until sometime tomorrow." Shaking the reins, he moved Prince toward the trail. "See you later. Tell the folks where I've gone, would you?"

By late afternoon, Prince's steady gait had him in Guymon. Mat looked at the buildings and the businesses with a keener interest. There was the now familiar courthouse, he noted with a smile, and a restaurant. He was hungry, not having packed any food for the trip. That would be the first stop.

The place was small but looked very clean. There were six tables with an odd collection of chairs for customers. Two men about his age were seated at the table nearest the kitchen, one wearing an apron. He nodded to Mat. "Hello, what can I do for you?"

"I was hoping to get something to eat. It isn't too late, is it?"

"All I have left is ham and beans this time of day."

"Then that's what I'll have." Mat took a seat at one of the tables and continued looking around. The other man, lean and on the tall side, was engrossed in a newspaper. Soon, the proprietor brought a plate piled high.

"I had a big slab of cornbread left so you get that too."

"Thank you. It sure smells good." Mat was famished by now. He quickly broke off some cornbread and began eating. The food tasted as good as it smelled. Alternating between ham, beans, and bites of cornbread, he soon made the plate of food disappear.

"Well, I guess you didn't like it very much," said the owner, serving Mat a large mug of coffee and taking away the empty plate. About the same height and build as Mat, he had an infectious grin. He wore a moustache and wire-rimmed eyeglasses just like Teddy Roosevelt's.

Mat smiled. "That was a really good meal, just what I needed."

"Haven't seen you around town before. Did you just move to Guymon?"

"No, I'm from Goodwell, came for the dance tonight."

"Oh. Well, we have some good ones here in Guymon. There's a big turnout every Saturday night."

The owner rejoined the other man. Mat sipped his hot, steaming coffee. Soon, the other two began conversing in German. The man with the newspaper was reading articles to the owner. "A terrible story here on the front page. It says the *Titanic*, a large British steamship, hit an iceberg and sank last Monday. They don't know for sure but maybe fifteen hundred people were lost. That was the maiden voyage for a ship that was supposed to be unsinkable"

The owner shook his head. "That's a tragedy, all those people. And it's scary to think about for someone like me who crossed the Atlantic just a few years ago. But you know what I think? Germany is the only country that could build an unsinkable ship."

"Mmm, here's a story you'll like: 'A wedding chivaree went very wrong last Saturday out near Optima. Friends of a newly married couple ambushed them on their wedding night, just as they were getting ready for bed. Barging into the house, the men seized the groom, who was wearing only his shirt, and headed for the stock tank to give him a ceremonial dunking. But they didn't reckon with the bride. Tall and strong, she quickly dispatched her female tormentors. Then, she grabbed an extra buggy whip and vigorously attacked the men who held her husband. In the face of the whip lashes being rained down upon them, they retreated back to town.'"

The restaurant owner was holding his sides from laughter. The other man dropped his newspaper and was literally shaking up and down. "They didn't reckon with her spunk!" he exclaimed.

"No, they sure didn't," exploded the owner. "Boy, oh boy, she must have really been looking forward to being married!"

"She had to be. What a lucky man!"

Mat laughed out loud.

The owner swung around and looked at Mat. "*Sprechen sie Deutsche?*"

"*Ja,*" Mat replied, "but English was so hard to learn, I always speak it unless I'm talking to my parents."

"Join us," invited the owner, standing up. "My name is Gus, Gus Schubert," he said, extending his hand. "This mad man who's been reading the wild story is Joe Loesel."

"I'm Mat Welli." They shook hands all around and sat down.

"I didn't mean to eavesdrop but that was some story."

"Don't worry about it. Joe always has a good one he heard or read about in the newspaper. A man should have a good laugh a couple times a day. I think it's healthy. So you're from Germany and came all the way to Oklahoma for tonight's dance, eh?"

Mat chuckled at the exaggeration. "Our family came to America from Austria-Hungary. But my grandfather's family moved there from Germany about fifty years ago."

"Where did you learn English? You don't sound like someone from around here."

"I learned it in school when we lived in Youngstown, Ohio. Are both of you from Germany?"

"Our family moved out here to Optima two years ago from Lansing, Michigan," said Joe. "My folks came from Bohemia. Gus, you came directly here from Germany, didn't you?"

Gus nodded, but before he could reply a tall young woman dressed for Western style riding came into the restaurant. "Oh, there you are, Joe," she said, walking over to the table. "Hello, Gus. Joe, Mother wants to know if you're gonna' be home or going out on the Rock Island next week."

"I won't know until later today or tomorrow when they post the work schedule. When are you going back to Optima?"

"Not until tomorrow afternoon." Her dark brown eyes were fixed on Mat. "Are you going to introduce me to your friend?"

"He ain't our friend. We just met him," cracked Gus.

"Rosa, this is Mat Welli. He's from Goodwell. Mat, this is my sister Rosa. She lives in Optima with our folks but works in Guymon."

"I'm happy to meet you, Mat. What brings you to Guymon?"

"I came for tonight's dance."

"Oh, I hope you enjoy it," she said with a smile. "I saw a handsome black horse out front. Is he yours?"

"He sure is."

"What a beautiful animal. Is he saddle-broke?"

"Yes, but I use him mostly with the buggy."

"He's tall. Pretty fast?"

"I've never raced him but I think he could outrun most horses."

"Well, some day he should race against my mare. I have to go for now," she said, moving toward the door. "Goodbye, Gus. See you later, Joe." At the door she stopped and looked back. "It was nice meeting you, Mat. Maybe I'll see you at the dance."

Joe shook his head. "If you ever race with her, Mat, don't bet anything. That mare of hers is one of the fastest horses in the Panhandle. Besides, she's a great rider. And she really knows horses for someone who's only eighteen. Why, she can handle a four-horse team as well as a man."

"I'll keep that in mind. No use wasting my money."

"Back to our introductions," said Gus. "Joe's right. I came here from Germany, a town named Jordansmuehl, which is in Silesia. I heard about the new towns that were springing up out here and decided to come west. Tried farming in Texas for a while but decided I wasn't cut out for that kind of work."

"So far you haven't poisoned anyone with your cooking," quipped Joe. "If you do, you can always fall back on your piano tuning."

"You tune pianos, too?" Mat was intrigued.

"Well, I don't like to brag, but I can fix and tune any piano made. And I can cook anything that won't bite back. Actually, I do get a lot of repeat tuning business. That's how I spend my Mondays."

"Do you also play?"

"Some, but I don't enjoy it that much after spending so much time tuning them. Now the violin, that's different."

Joe nudged Mat's arm. "They call them fiddles in Oklahoma, Gus. Fiddles!"

"I know, I know. When I play songs they dance to around here, it's a fiddle. But when I'm playing songs I learned in Germany, it's a *violin*."

"What about you, Mat? Do you play?" asked Joe.

"Yes, a harmonica. I've been playing at the country dances around Goodwell for a few years."

"You hear that, Gus? Mat's a regular musician. With me on a second harmonica and you on the fiddle, the three of us could start up a little group. Just have to get a guitar player to join us and maybe someone to play piano . . .."

Their conversation continued until nearly sundown. These three young men were a good cross section of the local population: Mat, the homesteader, Gus, a restaurant owner and tradesman, and Joe, a railroad worker. "It's getting dark," observed Gus. "The dance will start pretty soon."

"Where's a good place to stable my horse?"

"There's a small barn out back where I keep mine. You can put him in there. Joe, why don't you show Mat where it is while I close up? Mat, we'll see you later."

CHAPTER 14
DANCING AND ROMANCING

When the dance started, I made a beeline for one (who later became my wife) and asked her to dance with me. She hesitated a moment, then without a word got up and walked along with me. She knew my name and had seen me around Beaver, just as I knew who she was. Some months later she told me that her first inclination had been to refuse to dance with anyone who had the gall to request a dance without an introduction first, but she thought that anyone who had ridden (a horse) all day against that wind was entitled to the pleasure of dancing.

RECOLLECTIONS OF NO MAN'S LAND

Memoirs of Fred Carter Tracy[19]

Mat walked into the dance hall to find a large crowd already gathered. Most were all dressed up in their Sunday best with men in coats and ties, women in their finest long dresses, hair decorated with a variety of ribbons. They surrounded the floor, their lively chatter tinged with occasional nervous laughter as they awaited the musicians. Mat smiled at the holiday aura, recalling smaller but similar crowds at the dances where he played. There were cliques of men and women, groups of two or three women, knots of five or six men — laughing too loudly and constantly looking around at the crowd, and a few men isolated, self-conscious, and alone, feigning disinterest. Mat was alone but definitely not disinterested. He slowly maneuvered his way around the floor, stopping briefly, then moving again.

Even as an outsider here for the first time, Mat was certain their thoughts were similar to those of people attending the dances around Goodwell. *Should I ask her to dance or will she say no? Someone's wearing expensive perfume. I hope he's here tonight. Does he really like me? Maybe I'll meet someone new tonight. Whew, he put on too much bay rum!*

The hall was exactly that, a long, rectangular building with closets near the entrance. A young woman was already sprinkling the wooden floor with cornmeal to smooth its surface. Another was lowering and lighting the overhead kerosene lamps. There was a counter and a large pass-through in the rear, and behind that, a kitchen. Six narrow windows flanked each side of the hall. The sills were waist-high and the tops nearly reached the ceiling. Each had an opaque, dark green shade. Mat smiled at this better way of keeping out the daylight. Shades were a big improvement over blankets that were used at dances in someone's home. Through the crowd he could see a piano tucked into a corner near the kitchen.

One by one, the musicians came in. The crowd parted as a young man strode directly to the piano. Then came another one about Mat's age carrying a guitar and a banjo. He leaned the banjo against the wall and began tuning the guitar to the piano.

"Better hope that pie-anna's in tune or you guys are gonna' sound awful," shouted one wag.

"So that's their problem," cracked another. "Well, why don't they have old Gus come over and fix the dang thing?"

Then the fiddler came in. An older man with a large, full mustache, his manner had a quieting influence. At his side was another about Mat's age who didn't seem to be carrying anything. *Must play the harmonica,* Mat surmised.

The musicians grouped near the piano. "All right folks are you ready?" asked the harmonica player.

"Yes!"

"Then get ready to put on your 'Golden Slippers.'"

The fiddle player took the lead on this fast tune with an infectious beat and the floor quickly filled up with couples. Mat turned to the nearest woman. "May I have this dance?"

"Certainly."

They whirled around the floor, Mat expertly taking her through the steps. And then it ended, much too soon. "Thank you," he told her. She smiled back at him.

"Here's one your grandparents danced to. You know what to do," said the harmonica player. "Get set for 'Buffalo Gals.'" The dancers were right with him.

Mat watched, tapping his foot, loving the sound of different musicians playing another of his old favorites. "Hello, Mat. I see you made it."

"Hi, Rosa. Say, you look different, very nice." She was radiant. The long skirt, a lace-trimmed blouse with long, puffy sleeves, and ribbons in her hair had transformed the young tomboy into a delightful young woman.

"Thank you." Her dark brown eyes sparkled at the compliment.

The next number was a sprightly waltz. "Would you like to dance?"

"Yes, very much."

Mat whirled her around the floor as several other dancers admired their elegant style. After two more numbers they took a break.

"Thank you, Mat. You're an awfully good dancer. Where did you learn?"

"I play harmonica at the dances around Goodwell. I don't get to dance very often but I've learned a lot just from watching as I play."

"Oh, that's very interesting. How many musicians?"

"Mostly just me and a fiddler. Sometimes we have another harmonica. This is a good group playing here. Having the piano and guitar really makes a good sound."

Rosa touched him on the arm and said, "Look who finally showed up."

"Are you two getting better acquainted?" asked Gus.

"Yes, we are," said Mat. "I see you brought your fiddle. Are you and Joe going to play with this group?"

"We fill in when they need to take a break," replied Joe.

"Joe, please dance with me," asked Rosa. She and Joe moved out to the strains of "Sidewalks of New York."

"You and Rosa are good dancers," observed Gus.

"Thank you."

"I kinda envy you folks who can dance to any song. I'm one of those who can only do a slow waltz. While you and Rosa were dancing, I overheard several women asking about you."

"Really?"

"Oh yes. They always notice someone new, especially if he's a good dancer."

"At Goodwell we have the same crowd every Saturday night, hardly ever anyone new."

The hours flew by. At midnight, Gus and Joe were playing for the second time while the other musicians took a break. Mat kept dancing with many women, and several more times with Rosa. Then it was daybreak but the dance didn't end. The young women who lit the lamps and kept the floor smooth with cornmeal began pulling down the window shades to keep out the daylight. Again Mat smiled.

Pulling shades down worked much better than hanging blankets over the windows like folks did in a farm or ranch house.

Finally, the leader called, "Last dance!"

"Will you dance this with me?" Mat asked Rosa.

"Yes, I love this song."

They moved onto the floor while the musicians played "After the Ball is Over."

"This is a beautiful old song. You should hear Gus play it. He plays it so well you never want the music to end."

The music stopped but the dancers remained on the floor, reluctant to end the night and face the bright sunshine that awaited them outside. Little by little, however, they slowly moved to the door.

"It was nice meeting you, Mat. Thank you for the dances," said Rosa.

Joe shook Mat's hand. "It was really good to meet you. Bring your harmonica next time."

"I'll walk with you to get your horse," added Gus.

Shortly, Mat had Prince hitched up and was headed back to Goodwell, tired but happy. Going to Guymon had been a good idea. The horse's fast pace had him home before noon. After giving Prince a quick rubdown and some grain, Mat went inside and stretched out on the bed, still fully dressed.

When he awoke, it was nearly dark. He went out to the barn, checked on Prince, and gave him some water. Then it was back to bed. Tomorrow there would be more work around his new place.

"Mat, are you up? Mat?" This was followed by loud knocking.

Still yawning, Mat stumbled to the door. It was George.

"*Haf gut schlafen?*" George asked brightly.

"I slept well, but I'm still tired."

"Dancing all night long will soon have you worn out. That's more work than playing the harmonica, isn't it?"

"Yes, it is," Mat mumbled.

"Well, get dressed, saddle up your horse, and we'll take a closer look at our new land. If we're going to raise cattle, we need to fence about eighty acres of the best grassland. That'll leave half this spread for crops."

Back at the house after riding over nearly every acre, George had a plan. "Looks like we should fence the south half. That's the roughest part of the break but it's good grazing land. The north is fairly level ground. You could see where they used to raise broomcorn. Then, we need to get someone to fix the windmill if we can't do it ourselves. And we better add a dugout onto the house. That will give you a storm shelter and a place to keep root vegetables. Gotta' make some repairs on that barn too."

"Anything else?" This was going to be a busy period that would take them right into broomcorn planting and the summer wheat harvest. Putting in a fence, especially around eighty acres, was hard, backbreaking work, a job despised by homesteaders and ranchers alike. There would be one and one half miles of it. Mat didn't know what was worse, digging postholes by hand every few feet with a two-handled posthole digger or placing the heavy corner posts and their anchors. No, there was something even worse, the final steps of stringing, steepling, and stretching three strands of wire with razor-sharp barbs. Their friend Joe Udry liked to say: "If a man ain't careful with that wire he'll look like he's been in a fight with three wildcats all at once."

"Yes, there's more," George continued, looking up at the sun that was now directly overhead. "Put up your horse, then come over to the house. Your mother still has coffee left. After dinner we'll take the wagon into town and get a load of fenceposts at the lumberyard."

Mat smiled as he walked Prince toward the barn. Dinner was the best part of his father's plan.

The week passed, each day filled with backbreaking work. George would dig for a while, and then Mat would take over. When a hole was about two feet deep, they put in a post, packed dirt into it, and tamped it with a pole. Then, they moved on. "Glad we're not doing this in summer," said George after a long pull from the water jug.

Mat frowned and kept digging. "It's hot enough, now."

Through the week they slowly worked their way around the eighty acres that would become fenced grazing land. Looking back, it was encouraging to see the lengthening line of fence posts but there were still many more holes to dig. There would be more than 500 fenceposts when they were done. On Friday the work got even harder. After digging down a foot they would hit dry hardpan.

"We'll have to bring water tomorrow and soak the holes in this stretch before we can finish them," said George, "unless nature gives us a hand."

"Think it'll rain?"

"The sky looks kinda strange in the southwest. If it's raining hard tomorrow, I'll stay home and get caught up on harness repair. Gotta' get that done before summer and besides, it would be good to work sitting down for a change."

Mat was awakened by the crash of earsplitting thunder the next morning, even better, the beat of heavy raindrops on the roof. *Good, no work today.* He started to go back to sleep but bolted upright. *If it's raining here, it might be raining all the way to Guymon. The trail could be nearly impassable.* He jumped over to the window and looked out toward the northeast. *Blue sky on that part of the horizon. If the rain doesn't move up that direction, the trip wouldn't be too difficult. Such strange country!*

An hour before sundown, Prince's steady gait had them in Guymon. The day had turned out fine, except his back, shoulders, and arms ached from a week of digging postholes. No matter, a *schottische* followed by a fast polka would limber him up.

"I see you made it back to town," smiled Gus. "Thought the rain down your way might keep you from making the trip. Even from here I could see the lightning flashes and hear the thunder rumble."

"It rained hard around Goodwell most of the morning but I could see blue sky up this way. Sure enough, the trail was dry after a couple of miles."

"Hungry? I got ham and beans left."

"Sure. Say, where's Joe?"

"He went out on the Rock Island a few days ago. Probably be back later tonight."

"All right if I put my horse in that little barn in back?"

"By all means, anytime. My Coalie is the only horse that's stabled there now."

"Fine. I'll see you later."

Walking into the hall, Mat didn't feel like a stranger tonight. Several men and women recognized him and smiled. Soon the music started and he moved out onto the floor, at first with women he danced with the previous week. Then he began making new friends.

Rosa came into the hall, looking around with interest. She saw Mat near a window and came directly over to him. "Hello, Mat. It's good to see you again."

"It's good to see you. Would you like to dance?"

They moved out on the floor, danced two waltzes and a *schottische*. As they started off the floor, the musicians began playing the "Beer Barrel Polka." Laughing merrily, Rosa exclaimed, "I love this crazy old song. It always makes me laugh."

"Well then, we'd better dance it too!"

The evening went on and Mat continued to dance with Rosa and many others. No woman turned down his request for a dance.

"You're certainly making yourself known."

"Hello, Gus. Gonna' fill in for the fiddler again tonight?"

"Sure, but hold my violin for a while, would you please? There's a slow waltz and I see someone I want to dance with."

Mat saw that Gus was a better dancer than he professed. He had good rhythm; he just needed more practice. "Hi, Joe," he heard someone call. Joe Loesel walked onto the floor accompanied by a very attractive woman. They whirled around to the stately old waltz and Mat followed their every move. *She's a fantastic dancer. How does he know her? She's more than attractive. She's a real beauty.* His thoughts tumbled over each other.

As the waltz ended Joe and the mystery woman came off the floor, walking directly toward Mat. *Is he going to introduce me to his friend? I better be extra polite.*

"Good to see you, Mat. Laura, this is Mat Welli. He came up from Goodwell again for the dance. Mat, this is my sister Laura."

"How do you do, Mat?"

"Fine, happy to meet you, Laura. I didn't know Joe had a sister. I mean, I didn't know he had *another* sister."

"Oh, you've met Rosa, then." Her dark brown eyes met his in a manner almost challenging. Or, was it only merriment? "Do you play the violin, Mat?"

"No, I'm just holding Gus Schubert's fid — uh, violin for him."

"Looks like Gus is going to dance another number. Want me to hold his fiddle, Mat?"

"Thanks, Joe. Uh, Laura would you care to dance?"

"I'd be delighted."

They moved onto the floor to another waltz, this one sprightlier. Although smiling, she was silent throughout the dance. Mat didn't trust himself to speak. As the song ended, he kept her on the floor. "You're a marvelous dancer, Laura."

"Thank you. That's a nice compliment from someone who dances as well as you."

"Then, let's dance another."

"Good."

Mat kept her on the floor for a third, then a fourth dance. By then, it was as if they had danced together for years. Moving as one, they received admiring glances from other couples. Joe and Gus applauded them when they finally came off the floor. "Beautiful dancing."

Midnight approached. Mat continued dancing with others and with Rosa. But each turn with Laura was for two or three dances. When they started pulling down the shades, Mat sought her out again.

"I really enjoy dancing with you, Laura."

"Why, thank you again."

Her eyes were mesmerizing, perfection that accompanied her fine, light brown hair decorated with ribbons that matched her white, high-necked blouse.

"Last dance!"

They moved out gracefully as the musicians ended the dance with "After the Ball is Over." At times, Mat thought he could hear her humming the tune.

And then the music stopped. They smiled and said nothing for a few seconds.

"Thank you for all the dances, Mat."

"You're welcome and thank you!"

"Will you be back next Saturday night?"

"Yes."

"I'd like that."

As they walked to the door, Rosa, standing nearby, called, "Thank you again for the dances, Mat." Unnoticed by him, the smile left Laura's face.

The ride back to Goodwell was pure pleasure. The long, unbroken stretch of prairie was beautiful. Everything was beautiful. *I'd like that. She said: I'd like that . . . I'd like that.*

CHAPTER 15
COURTSHIP AND CONFLICT

"I'm six years older than you, Rosa. Wait your turn. You have plenty of time to find a man!"

Laura Loesel to sister Rosa, 1912

Mat awoke late Sunday afternoon with a rush of pleasant memories. Soon, however, it dawned upon him that while *everything is beautiful*, his life had suddenly become very complicated. *Not one but two interesting women! But why do they have to be sisters?* Another flash of reality followed closely and it, too, prodded him for a decision. *What about playing and singing at the dances around Goodwell? Could he give that up, something he enjoyed so much? And all the friends he's made, especially his friend Ray Fisher? Are they to be simply abandoned? I've been an adult for less than a month and look what I've gotten myself into!*

That evening he walked across the fields to the home place, meeting Annie just coming in from milking the cows. "Well hello, stranger. What have you been up these past two weekends? Met anyone interesting?" she giggled.

"Maybe," he replied, relieving her of one of the heavy milk buckets. "Where's the dance going to be held next Saturday?"

"At the Udry's. It was supposed to be at Howard White's place but he has to go to Optima for a wedding. So, Rosina and Joe volunteered their barn."

Mat nodded. "Maybe I'll be there," he said, opening the door as they entered the house.

"Well, it's the man from Guymon!" teased George.

"Hello, everyone. Why hello, little brother!" replied Mat, doing an exaggerated handshake with Michael.

"Well, if the weather's good, we should finish up that pasture fence in just a couple more days. Then, we'll have to buy some weaned calves to put on it," said George.

"But who from?" Mat wondered.

"I know what you mean. The Stonebreaker Ranch is out. Even if they would sell to us, which isn't likely, I wouldn't buy from them!"

"Where then? From Joe Udry?"

"No, he doesn't have that big a herd. Who else do we know who owns lots of cattle?" smiled George, pointing in a southerly direction.

Mat smiled. "Of course."

On Wednesday, George, Mat, and Michael drove the wagon down to the ranch house in Texas. Upon seeing them, the rancher laughed. "I hope you're not here to tell me the windmill is broke down." After shaking hands, he asked, "What can I do for you?"

"We claimed some more land and have fenced off part of it. Now we want to buy some weaned calves to put out to pasture," replied Mat.

"How many would you want?"

"We think about thirty or forty to start with."

"That's no problem. I could sell you several times that many. The last I heard, market price is about four dollars a head for calves. Would that be agreeable?"

After consulting with George, Mat replied, "That's fine. We'll take forty head. When could we pick them up?"

"Come down to the windmill about noon the day after tomorrow. Me and a couple of the hands will have them cut out of the herd for you. One more thing, have you ever driven cattle?"

"Only tame old milk cows," laughed Mat.

"Well, these young critters are gonna' be kinda' skittish. And even though they're weaned, they're still gonna' miss their mommas for a while. So, tie one of your tame old milk cows onto the back of the wagon and bring her along."

"Really? Why?"

"Well, when you get ready to move them out, just drive your wagon in a circle around the calves then head back to your place. Urge them on a bit and they'll follow her like she's their new mom. But one of you should be on horseback just in case some of them try to stray on the drive back to your place."

"Well, thank you for the sale and the good advice. We'll see you day after tomorrow."

On Friday, George drove the wagon down to the windmill with Old Red, their tamest milk cow, tied on behind. Michael and little Mary, who had just turned seven, rode in the back. Mat was riding Prince. The rancher and two of his hands were on horseback and had herded forty calves together just north of the windmill. After paying for them, it was time for the nearly two-hour drive back home. George drove the wagon over where the ranch hands had them gathered, circled the little herd, and then moved out. "Heyah! Heyah!" yelled the two cowhands. Sure enough, with their cries and a little urging from Mat, the calves started following along.

"Good luck to you! Come back any time you want more calves," called the rancher, waving to them.

"Thank you!" replied Mat, as he and Prince brought up the rear. "Hey, just as you said, they're following the lead cow!"

Sure enough, the herd of calves followed Old Red as she calmly plodded along behind the wagon. Still sitting in the wagon bed, Michael and Mary laughed and joked about which calves would be their favorites and the names they would give them. Mat followed, smiling at the strange little procession. Eventually, they passed by the family home and then descended down into the break to Mat's place. Michael jumped off the wagon and ran ahead to open the pasture gate. Then, George drove the wagon into the newly fenced pasture, making a wide circle, the forty young calves following along to their new home.

After moving the wagon out of the pasture, George and Mat admired their newly acquired herd, which was exploring the surroundings and sampling water from the stock tank. "Well, we're more than just homesteaders now. We're stock-raisers, too," said George, with satisfaction. Then he added dryly, "It also gives us something more to worry about. Now we can start worrying about cattle prices right along with wheat and broomcorn prices, drought, blizzards, and hailstorms!"

Mat laughed. "Yeah! I guess we've taken a big step forward."

"Tomorrow's Saturday. You going to Guymon again?" asked George.

"I may be going there every Saturday from now on. But I need to go to the dance at Udry's tomorrow so I can talk to Ray Fisher about taking over the music."

"That's good. You shouldn't just quit going to those dances all of a sudden and have him and the other folks wondering what happened to you."

Mat arrived early at the Udry place. It seemed strangely unfamiliar after spending the past two Saturdays in Guymon. Ray Fisher arrived shortly after Mat. "Well, look who's back! Did you get tired of Guymon so soon?" he laughed, extending his hand.

"No, I just thought I'd better show up here before you and everyone else forget who I am. Actually, I wanted to tell you in person that I may start going to Guymon every Saturday from now on."

"Well, sounds like you've had some real adventures up there. Let's hear about them."

Mat summarized the past two weekends, ending with, "There's two women who are very interesting, but they're sisters."

Ray shook his head in mock sympathy. Then, in a more serious tone, "You have to do what's best. We can carry on with the music here. I had to make a decision about coming out here with my folks. There was a nice gal in Missouri who was sweet on me. But because of my Dad's bad leg I felt I had to come out and help them get started. Had to leave her."

"Think you'll go back to Missouri some day?"

"Probably not. We wrote regularly for a while. Then the letters got farther apart and finally stopped all together."

Despite looking forward to the following Saturday dance, Mat didn't arrive in Guymon until early evening. It had been a busy week at home and he felt almost too tired to go. However, the approach of sundown and thoughts of dancing restored his energy. He put Prince in the small barn with Gus's horse Coalie, noting that Gus had already closed his restaurant.

Upon entering the dance hall he saw Gus and Joe and walked over to them. "Well, hello!" they greeted, extending their hands. "We missed you last Saturday," said Gus.

"I had to go to the Goodwell dance. The fiddler is taking over as the music leader and I wanted to talk to him about it." Mat quickly scanned the room to see who was there. He saw Rosa with a group of women and smiled to her. She smiled back and gave a small wave. But Laura was nowhere in sight.

When the music started, Mat asked Rosa to dance. "Thank you, Mat. You're such a good dancer, and it's a pleasure." They moved out to "Sidewalks of New York," making a handsome couple. When the number ended Rosa told him, "We missed you last weekend, Mat."

"Had to take care of several things in Goodwell." Then, to switch subjects, "Tell me, Rosa, how you get in here so early for these dances? Don't you have a ten-mile trip from Optima?"

"No, I work as a maid at the hotel. So, I'm already in town when the dance starts. And from my folks' place it's only about seven miles. That's an easy run for my horse Bobby."

"I see. All of you live there?" Mat gestured toward her brother Joe.

"Yes, Mom and Dad, Joe, and I."

They danced another number, Mat restraining himself from asking why she didn't name Laura in the family group. "Thank you so much, Rosa," he said when the song ended. Gus and Joe came over to talk while Rosa moved off to dance with another man.

"So, are you going to bless us with your company every weekend from now on?" asked Gus.

"Maybe so," chuckled Mat, "if only to hear your eloquent choice of words."

"Don't encourage him, Mat. He makes enough flowery speeches as it is," cracked Joe.

"Hey, there's a nice waltz. I'm gonna' go dance," said Gus, moving off to the strains of "Over the Waves."

"Laura is supposed to be here. Maybe she's working late," said Joe.

"Where does she work?"

"She works at the hotel as a maid — the same as Rosa. But she moved to Guymon shortly after we came out here because she was twenty-one. She also does housecleaning for the woman who owns the place where she lives."

"When did you and your folks move out here?"

"In April of 1910."

"Is that when you started working for the Rock Island?"

"That's a long story. When we got out here there wasn't much good farmland left. The place we claimed west of Optima was poor land for farming, much better for grazing. Dad farmed when we lived in Michigan and didn't know anything about raising beef cattle. After a few months things were so tough I took a job with the Rock Island as a section hand doing track repair. Laura and Rosa took jobs at the hotel as maids in order to help out. Later, the Rock Island made me a crew supervisor."

"Track repair? That's hard work, just as tough as farming or ranching," replied Mat. "Laura just came in," he observed, pointing toward the door. At the same time he did some quick math based on Joe's comment about her moving to a place in town in 1910 because she was already twenty-one. *She must be at least two, maybe three years older than I am. Ugh! There are names for men who get involved with older women and they aren't nice. People say those men are looking for money, or worse, a new mother!*

"Hi, Joe. Good evening, Mat," Laura greeted them.

"This is a nice old song. Would you like to dance?" asked Mat.

"Yes, thank you."

They made a fine couple, whirling about ever so gracefully to the sprightly number. Mat could see that Rosa was watching them closely. When the song ended, Mat thanked her, saying, "You're a great dancer, Laura. It's a pleasure dancing with you."

"Well, thank you!" Her eyes looked directly into his, lingering a bit.

Gus rejoined the group and greeted Laura with, "Hey! You're kinda' late tonight. Working extra hours?"

Laura laughed. "No, I just got to talking with Mrs. Harris and lost track of the time. She's been so lonely since her husband died last year."

Mat spent the remainder of the night dancing and talking with Laura, Rosa, and several other women. Between dances he laughed and joked with Gus and Joe. On the ride back to Goodwell he pondered his situation. *There are two women. Both are excellent dancers and fun to talk to. Rosa is only eighteen. That's what Joe said when I first met her a few weeks ago, so I'm three years older. Laura is also a fantastic dancer and seems so intelligent. It makes her interesting and a bit mysterious. Only she's at least two, maybe three years older than I. But she doesn't look any older. She really doesn't! And they're sisters! What to do? Just go back to the dances at Goodwell?*

Mat spent the week wrestling with the conflicting aspects of his situation. Finally, Saturday afternoon arrived and he had Prince hitched up and back on the trail to Guymon. The night was a repeat of the previous Saturday night. Except when it ended Mat asked, "Laura, may I escort you home?"

"Why yes, Mat. I'd like that. But it's only a short walk from here."

"That's fine."

They began walking, eyes adjusting to the brilliant sunlight of a new day. When they arrived at a large white house with a fenced yard, she turned and said, "Well, good night, or maybe good day would be more appropriate."

"There's one more thing I wanted to tell you. I would like to begin seeing and visiting with you every time I'm in town."

"Would you really? Well, I'd like to see more of you too, Mat," she said, tilting her head and breaking into a warm smile.

Mat cleared his throat before speaking. "Then I'll meet you here just before the dance next Saturday. Would that be OK?"

"Yes, but there's one more thing. I should introduce you to my mother and father. I'm going to Optima next Sunday and will be spending a few days there. If you took me, you could meet them."

Mat nodded. "That sounds like a good idea. I just hope they'll understand that I've been up all night dancing and not judge my conversational skills too harshly."

Laura laughed merrily. "They'll understand. They used to go to dances like these in the old country."

The following week everything seemed to go right. Mat was lively, talkative, and in fine spirits. Anna observed, "Mat, you seem to be all energy these days and so talkative!"

George looked directly at him and smiled. "Maybe he's met someone."

"Have you, Mat?" asked Anna.

"Yes, I have. Her name is Laura Loesel and she lives in Guymon. Her folks live on a farm near Optima."

"Loesel. That's a German name, isn't it?" asked Grandma Welsch.

"Yes, they moved here from Michigan but came to American from Bohemia."

"Have you met her parents yet?" asked Anna.

"I will next weekend."

Mat arrived in Guymon late the next Saturday. He quickly put up his horse, walked at a brisk pace to the house where Laura lived, and knocked. An elderly woman opened the door.

"Good evening, I'm Mat Welli, here to meet Laura Loesel," he said in his most dignified manner.

"Come right in. She's expecting you. Won't you sit down? I'm Mattie Harris."

Laura came out just as Mat had taken a chair. He got up quickly. "Good evening, Laura."

"Hello, Mat. It's good to see you."

"You look wonderful. Ready for dancing?"

She was truly radiant, wearing a long, elegant, ivory-colored dress that flattered her trim figure. Lavender ribbons set off her hair, which was done up in 1912's most fashionable style.

"Yes, thank you," she smiled, placing a valise by the front door. "We need to stop and pick this up before going to Optima tomorrow."

When they entered the dance hall, Rosa smiled and waved quickly at Mat. But seeing Laura on his arm, she was crestfallen and quickly retreated to a far corner of the hall, joining a group of women in conversation.

Mat danced only with Laura throughout the night. During the few breaks they stood on the side and talked with Gus and Joe. Rosa kept away but watched them closely during the dance. Mat noticed and felt sorry for her. *I hope Laura hasn't seen how closely she's been watching us!*

In bright sunlight the next morning they headed northeast toward Optima, Prince moving at a brisk pace. They spoke of light, entertaining matters during the early part of the trip. Mat wondered when or if he should bring up the differences in their ages. *After all, I am going to meet her parents. What if they ask how old I am?*

Laura provided the opportunity shortly after they were outside Guymon. "Look off to the northwest, Mat. See those breaks? There are lots of mustangs living there. People from Guymon drive out on Sunday afternoons to watch them. They're such beautiful animals, so wild and free."

"Ever been out there?"

"I went out there twice with Mr. and Mrs. Harris."

"When did you begin living with them?"

"In 1910."

"I see. But I'm curious. Why did you want to live in town instead of with your family?"

"Well, times were really hard when we came out here from Michigan. The land that my father claimed wasn't much good for farming. To help out, Rosa and I took jobs at the hotel and Joe went to work for the Rock Island."

"Well, that was a good thing to do."

Laura paused a moment. "There's a bit more to it. And since you're about to meet my parents, you should know that my father and I had a serious falling out."

"Oh?"

"Yes, when we all went to work, Joe would give half of what he earned from the railroad to my father. But he demanded all of what Rosa and I earned working as maids at the hotel. Since she was only sixteen he had the legal right to take it from her and she didn't argue. But he also wanted all of my wages even though I was over twenty-one. I offered to give him half just as Joe was doing but he wouldn't agree to that. We had a big argument and that's when I moved in with Mr. and Mrs. Harris." She looked at Mat a bit apprehensively.

"How are things with him now?"

"Polite but indifferent. The hostility is gone and I'm grateful for that. However, we aren't nearly as close as we used to be."

"Thank you. I'm glad you told me. Guess I'd better watch my manners closely today."

"Don't worry too much. He's a lot different with men than with women. He's just a man who still follows all the customs of the old country."

"All right. I understand. You know Laura, there's another thing to talk about. You mentioned that you were already twenty-one in 1910. But I just turned twenty-one last month. That makes me about two or three years younger than you." He looked straight ahead for a moment, then back at her.

"Well, I must confess to being very surprised. Your speech, manners, confidence, and bearing are that of someone older and more experienced."

"Thank you, but I'm newly twenty-one."

She laughed, and then put her hand on his arm. "I was born in September 1888. That makes me about two and one-half years older than you. It doesn't bother me if it doesn't bother you. Besides, someone with your looks and dancing ability should be able to have any woman he wants," she added softly.

"Thank you for the fine compliment. Maybe playing at the Goodwell dances helped me. No, the age difference won't be a problem for us!"

"Just one more thing, is your brother Joe older than you?"

"Yes, by two years. But my father is also named Joseph so around home we call my brother Young Joe."

"What's your mother's name?"

"Antonia."

Soon they arrived at a fork in the trail and Laura pointed to a house about a quarter of a mile to the south. "That's where we're going."

Mat pulled up in front of a house that looked much like that of his parents, with a dugout added on, a barn, and other outbuildings. "Mmm, it smells like Mother is making a tasty Sunday dinner. She'll be surprised to see we have a guest."

"Not too surprised, I hope," laughed Mat, as they walked into the house.

"Mother, Father, I've brought company. This is Mat Welli," she announced, following it with, "Mat, this Joe Loesel and Antonia Loesel, my father and mother."

Mat was surprised at how calm he felt.

A bear of a man with a broad smile stepped forward and extended his hand. "It's good to meet you, Mat. Young Joe has told us about you but this is a nice surprise," he said, pumping Mat's hand vigorously.

Mat smiled. "Thank you. It's good to meet you."

Joe continued, "And this is my wife, Antonia."

Mat nodded to her saying, "How do you do, Mrs. Loesel? It's an honor to meet you." He couldn't help but notice the differences in their appearance. Joe was tall, robust, and hearty with graying hair and a large, full mustache. But Antonia was short and slender with dark eyes and hair. She moved across the room with the grace of a ballet dancer.

Antonia smiled. "Thank you. It's nice to meet you too, Mat. Dinner will be ready soon, please sit down. Rosa and Young Joe are out tending the horses. They'll be with us too."

Joe and Rosa came in just as the others were sitting down. "Hello Laura, hello Mat," said Young Joe.

"Hello Mat," said Rosa, seeming not to notice Laura's presence.

"So tell us about yourself, Mat," said Joe, passing around a huge platter of fried chicken, and then reaching for the potatoes and gravy.

Mat summarized his family's present life and briefly touched on how and why they decided to move to America, first to Ohio, then to Oklahoma.

"That's much like our story. Only difference is that we came from Bohemia to Michigan in 1890. Then we decided to try homesteading out here in 1910," said Joe.

"What part of Michigan?" asked Mat.

"Our place was just outside Lansing."

When the hearty Sunday dinner was completed, Antonia said, "Laura, you can entertain Mat in the front room this afternoon. The rest of us are going outside and look over the garden."

"Mother, do you still have the stereoscope and all those pictures from Europe? I want to show them to Mat."

Antonia motioned Mat and Laura to follow her to the living room. "I'd almost forgotten we had them," she said, walking over to a large humpbacked trunk. She opened it, saying, "Mat, I hope the mothball smell won't knock you over." She took out a violin case and several quilts before finding the pictures. "Here we are, the Holmes Stereoscope and our box of pictures. You're right, Laura, these are all scenes from Europe. Enjoy yourselves."

"Who plays the violin?" asked Mat.

"Mother. She's an excellent violinist. She also has a gorgeous soprano voice."

"That good?"

"Yes. In fact, she wanted to study music when she was young but her parents wouldn't allow it."

"Did they think that only men could be musicians?"

"That's exactly right. How did you know?"

Before Mat could answer, Rosa walked into the room. She seemed to be searching for something.

Finally Laura asked, "What are you looking for, Rosa?"

"My riding gloves."

"They wouldn't be in here," said Laura, her cheeks beginning to flush.

"I guess not." Rosa walked out of the room at a snail's pace, lingering at the door.

"About studying music, it was the same where we lived in southern Hungary. Just men were musicians who played outside the home," said

Mat. "These pictures are fantastic. The mountains stand out and seem so real."

"Here's one with several people in it. See how lifelike they are," said Laura, handing the stereoscope to Mat. They continued talking and looking at the large collection of pictures. Then they heard the back door slam and someone walk into the kitchen, take a dipper of water out of the bucket, and drink it. Then there was a long silence. "What are you doing, Rosa?" Laura asked, even more irritated.

"Just getting a drink of water," was the soft reply. After a lengthy silence, Rosa left the kitchen. Mat and Laura resumed the picture viewing.

"These are wonderful pictures, Laura. I never saw any mountains when we lived in Europe. This is a real treat," Mat told her.

After more time passed Laura looked up and asked, "What do you want *now*, Rosa?"

"Mother said she was thirsty so I offered to get her a drink."

"Well, the water bucket is in the kitchen, not here in the living room." Laura's exasperation was beginning to show.

It was getting close to sundown. "I should head back to town," said Mat.

"Are you going all the way back to Goodwell tonight?"

"No, just to Guymon. Gus said I could stay at his place tonight."

"I really enjoyed our time together."

"I did too. I'm already looking forward to next Saturday."

"As am I," she said, flashing a warm smile and touching his arm.

"Mat, would you give me a ride back to Guymon? I need to go out on the Rock Island tomorrow and it will give me a good head start if I'm already there," asked Young Joe.

"Certainly!" replied Mat. Then, "Mr. Loesel, Mrs. Loesel, I really enjoyed your hospitality. That was a fine meal!"

Antonia smiled, "You're most welcome."

"Come back any time," said Joe, his mammoth hand engulfing Mat's and shaking it vigorously. "Tell me, Mat. Does old Gus still like his beer?"

"He does when he can find it," laughed Mat as Prince began pulling away for the trip back to Guymon.

On Monday morning Gus, Joe, and Mat awakened early to face the new week. All were in a jocular mood and the quips and laughter came easy.

Such was not the case at the homestead west of Optima. Despite Mat's hopes at the dance Saturday night, Laura had, in fact, noticed how Rosa was practically stalking them. *And all those trips into the living room yesterday, they were such weak pretenses! In fact, they were inexcusable!* The more Laura thought of it, the more incensed she became. After her father left the house for an early morning trip to Optima, things boiled over.

"Rosa, you were spying on Mat and me at the dance Saturday night! And those silly excuses for coming into the living room yesterday, can't I entertain him without you snooping around?" Laura could feel her face flush as her anger exploded.

"I'm your sister, Laura — I live here too, remember? Besides, I met him before you did."

"I'm six years older than you, Rosa! Wait your turn! There's lots of time for you to find a man. You're only eighteen."

"Girls! Girls, this isn't right!" pleaded Antonia.

"Mother, tell her how it is. Please!" urged Laura.

"Mother, I'm telling the truth. I met Mat before Laura did," said Rosa, tears streaming down her face.

"But I'm the one he asked to come courting," countered Laura. "I think his choice counts for a lot!"

"Mother, please," sobbed Rosa.

"Mat seems to be a fine man and I can see why you're attracted to him," replied Antonia, sympathetically. "But Laura is right. She's six years older and she should be the first to marry. I'm sorry but that's the way it is." She put her arms around Rosa and with a quick wave motioned Laura out of the room. Rosa cried long and piteously, sobs wracking her body and Antonia's. "Time will heal things, honey," she said, patting Rosa's cheek. "You're a very pretty young woman. You'll find a man for yourself. It's just a matter of time."

CHAPTER 16
STRICTLY MODERN

The public of the nineties had asked for tunes to sing.
The public of the turn of the century had been content to whistle.
But the public from 1910 on demanded tunes to dance to.

Edward B. Marks, noted music publisher

"Folks, we're gonna' start things off a little differently tonight," said the music leader. "You've been wondering why these two big tables are set up here at the end of the hall. Well, we're gonna' start playing more of the newer music, especially ragtime, and that means learning some new dance steps. But you won't have to buy dance manuals to learn the numbers. No sir! We have a couple of fine dancers who will show you how to do them. For some time we have been practicing on weekends. Guymon has its own exhibition dancers now, just like the ones in the big city ballrooms back East. Mat and Laura, come on up here."

With Laura holding his arm, Mat came forward to a smattering of applause. The dancers weren't used to changes in the routine, especially such dramatic ones. They mumbled and whispered their concerns. They knew this couple to be excellent dancers but such a change had to be seen before it could be accepted.

The leader continued, "You've probably guessed by now that these tables will form the stage where you can watch them. Go on up

Mat, Laura. And one more thing, you'll see that the piano is the key instrument for this type music and several other numbers we'll play tonight. That's another big change. We'll begin with the 'Foxtrot.'"

Mat stepped on a wooden chair and up onto the table. Then he helped Laura up. They looked for friendly faces in the crowd gathered around the stage and smiled to them. When the piano started they began the lively dance, demonstrating the same skill that many in the crowd had admired over the past six months. As the song progressed, two couples moved out onto the dance floor to try the number for themselves.

"All right, we're changing things with a song called 'Argentine Tango'," said the leader. The crowd watched Mat and Laura dance to the rhythmic, sensuous number but no one ventured out to the floor. "OK, now for an old one. Put on those 'Golden Slippers.'" Everyone moved onto the floor, happy to dance a familiar number. Mat and Laura continued dancing on the makeshift stage. After an hour the crowd was animated, the atmosphere nearly that of a holiday as the merrymakers began to enjoy the new routine.

During a break Gus and Joe approached the couple newly designated as exhibition dancers. Both were beaming. "You sure surprised us. You're really good up there. I've read newspaper stories about ballroom dancers who help folks learn new steps but I've never seen it done before," said Gus.

"You did well up there. I'm proud of you, Kid Sister," Joe said to Laura, then turned and clapped Mat on the shoulder.

"Thank you so much," said Laura, beaming as she took Mat's arm. Being together now seemed the norm and being apart almost unnatural.

"Yes, my thanks too. You never know how things will work out but the folks seem to like this a lot now," replied Mat.

Once again, Mat would be a focal point at dances. But instead of leading the music with his harmonica, he and Laura, his dance partner, led by demonstrating the latest dance steps. The resulting public approval would significantly strengthen the bonds that made them a couple.

Just before World War I began in 1914, many dance manuals were published to satisfy the public desire to learn the latest numbers. In addition, numerous exhibition dance couples both entertained and taught new dance steps. The best-known dancers were Irene and Vernon Castle, who published *Modern Dancing* in 1914. After 1920 the need for manuals and exhibition couples diminished. People could see the dances in movies or practice them at home to phonograph records and radio broadcasts.[20]

Later that evening, Gus announced a trip he had planned. "I'm going back to Jordansmuehl to see my family. Haven't been there since I first came to America."

This surprised both Mat and Joe. "How long will you be gone?" asked Joe.

"About two months. I should be back the middle of November. Mat, could I leave my horse at your place while I'm gone?"

Mat nodded. "Certainly." This was turning out to be a night with interesting news. Then he and Laura returned to the stage. Rosa only watched from a far corner, a look of despair on her face, declining all invitations to dance as she had since the evening's activities began.

On a Sunday afternoon in November, Mat and Laura went for a picnic in the breaks north of Guymon. "This is my favorite place, especially this time of year," she said.

"It's my favorite time of year too, sunny and just cool enough for a light jacket in the morning," Mat agreed, reveling in the warm sun beaming down from a sky that was exceptionally clear and blue.

"Let's stop over there. That's the place where we watched for wild horses when I used to come out here with Mr. and Mrs. Harris."

Mat smiled but said nothing. *My dad and I always watch for wild horses and stray cattle, but for a lot different reasons.* He reined in Prince, and then helped Laura down from the buggy. Her eyes locked with his as she descended but she said nothing.

Prince raised his ears and whickered, looking intently off to the northwest. Mat turned to look. "What do you see, old fellow?"

"Look! There are some horses now!" exclaimed Laura, moving closer to Mat and taking his arm. They watched as the mustangs grazed, fought, frolicked, and moved about, much as wild horses had done on the Great Plains since the days following the early Spanish explorers. "They're so beautiful and free!" She released Mat's arm and began humming a song, whirling and dancing in the gorgeous autumn sunlight. Finally, she laughed merrily and danced her way back to Mat's side.

Mat took her in his arms and they kissed, her arms now locked about him. This wasn't their first kiss but it was one much different from before. It was intense, meaningful, a harbinger of permanence. "Laura, I love you so much. Will you marry me?"

"Yes, Mat, my love. Nothing could make me happier," she replied as they kissed again.

After the embrace they strolled, hand in hand, laughing, making small talk, and then discussing more serious matters. "What do you think about April for a wedding? That would be a year since we first met," said Mat.

"Yes, in the spring. It would be a beautiful time. But let's not tell anyone until after the first of the year."

"Even our parents? You think that's best? Why?"

"It gives us more time to be a single couple, more time to think about all this. And maybe my father will be more agreeable after he gets to know you a little better."

Mat thought for moment. "That's a good idea."

For the remainder of 1912 and early 1913 they continued to demonstrate new dances on Saturday nights, becoming a "resource" for those eager to learn the new dances that were coming into vogue. In mid-February they awed the crowd with another new tango.

They visited her parents every other Sunday. Antonia was always happy to see them. Joe remained somewhat aloof to Laura but warmed to Mat and they had long, jovial conversations. The reception from Mat's parents was effusive. "She's beautiful, Mat. And she seems so wise," Anna told him the day after meeting Laura.

George only smiled in a manner that said, "Well done, son."

In late February they told family and friends of their wedding date. "It will be April 20. That's the Sunday when Father Monnot will be in Guymon," Mat explained. "Will you stand up with me, Gus?"

"Mat, I've been away from the church since I came to America. Better have Joe Loesel stand up for you. I'll be there. I just hope the walls don't cave in when I walk through the church door!"

When the day arrived, the entire Welli family and several friends attended. With one exception, so did the Loesel family, including Rosa. "Your father hemmed and hawed about it all week, then at the last minute decided he wouldn't come," Antonia whispered to Mat and Laura, who exchanged knowing glances.

After his benediction ending the mass, Father Monnot told the parishioners: "The service is over but there's much more of the Lord's work to do this day. We have four children to baptize. And there are three couples to join in holy matrimony."

Mat and Laura were the last couple to come forward. Laura was dressed in her usual elegant manner, a long white dress with a high neck set off by matching white ribbons in her hair. Mat wore a black suit with trousers matching the jacket. His necktie was borrowed from the photographer who would take their wedding picture. They stood before the altar with Joe Loesel and Laura's friend Hanna Roddes as witnesses and repeated the wedding vows.

And now they were husband and wife. "Mat, I'm so happy for you! Laura, you're just beautiful!" exclaimed Anna, first of the well-wishers. At the afternoon reception the two families and their respective friends became better acquainted, urged on by Anna and Antonia. Antonia was especially heartened to see Rosa enjoying herself, a pleasant surprise. Now she was glad she insisted that Rosa attend the wedding. Rosa and Mat's sister Annie immediately became friends and when the day's festivities ended, they agreed to visit whenever possible.

"Hello in there! Anybody home?" the newlyweds heard one Monday afternoon in late June.

"Mat, is that Gus?" asked Laura. She hurriedly finished clearing the noon-meal dishes from the kitchen table.

"Come in, Gus, it's great to see you," said Mat, grabbing his hand.

"I just finished tuning a piano this morning for the folks who live a mile east of here. Figured I might as well stop in and see how married life is agreeing with you."

"Hello Gus, would you like some coffee or a drink of water?" Laura greeted him. "And please sit down," she added quickly.

"Sure, a drink of cool water sounds good. But I can't stay too long. Have to get back to Guymon and tune another piano early this evening. Haven't seen you at many dances since you got married. They sure could use your help demonstrating some those new numbers they're doing now days."

"It's been busy around here, getting ready for the wheat harvest and taking care of the livestock," Mat replied.

After an hour of revisiting old times and getting caught up on news, Gus stood to leave. "I'd better be moving on. There's that last piano to tune and I've got to get the restaurant ready to open up tomorrow. Goodbye, Laura. Say, get Mat to bring you to a dance."

"Before you go, I want to show you something down at the barn," said Mat. The two men proceeded at a leisurely pace, joking and laughing.

"What did you want to show me?"

"Actually, I need a favor," Mat said softly, reaching under the seat of the buggy. "Could you mail this letter for me? Right now Dad and I are really cash-poor. I don't even have the price of a postage stamp. Laura wrote this to some friends in Michigan three weeks ago and now she's wondering why they haven't answered."

"Oh. Well, give it me and I'll take it to the post office." Then, looking closely at Mat, "I could lend you twenty bucks until the wheat harvest. Would that help?"

"It sure would. You know, I even worked some on the new building they were putting up at the college in Goodwell."

"No, didn't know that. How was it?"

"I was helping dig trenches for the foundations. That's tough work! But the worst part was the foreman. A man couldn't even straighten up and wipe the sweat off his face without that guy yelling at him, 'Get back to work!'" Mat said, recalling his hellish two weeks as a construction worker.

"Really? Did he use to work as a prison guard?"

"You'd think so. He even yelled when we stopped to get a drink of water. He'd say, 'Just drink enough to wet your mouth and lips. Don't drink so much you have to stop work and go to the toilet!'"

Gus leaned forward. "He actually said that?"

"That he did!"

Gus roared with laughter. "Ohhhhh, that's good! I gotta' tell Joe Loesel that one. Maybe he can use it to get more work out his section hands. The Rock Island might even promote him!"

Mat brightened considerably. "Just lend me ten dollars. I hate to owe more than that," he said, still chuckling from Gus's reaction. "I've been thinking about selling Prince, too. He should be worth quite a bit to the right man."

"Well, Joe Lacey was in Guymon this morning, said he would be in Goodwell tomorrow and Texhoma the day after that. As horse traders go, he's as honest as any and more honest than most. He has an eye for good horseflesh and he's always trying to get me to sell Coalie to him. Are you sure you want to sell Prince? He's family, isn't he?"

"After two years he really is. Things will be all right after the wheat harvest but it's several weeks away. But now I don't have a cent to my name except the ten dollars you just lent me. Maybe I could trade for an old plug and get some cash to boot," Mat said, his voice trailing off.

"That would be your best bet if you're bound to do it. Well, gotta' be going now," said Gus, starting for his buggy. "Come to Guymon and see us sometime, folks," he called as Coalie pulled away at a brisk trot.

For the first time in several weeks, Mat felt relief from the temporary but severe financial pinch. *Maybe tomorrow I can get things in a little better shape.* Once back in the house, he found his harmonica. "What would you like to hear, Laura?"

The next morning Mat set off on the three-mile trip to Goodwell, carrying a list of items needed in the kitchen and in the barn. As he neared town, his eyes focused on Prince. *What a beautiful horse and such a friend.* He considered turning around but reluctantly discarded the idea. *Must go on.* After getting a few supplies at Blake's Store he spotted a horse trader setting up nearby.

"Hello, looking for a horse?"

"I might be," said Mat, taking his time in getting down from the buggy. He slowly walked around, taking a casual look at the string of nine horses. Then, as he had seen George do, he began inspecting the mouths and ears of some. Next, he checked their legs for scars and possible joint problems. He said nothing, and then finally asked, "How old is that short, stout horse?"

"Oh, he's just under three years. Kinda' surprised you asked about him considering the kind of horse you already own."

"What's he worth?" Mat continued.

"Oh, twenty-five dollars, I guess. He's kinda' slow and poky but strong. He'd be a good horse for pulling a buggy or for a young kid to ride. Are you sure I can't interest you in another one?"

Mat walked around the string, looking them over for a second time. Finally, just as the trader seemed to have given up hope on making a sale, Mat asked, "How much boot would you give me for my horse in a trade for that first one?"

The trader's jaw dropped but he said nothing. He looked Prince over thoroughly, at the same time trying to mask his admiration for the tall, black gelding. Finally he looked at Mat and said, "My horse and fifty dollars."

"Your horse and $100," countered Mat.

The trader took another look at Prince. "My horse and seventy-five dollars."

"Make it eighty-five dollars and we've got a deal," replied Mat, sensing the trader's interest. *Might as well have seventy-five dollars for myself and ten dollars to repay Gus.*

"All right, it's a deal," said the trader, reaching into his money belt. "Eighty-five dollars and my horse Chunk."

After hitching Chunk to the buggy, Mat walked over to Prince, gave him a turnip, and patted him on the neck. "So long, old fellow." Then, after a quick handshake with the trader, he headed home, tears blurring his vision until he reached the bottom of the long break where he would turn east toward wife and home. Once there, he quietly put Chunk in the barn and went into the house with the flour and sugar Laura needed. *I'll tell her about the trade tomorrow, not today.*

Mat and Laura received a warm reception when they began attending the Saturday night dances again. Folks had grown to like the idea of having a couple demonstrate new dance steps. In December 1913, they awed the crowd with a Brazilian tango known as the "Maxixe." "Fabulous! Bravo! Well done!" were the accolades.

The ride home the next day gave them an opportunity to reflect on their time as exhibition dancers. "This was great. The folks there really enjoyed it and so did I," Mat said with enthusiasm.

Laura agreed. "It's been a marvelous experience. I'll always remember how romantic and exciting this has been."

"You make it sound as if this was our final performance."

"I'm afraid it is," she said with a dreamy smile. "The dresses I wear to dances are getting way too tight. I could hardly button this one."

Mat smiled and squeezed her hand. "I hope it's a boy."

CHAPTER 17
NEW HOMESTEADER FAMILY

WHEREAS, A certificate of the Register of the Land office at Guthrie, Oklahoma has been deposited in the General Land Office, whereby it appears that pursuant to the Act of Congress May 20, 1862, "To Secure Homesteads to Actual Settlers on the Public Domain," and acts supplemental thereto, the claim of Mathias Welli has been established and duly consummated, in conformity to law, for the Northwest quarter of Section Twenty Eight in Township One North of Range Fourteen, one hundred sixty acres.

IN TESTIMONY WHEREOF, I Woodrow Wilson, President of the United States of America, have caused these letters to be made Patent and the Seal of the General Land Office to be hereunto affixed. GIVEN UNDER MY HAND, At the City of Washington, the Fourteenth day of October in the year of our Lord one thousand nine hundred and Sixteen.

Homestead Patent, Texas County Oklahoma

"Are you sure? Should I go get Grandma Welsch?" asked Mat, a stricken look on his face.

"Yes, I'm positive," replied Laura. "I feel just the way Mother told me I would."

"I'll be right back!" exclaimed Mat, hurrying out to hitch Chunk up to the buggy. "Giddap," he shouted, slapping the reins. With agonizing slowness Chunk began to move. "Go!" shouted Mat, slapping the reins again. Finally the horse broke into a trot toward George and Anna's place. *I should have kept Prince and let someone else have this slowpoke!*

Once there, he bolted into the house. "Grandma, it's Laura's time. Come quick! I've got the buggy outside so you won't have to walk."

Grandma Welsch arose from her chair. "I'll get my kit. Anna, do you want to come along?"

"Of course. I'd love to be there when my first grandchild is born. Annie, take care of the children. If we aren't back by sundown give them their supper. And one more thing, tell your father and Mike where we are when they get back from town," Anna instructed as they hurried out of the house.

Despite the additional passengers, the sturdy Chunk made good time back to Mat's place. The anxious trio hurried into the house to find Laura surprisingly calm. "How are you?" Mat asked, taking her hand.

"I'll be all right."

"Is there anything I should do, boil water or something?" Mat asked, still frantic.

"No, we won't need any boiling water. Go put up your horse, rub him down, and give him some grain. And take your time about it. We'll call you in later," chuckled Grandma Welsch.

"Things will be just fine, Mat," said Anna, giving him a reassuring pat on the shoulder.

Mat hurried off to tend the horse. But after an hour of rubbing, combing, and currying Chunk he went back to the house and sat on a stool just outside the door. It was strangely quiet inside, a serenity that matched the clear, early spring afternoon. Finally he heard excited voices and then a baby's cry! He stood up, but just as he began pacing, Anna opened the door. "Come in, Mat," she said excitedly. "You have a son!"

Mat bolted into the house and rushed to Laura's bedside. She smiled up at him and repeated the news, "We have a son, Mat."

Grandma Welsch was holding a tiny bundle, rocking and swaying. "He's a fine, strong baby, Mat. Take a look. Better yet, hold him for just a bit."

Mat took the small bundle and peered at the tiny face and hands. "He's so light — easy to hold," he said, extending the baby close to Laura for another look.

She nodded. "Such a beautiful baby. What will we name him, Mat?"

"I was thinking of George for a first name and Joseph for a middle name. That way he's named after both his grandfathers."

"That's good. I like that."

"He's also named after his great-grandfather, George Welsch," Anna added with a smile, and then continued, "And you know what Mat? His March 14, 1914 birth date is just two days after your father's fiftieth birthday."

"Maybe we should call him George III. There are already George, Sr. and George, Jr. at your house," Mat replied.

A few weeks later the new family heard a booming voice call, "Anybody home in there?"

"That sounds like your father," said Mat, hurrying to the door.

"Hello Joe, Antonia," he greeted the couple. "Come right in."

Laura ran and hugged her mother. "It's so good of you to come. Hello, Father."

"We got your letter telling us about the baby and are just so thrilled," said Antonia. "Imagine, our first grandson! We just had to come and see him."

"Yes, Laura. It's a big event for you and Mat. Your mother and I are very happy for you," Joe said earnestly, looking directly at her for the first time in years.

Laura went to the crib and brought George III over, handing him to Antonia. "Oh, he's precious. Such a beautiful baby," she cooed. "George Joseph. That's a fine name for our first grandson, don't you think, Joe?"

Joe nodded and extended his finger toward the baby's hand, which immediately grasped it. "My word! He's got a strong grip already."

The remainder of the Sunday afternoon was festive, the house filled with laughter and spirited conversation. As the day's end drew near, Joe got up, saying, "We should go, Momma. It's getting late."

"Are you going all the way back to Optima tonight?" asked Mat.

"No, we'll spend the night with friends in Guymon and go on home in the morning," replied Joe. "It makes it easier on the horse," he added with a smile.

After they departed, Mat observed, "You and your father seem to be on good terms again."

"Yes, he can be kind of unpredictable."

Soon, spring turned into the busy season of long days filled with broomcorn and milo planting. After this came the all-important wheat harvest, days of cutting, binding, and stacking the wheat bundles, followed by the appearance of the threshing crew. The days were long, as this was in addition to the constant chores of milking cows and looking after the beef cattle. However, the summer of 1914 would be memorable for other reasons, as international events added a level of intensity to the family gatherings.

One Sunday in August 1914, Mat and Laura arrived at George and Anna's place with several newspapers. "There's war in Europe," Mat told them grimly, after the initial greetings and marveling over George III, now five months old.

"Really? Where in Europe? How did it start?" asked George apprehensively.

Mat checked to make certain he had the papers in order. "From what it says here, it all started in Sarajevo when the Austrian Archduke Ferdinand was assassinated by a Serbian. So, Austria-Hungary declared war on Serbia. Then Russia declared war on Austria-Hungary," he said, looking up at George.

George nodded and frowned. "Then what?"

"Well, let's see, oh yes, then Germany declared war on Russia and so France declared war on Germany and Austria-Hungary. Germany invaded Belgium and then Great Britain came in on the side of France and Russia. Sir Edward Grey, the British foreign minister, said, 'The lamps are going out all over Europe; we shall not see them lit again in our lifetime.' There will probably be more countries declaring war before long," Mat commented after reading additional excerpts from articles emblazoned with their bold headlines. "I'll leave the Optima paper here so you can read it for yourself. There's a column on the front page that's in German."

George sat momentarily in a stunned silence. Finally, he said, "You hear that, Anna? There's war all over Europe now. You might know it would start with something between Austria-Hungary and Serbia!"

"We haven't had a letter from your brother Joe for quite a while. I hope he and Augusta are safe," Anna replied.

"That's right. I'd better send him a letter. For us it's good to be in America but I can't help but worry about the family still in Dunacseb," he added glumly.

But the gloomy atmosphere quickly brightened when they heard hoofbeats outside, followed by loud, girlish laughter. In walked Annie, followed by Rosa Loesel. "Sis, I didn't know you were here," laughed Laura as she gave them both hugs.

Mat greeted Rosa with a cautious smile and nod. *It's really good to see her and Laura on friendly terms again.*

"Well, I promised Annie I would come visit her some time and I was going to stop at your place later so I could see my first nephew. I rode Bobby down here from Guymon this morning."

The seasons changed but the family's concerns about the war in Europe became a constant source of conversation. Unfortunately, much of it was based on sketchy information. News in the local newspapers dealt mostly with the situation in France. Information about the war in Austria-Hungary was scarce except for a few accounts of battles between the Austria-Hungarian and Russian armies.

One Sunday in February 1915, Mat and Laura were again at George and Anna's home. As had become routine, Mat brought the latest Goodwell, Guymon, and Optima newspapers. Seated at the kitchen table with Laura, his parents, and his grandmother, he would read them aloud in German.

But this Sunday George had some welcome news. "I got a letter from Joseph yesterday. However, it's dated November 20. I wonder why it took so long to get here. Anyway, he writes that he and Augusta are in good health and feel reasonably safe. Now listen to what he writes: 'Two months ago we saw long lines of Austrian troops passing by, headed toward the Serbian border. We heard later that they invaded Serbia and shelled Belgrade with their artillery.'"

George frowned and looked up at Mat. "It was good to get Joseph's letter but this is very old news."

"Yes, it is. The invasion of Serbia was one of the first battles on the Eastern Front. And it's still the same with the newspapers. Most of the news is about the Western Front, where France and Great Britain are fighting the Germans."

George smiled. "You have a good head for all this news, geography, and history."

"Well, I guess that extra time learning history as an altar boy did some good after all," Mat laughed.

Suddenly, their laughter was drowned out by that of the children. "Mother, look! George III is walking!" exclaimed Katie.

The adults turned in their chairs to better see the living room area. "Watch, we'll start again," said Mary. Then, she sat the baby down by a chair and called their dog Towser over. Using the chair, George III pulled himself up, and then placed his right hand on the back of the dog's neck. He took a tentative step and the dog moved with him, then another step and another. The dog remained close by for support, helping George toward the kitchen table.

"Oh look, Mat!" exclaimed Laura, grasping Mat's arm. "George, you're walking. Are you coming over to see us?" she asked with a bright smile.

Annie, Mary, Katie, and the twins, Johnny and George, Jr. were doubled over with laughter at the sight. "Good dog, Towser!" shouted Johnny. Annie's infectious laugh soon triggered more laughter from the adults. "Towser, you're such a good teacher!" she exclaimed. Then, seeing Mike come in from the barn, "Mike, watch how little George is learning to walk!" The show was repeated for his benefit.

Mat and Laura exchanged knowing smiles. *Despite the concerns of war, life goes on.*

The United States remained neutral in the conflict despite propaganda efforts by both the Allies (Great Britain, France, and Russia) and the Central Powers (Germany and Austria-Hungary). Further, at least in principle, it attempted to maintain trade relations with both sides. A year before the war began, U.S. exports were worth $691 million. In the twelve months ending June 1916, the figure had reached $4,333 million. As a practical matter, however, trade, especially in munitions, was almost entirely with the Allies. Early in the war, the British Navy established a suffocating blockade that kept nearly all shipping from reaching German ports.

In early 1915, two thirds of the U.S. population had no strong feelings either way as to favoring either the Allies or the Central Powers. However, of the one third with an opinion, most favored the Allies. But the nation's mood was about to change. This change would soon have a major impact on Mat's friend Gus Schubert. Ultimately, it would also impact the entire Welli family.

In response to the British blockade and to prevent delivery of munitions to Great Britain, German submarines preyed on merchant ships in the North Atlantic. On May 1, 1915, the British ocean liner *Lusitania* sailed from New York with a crew of 703 and 1,257 passengers, including 197 Americans. She was the Cunard Line's largest and most modern passenger ship. Passengers believed that German U-boats would not attack an unarmed ship carrying women and children. However, on May 7 just off the Irish coast, she was struck by a single torpedo and sank in less than twenty minutes. Of the 1,200 lives lost, 128 were Americans.

The resulting outcry condemned Germany in the eyes of the world, including the United States. On May 13, 1915, *The New York Nation* stated, "The torpedo that sank the *Lusitania* also sank Germany in the opinion of mankind. . . . It is at once a crime and a monumental folly." A day later, *The Optimist*, a weekly paper in Optima, Oklahoma, carried the headlines: "German Torpedo Sinks *Lusitania* — Naval Experts Think The Vessel Lasted But Thirty Minutes After Being Struck." In Washington, D.C. the German ambassador to the United States telegraphed Berlin, "Our propaganda in this country has collapsed!" President Woodrow Wilson insisted on maintaining American neutrality, saying, "A nation can be too proud to fight."

In 1914, 9 million of the U.S. population spoke German and another 15 million, almost a quarter of the total population, were of German stock. Germans, stable, hardworking, and civic-minded, had long been at the heart of American development. The first thirteen families had arrived in the New World on October 6, 1683, on the *Concord*, their own *Mayflower*. German-Americans were in the forefront of assimilation, through marriage and acceptance of the English language and involvement in business and community life.[21]

But not all German-Americans kept silent about their allegiances to the homeland. In fact, Mat would soon learn that some were quite outspoken on the subject. One morning late in May 1915, he and Laura stopped at Gus Schubert's restaurant on the way home from a weekend visiting her parents. They entered just as Gus was telling three departing customers, "It would be foolish to think Germany won't win this war. They have too much military power."

He brightened and his tone softened upon seeing Mat and Laura and he motioned them to a table. "Oh, some friendly faces! And you have the baby with you too. Want something to eat or just coffee?"

After taking seats Mat replied, "Just coffee. Sounds like you were having a lively discussion about the war."

Gus returned with two steaming cups and sat down, wiping his hands on the apron he always wore. "It seems as if most people around here favor Great Britain and France."

"Well, more than one hundred Americans died when the *Lusitania* was torpedoed by the German U-boat. That's had a big effect on what people think about Germany," replied Mat. "And just last month, they used poison gas against British and Canadian troops. You need to be careful how you talk about the war now, even though America isn't in it."

"Remember when I made that trip back to Germany two and one half years ago? I saw the industrial and the military might they have. They'll win this war. And if the United States is foolish enough to join in, they will get a bad beating by the German army," replied Gus. "But enough about that. How long are you in Guymon?"

"We're on our way back to Goodwell after visiting Laura's folks in Optima. We thought we'd stop for a short visit."

"There's a movie playing at The Dime Theater that Joe Loesel and I are going to see tonight. Let me get that newspaper ad," said Gus, walking over to one of the tables near the kitchen. Returning, he continued, "Here. It's right on the front page of last Thursday's *Guymon Democrat*: Jess Willard, the Heavyweight Champion, Presenting 'The Heart Punch' at The Dime Theater on Monday, May 31, 1915 — Admission 10¢. Why don't you and Laura come see it too?"

Mat thought for a moment and replied, "Well, I've never seen a moving picture before. This is a movie with Jess Willard, the heavyweight champion of the world? I'd really like to see it. Laura, would you?"

Laura shook her head. "I wouldn't care for a story about boxing. Maybe I could visit with Mrs. Harris while you men go to the movie. I'd like to have her see the baby."

"Is someone looking after your place and your livestock?" asked Gus.

"Yes, my brother Mike. I told him we'd be home today but I know he wouldn't mind taking care of the place for another night. He says he likes to because it makes him feel grown up," replied Mat.

"Well then," Gus continued, "you could stay at my place with me and Joe after the movie. Can Laura stay with Mrs. Harris for the night?"

"She'd like nothing better. She's always happy to have company," Laura replied quickly.

The "Heart Punch" was a one-reel film starring Jess Willard, who became the world heavyweight boxing champion after defeating Jack Johnson in Havana, Cuba on April 5, 1915. It was made in late 1914 but not released until the following February. In the film Willard is identified as a promising fighter by a promoter and signs a contract to fight a well-known boxer, even though his wife is fearful that he might be seriously hurt.

Several hours later, Gus, Joe, and Mat were back in Gus's restaurant. "Take a seat at the back table. I have a little something for us to drink," said Gus. He returned with three bottles of beer.

"Well now, that's a treat, especially in a state that's dry," cracked Joe. "Where did you get it? Texhoma?"

"Piano tuning gets me around and I meet some interesting people. The folks I tuned one for last week paid me with beer. I told them it was just as good as cash money," laughed Gus. "Mat, how did you like your first movie?"

"It was kinda' short but very interesting. I wonder if the Jess Willard in the story kept the promise to his wife."

"The promise not to fight again?" asked Joe.

Mat nodded. "His wife didn't want him to fight in the first place but they needed the money because their baby was sick so he went into the ring. I guess he did the right thing in the end."

"You followed the story pretty well, Mat. Was this really the first movie you've ever seen?" asked Gus.

"It sure was."

"Well, there's something new being invented all the time. I think we'll probably see lots more new gadgets in our lifetimes," said Gus. "Did you guys ever hear the story about the old-timer and the phonograph player?" Without waiting for a reply, he continued, "Well, there was this old guy who was afraid of anything newfangled. He just didn't trust new machines. Finally, the storekeeper who was trying to sell him a phonograph got him to sit down and listen. He cranked up the machine, turned it on, and a loud John Philip Sousa march started blaring away. The old-timer jumped up and ran out of the store, shouting, 'Ye Gods, here comes a brass band and I left my mules untied!'"

"Oh, I get it. He must have thought it was a real marching band," Joe deadpanned, giving Mat a conspiratorial glance.

"Yes, I suppose that's what he must have thought," Mat agreed, nodding his head solemnly.

"You two keep talking like that and the beer supply is going to get awfully short awfully soon!" exclaimed Gus.

Joe and Mat roared with laughter. It was going to be quite an evening.

CHAPTER 18
BITTER FRUIT

Instead of rebuilding the old house you could replace it with one from Sears or Montgomery Wards . . . just order the kind you want from one of their catalogs. The pieces are precut and numbered. They even send paint and nails out to you on the Rock Island.

Howard White, family friend, 1915

"Looks like the wind's blowing up a storm," said the storekeeper as he helped carry Mat's groceries out to the wagon. "So far, this has been a cool month as August goes but today's kinda' hot and sticky. We've had some strange weather in 1915. The whole year has been real hard to predict."

"You're right, I'd better hurry home," said Mat as he began loading the flour, coffee, canned goods, and other supplies into the wagon. "Thanks for helping me carry this stuff out, Mr. Cartwright."

"That's a service for cash customers only," chuckled the older man. "Those who put it on the books have to carry for themselves."

As Mat headed out of town he looked off to the southwest and saw a wall of ugly, gray clouds approaching. After nine years in the Panhandle he knew all the signs of a storm. "Get up, Chunk!" he said, slapping the reins. The horse broke into a brisk trot, moving with an uncharacteristic urgency. *Maybe old Chunk knows something I don't.* "Good boy, keep up the pace!"

A mile out of town the fast-moving storm clouds blotted out the hot sun, providing relief from the heat. Then, Mat felt a sudden cold breeze. *Those clouds must have hail in them too!* Two miles to go. The race was on. They were pelted with blowing dirt and debris whipped up by winds growing in intensity. A lone jackrabbit crossed the trail in front of them, scurrying to a safe place. Even though there weren't any trees, Mat could hear the wind beginning to roar. "Come on, Chunk!" he shouted, slapping the reins. Nearly continuous thunder rumbled in the distance and brilliant flashes of lightning added to his urgency.

After several minutes he could see his place, home with Laura and the baby, just a half mile to go. Chunk was galloping faster than Mat had ever seen him move. "Good boy! Keep it up!" he shouted, adding an unnecessary slap of the reins. *Less than a quarter mile to go. I hope Laura and the baby went to the cellar!* "Oh no!" He stared in horror as a funnel cloud descended just ahead of the cloud bank, heading straight for their place. "Go, Chunk!" Blinding rain poured down as if making up for a summer-long drought. Sharp bolts of lightning immediately followed by crashing thunder added to his feeling of nearly total senselessness.

The storm front passed quickly and Mat frantically looked at the homestead. To his horror he saw that the house had been moved nearly a quarter turn on its foundation. It now faced almost due north instead of east. "Oh, no! Please, no!" There was a sharp dip in the house's roof line, giving it the appearance of a large animal with a broken back. The windmill, the barn, and other outbuildings appeared to be untouched. As the wagon pulled up by the house, he could see some of its siding buckling and breaking loose from the strain.

"Laura! Laura! Are you all right?" No answer. The only sound was that of raindrops still splattering on the roof and on his hat. He leaped from the wagon and ran into the house, calling her name. But it was silent save for the ominous groans of severely strained lumber. Rain was leaking through the damaged roof, falling on the still smoldering kitchen stove, which was lying on its side. "Laura! Where are you?" He quickly looked through the storm-wracked house but to no avail. *Maybe she made it to the cellar!*

He ran from the house still calling her name and opened the cellar door. Quickly descending into its dim interior, he saw her huddled in a corner of the low platform where they stored vegetables. She was holding George, who was quietly sobbing. "Laura, are you and George all right?"

"Yes, I think so. Mostly we're all right," she replied softly, then stood up.

"Thank heaven you're safe!" he exclaimed, taking her into his arms. She winced at the contact. Even in the scarce light of the cellar he could see large burns on the right side of her face and on her right arm. "Let's get you upstairs," he said gently as he picked up George. There, he saw that her dress was also burned, its right side scorched and blackened. She stood mute, clinging to his arm and blinking from the bright sunlight that re-emerged as the clouds passed on to the east.

"Can we go in the house?" she asked.

"No, we better not. I'm afraid it's not safe. It's a total wreck inside. We'll go over to Dad's place and see if Grandma Welsch can do something for your burns. How bad do they hurt?"

"Not much at first but now they're beginning to," she replied, weaving unsteadily on her feet.

Seeing this, Mat quickly helped her into the wagon and made a closer inspection of seventeen-month-old George. "You're a very lucky boy. There isn't a mark on you," he observed with relief.

"Get up, Chunk!" As the wagon pulled away, Mat asked, "How did you get those terrible burns?"

She paused for a moment, replaying the frightening scene in her mind. "Well, I knew it was a bad storm because of the wind, hard rain, and all the thunder and lightning. When I heard a loud, scary roar, I knew we had to go to the cellar. I just opened the front door when George broke away and ran back to the kitchen. So, I went back for him. Just as I picked him up, the whole house seemed to lift and the kitchen stove came flying toward us. I tried to turn away but it hit me on the right side. I was getting ready to bake bread so there was a big fire going. We ran out to the cellar and when I looked back, the whole house seemed to be twisting and turning on its foundation!" Laura paused, then touched her head and immediately winced. "I have a huge knot on the right side of my head, too."

Quiet for a moment, Mat turned toward her. "That was a real close call. But you saved the boy's life and your own, Laura." They were silent for the remainder of the short trip to George and Anna's place.

"Let's get you inside, Laura!" exclaimed Anna. "Annie, take care of little George while Grandma and I see what we can do for these horrible burns." She continued murmuring sympathetically as they helped Laura into the house.

Grandma Welsch quickly got her kit. "Let's get her out of those clothes and treat those burns right away. I'll mix up some egg white and lard."

"The rest of you, outside," ordered Anna.

Once outdoors with the younger children, George asked, "How is the house, Mat?"

"It's still standing but in real bad shape. Turned almost a quarter turn on the foundation. And the roof is sagging so badly I don't know how long it will stay up."

George frowned. "It sounds like the next strong wind might blow the whole thing down. Did you go in?"

"Just long enough to see if Laura and George were inside."

"There's still plenty of daylight left. We'd better get over there and save as much as we can. Otherwise, you won't even have any clothes to wear. Mike, start hitching up our wagon! All of you kids except Annie come with us while your mother and grandmother take care of Laura."

Mat smiled inwardly. His dad's foresight and ability to quickly assess a situation, no matter how complex or unusual, was still a source of wonder. *Thank goodness Dad and Mother are close by!*

Once at the house, George walked around it, slowly shaking his head. His concern was intensified by ominous creaks as it swayed visibly in the wind. "All you kids stay outside. Mat and I will bring stuff out to you. We better get as much out as we can now before the roof falls in."

They spent the remainder of the afternoon taking out clothing, bedding, and furniture. Mat and Mike carried the heavier items out to the barn or to the cellar while Mary, Katie, Johnny, and George, Jr. placed clothing and other small items in the two wagons.

"I forgot how much we accumulated in the past two years," Mat remarked.

"Well, at least most of your things are out of there now," replied George. "I can't help but think that the next high wind will bring that roof down." Putting his hands on his hips, he stepped back and stared at the house. "It's gonna' have to come down, Mat. Then we can rebuild. All the horses in the county couldn't get it squared up on its foundation without tearing it up even more. But you and Laura and the baby are safe and that's the most important thing for now," he concluded as they climbed aboard the wagons.

One morning a few days later, a wagon pulled up at George and Anna's house. "Well, it's Howard White," said Mat. "Hello, Howard!"

"Hello yourself," smiled the tall, lanky visitor, shaking Mat's hand. "I saw that a storm hit your place and thought maybe you could use some extra food." He removed a large basket from the wagon and asked, "Did you all get out safely?"

"I was on my way home from town and didn't get there until right after the twister hit. Laura got burned pretty badly when the kitchen stove came flying across the room at her. It also hit the side of her head and left a horrible bump. She's been sleeping most of the time the past two days. She seemed a little better this morning but went back to bed right after breakfast. But George didn't have a mark on him, thanks to Laura."

"That was an awfully close call," Howard observed.

Mat agreed. "It sure was. I hope she gets better soon. Say! That basket of food. It's awfully neighborly of you. Howard, let's go in the house!" Inside, Mat continued, "This really smells good, fresh bread and something sweet and spicy like a dessert."

Howard removed the cloth from the basket and laughed as Katie, Mary, Johnny, George, Jr., and Mike quickly gathered around, attracted by the aroma of something good to eat. "I brought four loaves of bread and three dozen cookies. And for little George III, there's something extra special, a gingerbread man."

Mat interpreted Howard's comments for the family and asked Anna if it were all right to give cookies to the younger children.

"Yes, certainly," she replied. "And tell Mr. White that the woman who marries him some day is going to be very lucky!"

"What are you going to do for a place to live?" Howard asked after the children ran out of the house with their treats.

"The house has to be torn down because it's too badly damaged to repair. I really haven't thought much farther ahead than that," Mat replied.

"Well, I've got an idea if you'd like to hear it."

"Sure, let's sit down with the folks and talk about it. Just pause for a moment after you tell me something and I'll repeat it in German."

"OK, here's what you could do. Instead of totally rebuilding the old house you could just replace it with one from Sears or Montgomery Wards."

"Really?" Mat was incredulous.

"Yes, you could order the kind you want from one of their catalogs. I have copies of both of them. All the pieces are precut and numbered so you just follow their instructions in putting up the house. They even send buckets of paint along with the lumber and nails."

"Have you ever seen one of those houses?"

"Yes, I even helped put one up. In fact, so has Thomas, your neighbor to the east. I'd be happy to help you and I'm sure he would too."

"That sounds like a good idea! But one more thing, how does Sears or Wards get all that material out here. By rail?"

Howard nodded. "Yep, the good old Rock Island. All you'd have to do is go to town with some wagons and pick it up a few weeks after they get your order."

"How much would one of those houses cost?"

"Well, that depends on what you want. They run all the way from a few hundred dollars to a few thousand. Tell you what, I'll bring both my catalogs over tomorrow and you and Laura can pick out one you like."

By late September, Mat and Laura had a new home, one larger than the old one, with a living room, kitchen, and two bedrooms. With Howard White's help and that of several neighbors, the work went smoothly. There was only one hitch. "I'm sure I ordered white paint. Whoever heard of a blue house?" grumbled Mat upon opening the buckets. "Oh well, blue it is then! There are more important things to worry about, like getting moved in and getting back to regular family life."

But *regular family life* proved elusive. "Laura, it's been almost six weeks since you were hurt. Your burns have healed pretty well but you're still in pain. We'd better see a doctor about those headaches and the dizzy spells. It's not right for you to be fainting as often as you do!" was Mat's almost daily expression of angst.

"What could a doctor do for these scars on my face?" she would reply bitterly. "Or what could a doctor do for pain that moves around so much I can't even describe it accurately to you? Just get me something for pain at the drugstore in Goodwell. Why go all the way to Guymon and then have to pay a doctor to tell me 'get something for the pain'?"

"I feel terrible knowing how you're hurting," Mat would reply, trying to take her into his arms.

"No, you don't!" was her most frequent response, pulling away. "I feel so worthless!"

"Laura, you saved yourself and our son. It took a lot of courage to run back and get him when the house was just about to blow away."

Nothing seemed to pull Laura out of her melancholy. Even visits from her parents and sister provided only temporary respite. On one visit as Joe and Antonia Loesel were departing, Antonia confided in Mat, "I've never seen her like this before. In appearance she looks about the same but she doesn't act anything like the daughter I raised."

Extending his hand, Joe told Mat, "We know you're doing your best. We'd really like to help her if we could but I can't think of anything right now."

Summer and early autumn faded into the bleak days of mid-November 1915. In Europe the war had ground down to trench warfare with reports of casualties so high they were the focus of news accounts that Mat continued reading to George, Anna, and Grandma Welsch on weekends. On most of these days he made the trip to their place with only George III. Laura was becoming even more isolated and rarely left the homestead.

Mat returned home after a day of gathering feed for the milk cows from the north field. As the wagon pulled up near the house it was strangely quiet. Then, he heard George III crying and saw him at the screen door of the house. "Laura, Laura!" he called, becoming alarmed. Despite her depression, she usually came outside to meet him when he returned from the field or from town.

"Laura? Laura?" he called again, leaping down from the wagon and running toward the screen door. There was no reply, only the loud crying of George III standing just inside. Ominously, it was still locked. With a hard yank, Mat forced the door open and picked up George. "Where's your mother, son?"

"Laura, where are you? Laura?" he called, striding into the nearly dark house. *What's wrong, there isn't even a lamp lit!* "Oh, no!" he exclaimed upon seeing her lying on the kitchen floor. He put George down, knelt beside her, and took her hand. "Oh honey, did you faint again? Wake up! Please!" She lay motionless on the floor. He touched her neck and wrists, checking for a pulse, but couldn't feel any. "No, no! It can't. You can't. You can't be."

"Come on, little George, we're going to your grandmother's," said Mat, picking him up and running out to the wagon.

Shortly, he returned to the house, accompanied by George and Anna. After checking for a pulse, George looked up and shook his head saying, "She's gone, Mat." Then, examining her face, he pointed to deep wounds near her right temple. "Looks like she fainted then fell, hitting the corner of the stove and then the fuel box. She probably couldn't have tried to catch her fall and there would have been hard impacts as she hit the stove and the box. Look. There's blood where she struck them on the way down."

Anna gripped Mat's arm to steady him from the shock of his loss. "I'm so sorry, Mat."

A few days later, the Welli and Loesel families and Gus Schubert gathered at the Goodwell cemetery for the somber paying of last respects. "I don't know what I'll do. It's just me and little George III in our family now," said a grief-stricken Mat to George and Anna after the others had gone. "I should have done more for Laura. I should have made her see a doctor."

George put his hand on Mat's shoulder. "You can't help someone who doesn't really want to be helped, Mat. This is a terrible loss but don't go blaming yourself for it."

Hugging Mat, Anna told him, "He's right, Mat. You did all you could. You really couldn't force her to see a doctor. And don't worry about George III. He can stay with us as long as necessary. I think it will be good for you to spend some time alone. It may help in getting over your hurt."

CHAPTER 19
DISORDER ALONG THE BORDER

"If I have to defeat the American army I will!"
Pancho Villa, Mexican bandit, revolutionary

Mat spent the winter working hard to stifle his grief. Often he invented chores around the barn and livestock. Never before had old Chunk and the two workhorses, Bert and Bess, received complete inspections and been brushed and curried so regularly. Same for the cattle. The cows were always milked on schedule, occasionally ahead of time. The beef cattle were checked on and fed almost obsessively. But it was winter, a relatively slow period on a homestead. Invariably, the chores were done much too quickly and he had to return to the quiet, lonely house, a home in which the walls no longer rang with Laura's laughter, comforting words, and lively conversation, a home devoid of George III's cries, laughter, and first words.

Gus and Joe visited him on New Year's Day, 1916. But their time together was empty of the usual banter and boisterous camaraderie. There were awkward, almost embarrassing pauses in the conversation and Mat felt relieved when they left. But shortly after, he felt almost suffocated by the silence.

At times he simply had to get out of the house, for any reason. He made trips to Goodwell even if he needed only one item from the store. While in town there was the inevitable stop at the cemetery where he would gaze sorrowfully at the marble headstone, which read "Laura — wife of M. Welli — 1888-1915." *Yes, I'll come to Goodwell. But I won't go to Guymon. Guymon's for dancing and I've lost my beautiful dancing partner.* Finally, nearly blinded by tears, he would return home.

Daily trips to George and Anna's place were much more cheering. Sometimes Rosa was there visiting Annie as the two had become close friends. Today he walked in on a lively, almost whimsical family discussion.

"Mary, Katie, quit sneaking those kittens into bed with you," Anna was scolding, trying to suppress a smile.

"But Mother, little George likes to have them in bed with us," protested Katie.

"It's so cold outside," added Mary, gazing at Anna pleadingly.

Anna turned toward Mat in order to conceal her mirth. "Your father says no dogs or cats in the house overnight and he means it. They have fur to keep them warm and they know the way to the barn if it gets really cold."

"Even in the dark?" asked Katie.

"Yes, of course," replied Anna.

"How did you learn about this?" asked Mat, his curiosity piqued.

"Well, they start purring real loud after a few minutes in the nice warm bed with the kids. Dad is usually asleep so he doesn't hear it but a rule is a rule. Besides, someone as young as George III needs a clean place to sleep. The kittens might have fleas," replied Anna in a manner that seemed she was the one who most needed convincing.

"Hi, little George!" exclaimed Mat, picking up his son. Today was a bit brighter than most and soon winter would be over.

But for Mat, there were still the frequent trips to Goodwell, and the cemetery. In mid-March he watched a long train pull into the depot. Off stepped dozens of soldiers, marked by their broad-brimmed campaign hats, boots, and riding breeches. "Are we in the war now?" Mat asked. "And if so, how come you're headed west?"

"Yes, we're in a war but it's in a different direction," replied one of the young cavalrymen. "We've got a Mexican bandit to run down. A few days ago Pancho Villa and his band crossed the border and raided Columbus, New Mexico. They murdered eighteen Americans."

"Really? I haven't seen anything in the newspapers about it," was Mat's incredulous reply.

"It'll be in the papers soon enough, especially when we singe ol' Pancho's whiskers," chimed in another trooper.

"Where's Columbus?"

"Straight west of El Paso and Fort Bliss, Texas," was the reply.

"Well, this explains why your train is so long. Where are you coming from?"

"Fort Leavenworth, Kansas," they told him. "We got regular tourist cars for us to ride in, stock cars for the horses, and freight cars for the rifles, machine guns, ammunition, hay, grain, and baggage."

"How good are your horses?" Mat was now keenly interested.

"They're Thoroughbreds. All fine-looking, bright-eyed fellows," said one of the cavalrymen.

"All aboard!"

"Good luck, boys!" shouted Mat. He waved to them as the train pulled out, headed for Fort Bliss. *I'm really out of touch with things. Maybe I should go to Guymon and visit Gus and Joe, sometime next month, maybe.* He recalled reading something about Americans being killed in Mexico earlier in this year and other problems last year.

There had been serious friction along the Mexican border in 1915 with raids and murders on American soil by both Mexican bandits and the soldiers of General Carranza. U.S. garrisons were harassed at night, American soldiers shot at, and their horses and equipment stolen.[22]

Early in January 1916, the United States asked Mexico to punish bands of outlaws who had looted the Cusi mining property eighty miles west of the city of Chihuahua, but without effective response. A group of Americans went by train from Chihuahua to visit the mines. However, on January 10 the train was stopped by Mexican bandits. Eighteen of the Americans were stripped of their clothing and shot in cold blood in what became known as the "Santa Ysabel Massacre."

General Carranza told the U.S. State Department he had issued orders for the immediate pursuit, capture, and punishment of those responsible for the atrocity. However, no one was ever brought to justice.

Resolved to refresh himself, Mat looked at some news clippings saved from the previous year, before tragedy struck his household. *Yes! There's that one from the summer of 1915. Just like a story from a dime novel, except it's true! We loved hearing Joe Loesel read this one.*

COWED MEXICAN REGIMENT
Posse of Arizona Cowboys Cause Hasty
Release of Two Kidnapped American Youths

June 7, Nogales, Arizona – A posse of 10 American cowboys and miners galloped eight miles across the border into Santa Cruz, Sonora late today and, leveling their guns at the colonel commanding the garrison while 150 Mexican soldiers looked on, demanded the immediate release of two American youths. The boys were kidnapped early today by three of the soldiers on the Arizona side of the border.

The colonel gave up his 17-year-old prisoners, George Vaughn, son of the storekeeper at Duquesne, and Henry Chang, son of a Chinese-American citizen of Washington Camp, Ariz., without argument and the posse rode triumphantly back to the United States. Santa Cruz is garrisoned by the forces of Jose Maytorena, the (Pancho) Villa governor of Sonora. Washington Camp, where the Mexicans captured the boys, and Duquesne are border settlements twenty-five miles east of here. What was expected to be gained by the kidnapping of the boys was not ascertained.[23]

It would be good to see Gus and Joe again, he mused while scanning the clippings. But April came and went before Mat could bring himself to travel to Guymon, the place where he met, danced with, and married Laura. Finally, on a bright afternoon in mid-May he hitched up Chunk and made the trip. The perfect weather with brilliant sunshine and moderate temperature served to offset his misgivings about going. By the time he pulled up at Gus's restaurant, doubt was replaced by the anticipation of seeing old friends once again.

"I got nothing left but ham and beans this time of day!" was Gus's jovial greeting that had become a standard anytime Mat entered the restaurant. As usual, it was deserted this late in the afternoon. He got up from the table, wiped his hands on an apron, and shook hands. "It's good to see you again, old friend. Want some coffee?"

"Sure," Mat replied, sitting down. "Thought it was about time I got away from Goodwell for just a while and see how you and Joe are doing."

"Things are about the same. Business is still good here at the restaurant but the piano tuning has dropped off some. There have been a few Mondays recently where I didn't have any tuning jobs."

"Why is that?"

"I got into some arguments about the war on a couple of tuning jobs last winter. Guess that could be the reason. Oh, look who just walked in," he said, pointing toward the door.

"Well, hello!" exclaimed Joe Loesel. "Gosh, it's good to see you again, Mat. Been a long time!"

"Yes, at the funeral and on New Year's Day," said Mat, standing to shake hands. "I'm afraid I wasn't very good company then."

"Don't worry about it," said Joe, pumping Mat's hand.

"Looks like you brought lots of newspapers," Gus noted.

Joe placed them on the table and took a seat. "Ever since the raid down in Columbus, New Mexico they've had about three articles on the American army in Mexico for each one about the war in Europe."

"I saw a troop train in Goodwell back in March," offered Mat.

"According to the news, a big force went into Mexico right after the raid. Look at this picture in the Optima paper, Mat," said Joe. "They even have Apache scouts assigned."

"'Apache Scouts Helping General Pershing,'" Mat read aloud. "There are fifteen in this picture. I wonder if they're from Fort Sill."

"Fort Sill?" asked Gus.

"Yes, years ago a man told me the Apache scouts were stationed there."

"Well, this is mostly a cavalry operation. There was even a big battle with a cavalry charge," said Joe as he began reading. "Six troops of the Eleventh Cavalry, composed of fourteen officers and 319 troopers accompanied by thirty Apache scouts, marched all night to Ojo Azules, near Cusihuiriachic. At dawn they surprised 150 bandits encamped at the ranch. There was a running fight for two hours climaxed by a charge in a column of fours, using automatic pistols. The troopers killed forty-four Villistas while suffering no casualties. Afterward, an Apache scout shouted, '*Huli!* Real good fight!'"

"A lively story! Was Pancho Villa there?" asked Mat.

"It doesn't mention him. It says this was the Acosta, Dominguez, Angel band," replied Joe.

"Great story!" seconded Gus. "Maybe with this action in Mexico we won't be reading so many bad things about Germany in the papers."

"I don't know about that, Gus," replied Joe. Some people think Germany is supporting Mexico and causing the problems along the border. They believe that Kaiser Wilhelm wants to keep the United States busy in this part of the world so we won't join the British and French as allies in the war overseas.

"He's looking ahead. That's good thinking. But I hope Germany wins the war even if the Americans do join the British and the French!" exclaimed Gus.

"Gus, I'm glad no one but us heard that," snapped Joe, quickly looking around to make certain no one else was in the restaurant.

Surprised by both Gus's outburst and Joe's retort, Mat paused before speaking. Finally he replied, "Gus, all three of us here are Americans even if we can speak German. If America joins the Allies, we're still Americans. Our family left Germany and moved to Austria in 1863 because of Bismarck's war plans. Just three years later, one of my dad's older brothers died in the war that Germany declared against Austria."

Joe nodded, saying, "My family left Germany even before that, moving to the Bohemian part of Austria. Then, we came to this country in 1890. Gus, how many years have you been a citizen?"

"Since 1910," Gus replied, somewhat taken aback by his friends' reactions.

"A U.S. citizen for six years! Well, you'd better remember that or you're headed for trouble. There are people already watching for saboteurs or anyone who show signs of disloyalty. Last year some crazy

German professor back East tried to blow up the Capitol in Washington, D.C.," Joe continued.

"We're your friends, Gus. Listen to us," urged Mat, himself taken aback by the intensity of Joe's words.

"Well, maybe I'd better be more careful. Like I told Mat, the piano tuning is falling way off. I need restaurant customers to keep going here in Guymon," replied Gus, somewhat chagrined.

But Joe had a final admonition. He leaned forward. "Gus, if you're not careful about how you talk, one of these days you're gonna' be walking down the railroad track, kickin' horse apples, and sayin', 'Who woulda' thought it!'"

Their advice was timely and Gus followed their counsel. From then on he spoke only about crops, weather, horses, or cattle to customers in his restaurant. He talked about the news from Mexico but consciously avoided any conversation about the war in Europe.

At eight minutes past two o'clock on the morning of Sunday, July 30, 1916, a thundering explosion at the Black Tom munitions depot sent sleeping residents of New York City and surrounding areas tumbling from their beds.[24] Black Tom Island, connected to Jersey City by a long pier, was a depot for transshipping munitions to warring nations in Europe. The warehouses, holding more than one thousand tons of TNT, gunpowder, and shrapnel, went up in a blast heard as far away as Philadelphia and parts of Maryland.

Initially the explosion was thought to have resulted from spontaneous combustion. Later, however, it was attributed to sabotage. Gus Schubert was stunned when this news reached Oklahoma. *Joe and Mat really did me a favor. Such good friends!* He became even more solicitous of his restaurant customers.

Early in August 1916, Joe Udry had some valuable news for Mat. "The Lambirds are moving away so they're putting up their quarter for sale. It's good land and close by. You and your dad might want to look into it."

George was excited about the opportunity. "With another 160 acres we could raise a lot more wheat. It's a much better crop than broomcorn. That would give us 480 acres, 400 for wheat and 80 for grazing cattle and raising feed grain and fodder. Best of all, we can pay cash for it!"

By the end of the month George owned the quarter, having bought it for $2,000. The owner of the First State Bank in Goodwell congratulated Mat and George on their foresight. "I think this country will eventually get into the war. When it does, we're going to need lots of wheat," he told them, shaking hands when the deal closed.

EPILOGUE

Still a neutral country in 1916, the United States found itself attacked along the Mexican border and its port facilities in New York severely damaged by sabotage. Neither event, however, would have an immediate or full resolution.

Decades would pass before there was justice in the Black Tom sabotage. Not until 1930 was conclusive evidence developed linking a suspect "paymaster" for German agents. By that time, however, the man he was suspected of paying had been dead for two years.

Civil litigation of the Black Tom sabotage would stretch out for even more decades. On October 30, 1939, the Mixed Claims Commission awarded $50 million to American plaintiffs.[25] On January 6, 1941, the U.S. Supreme Court refused to review the case, letting the awards stand. However, final arrangements for payments were not completed until a post-World War II conference held in London with the Federal Republic of Germany in 1953. Final payments on the awards were made in 1979, sixty-three years after the sabotage.[26]

General John J. Pershing's Punitive Expedition into Mexico following Pancho Villa's raid also had mixed results. Pershing's force of 15,000 was evaded by Villa, who took refuge in the rugged mountain country of northern Mexico. However, Villa's band had been beaten and scattered, his veteran generals and colonels run to earth and killed or captured, eventually putting an end to serious border incidents.

The Punitive Expedition into Mexico in 1916 was a blend of old and new. The cavalrymen carried .45 caliber automatic pistols and some of the units were armed with machine guns. It involved the Army's first use of motorized vehicles and airplanes in a military campaign. There were also some noteworthy "lasts." The cavalry still used Apache scouts in their efforts to track down Pancho Villa. It featured the last cavalry charge and also marked the last time American soldiers went into combat wearing soft hats instead of steel helmets. This last horse-cavalry campaign of the U.S. Army became a metaphor for the ending of the Old West.

CHAPTER 20
HYPHENATED AMERICANS

"There are citizens of the United States, I blush to admit, born under other flags, but welcomed under our generous naturalization laws to the full freedom and opportunity of America, who have poured the poison of disloyalty into the very arteries of our national life; who have sought to bring the authority and good name of our government into contempt. . . . It is necessary that we should promptly make use of processes of law by which we may be purged of their corrupt distempers. . . . I am urging you to do nothing less than save the honor and self-respect of the nation. . . .Disloyalty and anarchy must be crushed out. . . . I need not suggest the terms in which they may be dealt with.

President Woodrow Wilson
December 1915 State of the Union address

November finally brought the long, bitter 1916 presidential election campaign to an end. Woodrow Wilson, the Democratic incumbent, ran against Republican Charles Evans Hughes. Most German-Americans were by now disillusioned with Wilson because of his attacks on foreign-born citizens. "Any man who carries a hyphen with him carries a dagger that he is ready to plunge into the vitals of this Republic whenever he gets ready," he reportedly said. However, even Hughes, aided by former President Theodore Roosevelt's claims of widespread disloyalty among "hyphenates," took up the same cry. Wilson won a close election based on the slogan "He kept us out of war."

For Anna, November brought on the need to cope with colder weather, not only around the homestead but also for the children's daily trips to school. "Mike, you're thirteen now and in your last year. You can drive Mary, Katie, and the twins to school in the wagon and put the horse in the stable they have there," George had told him in September.

"I like that!" Mike exclaimed, proud of the adult-like responsibility. And in the warm autumn days of September and October, it was a pleasant trip unless it rained. However, with winter coming on, there would be cold, bone-chilling rides of three miles each way.

But Anna reminded them of her solution to the winter cold. "We have extra blankets to put in the wagon. And when the weather gets real cold I'll start heating up that 'mountain rock' we keep in the garden." Everyone smiled. They knew wintertime was near when Anna had someone clean up the large granite rock and bring it into the kitchen to be heated in the oven overnight. "It won't help you, Mike, but at least the younger children will have it to put their feet on during the ride to school."

As 1917 arrived, international events were again the main topics of Mat's newspaper reading to George and Anna, similarly in his conversations with Gus and Joe. In late January it was reported that General Pershing's force was returning from Mexico. Pancho Villa hadn't been captured but his forces had been disrupted and decimated by the American Army. Further, more than 25,000 state militia troops were ordered back to their home states from the Mexican border.

On January16, 1917, Arthur Zimmerman, the German foreign minister in Berlin, sent the following telegram to Count von Bernstorff, the German ambassador to the United States:

Most Secret

For Your Excellency's personal information and to be handed on to the Imperial Minister in Mexico.

We intend to begin unrestricted submarine warfare on the first of February. We shall endeavor in spite of this to keep the United States neutral. In the event of this not succeeding, we make Mexico a proposal of an alliance on the following basis: Make war together, make peace together, generous financial support, and an understanding on our part that Mexico is to reconquer the lost territory in Texas, New Mexico, and Arizona. The settlement detail is left to you.

You will inform the President [*of Mexico*] of the above most secretly as soon as the outbreak of war with the United States is certain and add the suggestion that he should, on his own initiative, invite Japan to immediate adherence and at the same time mediate between Japan and ourselves.

Please call the President's attention to the fact that the unrestricted employment of our submarines now offers the prospect of compelling England to make peace within a few months. Acknowledge receipt.

Zimmerman

However, the telegram was intercepted by British intelligence, which deciphered and forwarded it to the U.S. State Department on February 24. Ultimately, President Wilson and Secretary of State Robert Lansing decided to release it to the public through the Associated Press.

The March 9, 1917 the *Optima Optimist*, a weekly newspaper read regularly by Mat, Gus, and Joe, had two articles with screaming headlines: GERMAN PLOT AGAINST UNITED STATES and GERMANY URGED MEXICO AND JAPAN TO FIGHT AMERICA.

Some pacifists and pro-Germans professed belief that the telegram was a forgery but Zimmerman admitted having transmitted it. Mexico denied ever being involved in the matter, while the prime minister of

Japan announced that if such a proposal ever came to hand, it would receive the contemptuous refusal it deserved.

Later in March, President Wilson told a newspaper editor: "Once lead these people into war and they'll forget there ever was such a thing as tolerance. To fight you must be brutal and ruthless, and the spirit of ruthless brutality will enter into every fiber of our national life, infecting Congress, the courts, the policeman on the beat, the man on the street."[27] In April he asked Congress to declare war on Germany, stating, "The world must be made safe for democracy."

Several weeks later, Mat was returning home from his daily trip to see the family, especially George III, who was now more than three years old. From a distance he saw a horse and wagon at his place. A little closer and he could see it was Gus. *Good, this should make for a lively time!* "Hello Gus," he called. But Gus responded with only a quick, perfunctory wave. *Now what?* Mat wondered.

Arriving in the yard, Mat commented, "Strange time of day to be coming around, but you're welcome anytime."

"I'm sure glad to hear that," Gus said softly, a stricken look on his face.

Mat looked at him, then at the wagon. It was loaded with boxes, clothing, and two chairs from Gus's restaurant. "What's up, Gus?"

"Trouble! Big trouble! Please, I need a place to stay, Mat!"

"How come? What happened?" Gus was usually jovial, brash, and very confident. Mat had never seen him like this.

Gus reached into his shirt pocket, pulled out a piece of paper, and handed it to Mat, saying, "This was nailed to the front door of the restaurant this morning."

Mat read the note silently, swallowed hard, and then read it aloud: "Attention German! Get out of Guymon or we will string you up. We mean it." Mat read it again. "Any idea who put this on your door?" he asked, handing it back.

"No, absolutely not."

"Did you have an argument with someone about the war?" Mat wondered if Gus had reneged on his commitment to avoid the subject with customers.

"No, certainly not, even though I've really been tempted since America got into the war. You should just hear how some of those people talk!"

"Let me see that note again." Mat alternately read it silently and aloud a few more times then gave it back. "I don't think it's a joke. I think you really do need a place to hide out."

"Thanks! I was hoping for that because I've got no where else to go." Gus smiled for the first time since finding the terrifying message.

"Well, let's put your stuff in the back bedroom. That's where George III slept before going to live with my folks. Then we'll stable the horses. I think we better hide your wagon in the barn for now. Oh, what about Joe Loesel, does he know about this?"

Gus shook his head. "He wasn't around. I think he's out on the Rock Island for a few days. I never even thought about telling him. I figured that your place would be the best place to stay since you live alone. Joe still lives with his folks."

"He'll be wondering what happened to you when he gets back to town. But I can tell Rosa the next time she comes down to visit my sister Annie."

Gus Schubert wasn't the only German in Oklahoma threatened with violence. A dentist in Oklahoma City suspected of disloyalty had his office wrecked. At Shattuck, the Defense Council compelled a man to kiss the flag and swear allegiance in public. At Bessie, a local citizen who defended a Farmers' Union official's right to speak was dragged from his bed in the early morning, coated with tar, and told to keep quiet. And at Elk City, a mob of patriotic citizens abducted a Socialist lecturer from police protection, tarred and feathered him, and ran him out of the county.[28]

Two weeks later, Rosa paid a visit and Mat told her of Gus's problems.

"Oh, I was wondering what happened to him! His restaurant has a sign in the window that says 'Closed.' No one in Guymon knows where he is. Joe will be so glad to hear that he's all right," said Rosa. "But what that note says, it's so frightening!"

"Rosa and I are going to a dance at the Udry place tonight. Why don't you come along too, Mat? You haven't been to one around here for such a long time," invited Annie.

"Well, I don't know," he replied, trying to think of a valid reason not to go.

"You've been alone for a year and a half," she added.

Mat paused, looking off into the distance. "I guess it wouldn't hurt. I'd get to see a lot of people for the first time in a long time."

Mat brightened upon arriving at the friendly, familiar Udry homestead. *That music! It brings back lots of good memories!*

"Hello, Annie! Hello, Rosa! Hey Mat, we can use an extra harmonica tonight," invited Ray Fisher.

"You don't need me. You've got a fine group already," countered Mat. "But it's sure good to see you again. Learned any new songs for the fiddle?"

"A few," Ray smiled. "I think you'll like them. Talk to you later."

Joe and Rosina Udry came over, accompanied by a younger man who bore a striking resemblance to Joe. Tall, handsome with chiseled features, dark curly hair, and a full mustache, he walked in a measured, almost military manner.

"Good evening, Annie, Rosa. Mat, it's good to see you again," said Joe. After they exchanged greetings with Rosina, Joe introduced the newcomer. "This is our son Frank, who's been visiting for a few days. He owns a farm at Iuka, Kansas."

"It's good to meet you," said Mat, shaking hands. "Where's Iuka?"

"It's in Pratt County, just five miles north of Pratt."

"I remember Pratt. The train went through it when we moved out here in 1906."

"That's how I came out here, on the Rock Island."

When introduced, Rosa simply nodded and said, "It's nice to meet you, Frank."

But Annie's face turned crimson and she had to suppress a giggle. "It's *wonderful* to meet you, Frank," she blurted, making a slight curtsey.

"Would you like to dance this number?" he asked.

Joe and Rosina moved on to greet newcomers. Mat turned to Rosa, "I've never seen Annie react like that before."

Rosa smiled. "She seems to really like him. I've never seen her that way before either."

"This is a great waltz, would you like to dance?" asked Mat.

As the evening wore on, Mat danced with several other women but mostly with Rosa. But Frank and Annie had become inseparable. They danced nearly every dance, displaying remarkable dancing abilities. During the infrequent breaks, they stood together talking animatedly. By dawn they were still together, having danced the entire night away.

When the dance ended, Mat told Rosa, "I wonder what she'll do now that it's time to go home."

"Me too," said Rosa. "But I need to go back to her place and get my horse. It's a long ride back to Optima."

They walked over to Frank and Annie. "Well, it's time to go," Mat said.

"You and Rosa go ahead. Frank and I are going to visit with his parents for a while longer. He'll bring me home later," replied Annie.

Mat and Rosa spent the trip talking about the instant strong attraction between Frank and Annie. "Frank has to go back to Kansas in a day or two," said Mat. "I wonder if they can stand being separated."

Long after the noon meal was over, Mat sat at the table talking about the war and other news with George and Anna. All the children were outside enjoying the brilliant, warm sunshine of late May. Anna kept going to the window. "I wonder why Annie hasn't gotten back yet," she would say, frowning and shaking her head in wonder.

Finally a wagon pulled up in the yard. In walked Annie, accompanied by Frank Udry. "Mother, Dad, this is Frank Udry, Joe and Rosina's son. We want to tell you something," she said nervously.

After everyone was seated, Frank cleared his throat. "Mr. Welli, Mrs. Welli, I want to marry your daughter and have come to ask your permission and blessing. I know we have just met but I have to go back to Kansas tomorrow."

Anna stood up. "Annie, I want to talk to you alone. Come out to the garden with me!" she said sternly.

Frank remained in the house with George and Mat, both of whom were surprised but not nearly as upset as Anna appeared to be. George got his pipe and made a lengthy production of filling it with tobacco, tamping it in the bowl, and lighting up. He took several long pulls before speaking. "This is very sudden Mr. Udry. But I do know your parents and they are among the finest people I've ever known. But I want to know about you. Can you support a wife? If so, how?"

"Mr. Welli, I have a farm of 320 acres at Iuka, Kansas. That's in Pratt County, five miles north of Pratt."

"We went through Pratt coming out here on the train," Mat quickly told George.

George nodded and continued. "How old are you?"

An intense discussion began immediately after Anna and Annie were in the garden and out of the earshot of anyone else. But Anna still spoke in hushed tones not much louder than a whisper. "Annie, you didn't compromise yourself, did you?"

"Oh no, Mother. It was nothing like that, I swear. But we got on so wonderfully. I've been going to dances for years now and haven't met anyone like Frank. He's kind, intelligent, very funny at times, and a wonderful dancer."

Anna took a deep relaxing breath, feeling some relief.

Indoors, Frank was telling George more about himself. "Mr. Welli, I'm thirty-four years old. I've been in the United States since 1908 and I'm a citizen."

George frowned a bit. "Our Annie is only twenty. Have you been married before?"

"Yes, but my wife passed away last year," replied Frank. "We were married for six years."

"Did you have any children?"

"No, she couldn't have children."

"Annie, marriage is a very serious step. Besides, this means that you would be moving a long way from here," Anna pointed out.

"I know, Mother. But I'm tired of doing all the work out in the barn with the cows. I'm tired of having to watch out for rattlesnakes in our garden and I'm tired of dust storms, grasshoppers, and hailstorms." She was almost in tears.

"I think you would be doing much the same thing as Frank's wife," said Anna, now sympathetic. "But I can't speak for the weather there in Kansas."

George took a couple of long pulls on his pipe then stopped to relight it.

While he was so occupied, Mat asked Frank about Iuka and Pratt. "They're both very nice towns. Pratt is bigger than Goodwell, maybe even bigger than Guymon."

Out in the garden Anna took Annie by the hand. "Annie, are you certain this is the right thing?"

"Yes, Mother. I've never been so sure of anything in my life!" She hugged Anna.

"One more thing. What did Joe and Rosina say about you two wanting to get married so quickly?"

"They were surprised. Just as you and Dad are. But they've known me for several years and thought it should be a good marriage."

George had his pipe going again. "Well, Mr. Udry, given your age you must have worked in the old country. What did you do there?"

"I was in the army."

"As an enlisted man?"

"No, I was an officer in the cavalry, an *oberleutnant*. I was stationed near Budapest."

George looked up and smiled for the first time. "It appears you have the means of supporting a wife and are able to take responsibility. But we need to see what Anna thinks."

Anna and Annie walked in arm in arm. Anna looked at George and nodded. He smiled and said, "Welcome to the family, Frank."

The next morning Mat took Frank and Annie to Guymon, stopping first to see Rosa and give her the good news. "I'm not surprised. I hope I get to see you again sometime," she said, adding her best wishes. Then they went to the courthouse to get a marriage license.

As they headed for the judge's office, Mat told them, "It's not too late to change your minds." They only smiled, determined to keep their date with the future.

With Mat and a courthouse employee as witnesses, the judge began: "This is to join Frank Udry and Anna Welli in holy matrimony on this twenty-first day of May in the year of our Lord 1917."

CHAPTER 21
FORTUNES OF WAR

The war would have a major impact on homesteaders and ranchers. Previously, news of events in far-off Europe or in Mexico was, for the most part, something that livened conversations. Now, with the United States in the conflict, America's young men were subject to the draft. Early in June 1917 nearly 10 million began registering.

Those not subject to the draft would find themselves in the middle of an almost unprecedented economic boom. The prices of wheat, corn, cattle, and hogs went up dramatically. On August 25, 1917, futures' trading in wheat was suspended at the Chicago Board of Trade, not to be resumed until June 30, 1920, when government price controls were lifted. The National Grain Corporation, part of the U.S. Food Administration, fixed the price of wheat at $2.21 per bushel.

"The banker was right, you made a good move buying that quarter of land last year," Mat told his dad.

George smiled. "A good crop and a good price all in the same year. That makes homesteading in 1917 worthwhile."

"It certainly does! The only sad thing is that our good friend Howard White has been drafted."

"His best hope is that they make him a baker or cook so he doesn't have to serve in the trenches," George chuckled.

Summer faded into the crisp days of autumn, a time of transition to winter. Horses and dogs grew shaggy coats and noisy ducks and geese passed overhead, bound for climes having milder winters. Busy cleaning and removing ashes from the stove, Mat heard Gus scream in pain. Worried that vigilantes had found him, he hurried outside.

"What's wrong, Gus?"

Gus was running toward the house, holding his left arm. "A snake bit me!" he screamed.

"A rattlesnake?"

"I don't know. He was down in a hole!"

"Let me see your arm." Sure enough, there were two fang marks on Gus's forearm. "Yep, it's a rattlesnake bite. You'd better go lie down."

Gus went to his room, moaning loudly from the pain. "It's swelling up something awful!"

"Why did you reach into a hole in the ground? This time of year snakes start looking for a safe place to spend the winter," chided Mat.

"I was chasing a rabbit. Thought we might like some cottontail with eggs for breakfast. He ran into the hole and I thought I could get him out," he said sheepishly.

"Just stay there on the bed. I don't have any whiskey so I'll have to go to Dad's place."

Mat told George, Anna, and Grandma Welsch of Gus's wound. "How bad is the swelling?" asked George.

"His arm is swelled up like a songbook that got left out in the rain."

George smiled at Mat's vivid description. "Well, whiskey is how everyone else treats snakebite. I have a couple of bottles. Let's go see if that will help."

"Do you know of any remedies, Grandma?" asked Mat.

"Well, put some of that whiskey on a rag and swab the bite marks before you start giving it to him. That's all I can think of. We didn't have problems like this in the old country."

George and Mat returned to the house to find Gus nearly panic-stricken. "I was beginning to think you weren't coming back," he said, visibly relieved. His arm, however, was now swollen so badly Mat wondered why the skin didn't burst.

"Here, Gus, drink some of this," said George, handing him a glass nearly full of whiskey.

"Ugh, how I hate whiskey. Will it help?"

"That's what everyone around here uses," replied Mat.

Gus took a small sip, made a wry face, and then downed the entire glass. "Ugh, that's awful-tasting stuff! Wouldn't beer work just as well? I love beer!"

George shook his head. "I don't know about beer. Besides, I don't have any."

After choking down another glass followed by a third consumed more slowly, the patient began to relax, humming a few bars of a song Mat hadn't heard before. Eventually, he calmed down and was the rowdy, boisterous Gus that they knew. He even began telling some old jokes.

"I'll go back home, now. See if you can get him to finish the first bottle today. Start him on the second one tomorrow," said George.

"Dad, do you think it will save him?"

George shrugged. "Bad business, those rattlesnakes. Well, if it doesn't work, I guess we'll always wonder why it didn't!" he mumbled, heading for the door.

Mat stayed near the house the next day. Each time he found Gus awake he gave him a shot of whiskey. Late the following morning Gus sat up and looked at his arm in amazement. "Mat, the swelling has gone down!"

Mat came into the room. "How do you feel?"

"Not too bad, except for a headache from all that whiskey! But for the first time in three days I think I'm going to make it."

As winter drew closer, Mat decided to make another trip to Guymon. The dance at the Udry place last May had renewed his interest in dancing and companionship. This Saturday night in November was his first visit to the place where he had met Laura. *It seems so long ago, 1912.* Just seeing the hall brought waves of memories and he could almost hear her laugh. *But it's time to move on. She's been gone for two years now.*

Mat entered and looked around at the familiar place. It was mostly the same old crowd, and a few new faces, same sounds, and mostly the same music, he noted. Several recognized him and nodded or spoke. But Joe Loesel wasn't there and neither was Rosa, not yet anyway. He danced a waltz with a woman he'd danced with a few times years ago. Between numbers two men worked their way over to him and began a conversation.

"Haven't seen you around for a spell," said one. His companion said nothing but gazed at Mat intently.

"This is the first time I've been here in a long time, more than two years."

The companion betrayed the reason for striking up the conversation. "We haven't seen ol' Gus around for quite awhile either."

His guard up, Mat shook his head. "Me neither. He seems to have just dropped totally out of sight. Excuse me, I see someone I want to dance with."

An hour later, Joe Loesel came in and greeted Mat warmly. "It's really good to see you Mat! I'm glad you're getting out again." Then, in a lowered voice, "How's Gus doing?"

"He's good but he gets bored with life on a homestead. He says he's a townsman, not a farmer. And he proved it a few weeks ago when he got himself bitten by a rattlesnake." After filling Joe in on the details of the bite and Gus's near-miracle recovery, he said in a lowered voice, "See those two men over by the door, with their backs turned toward us?"

"Yes."

"I wasn't here very long before they came over and asked about Gus. I told them I hadn't seen him, said that he seemed to have just faded away."

Joe turned back and muttered, "Those guys asked me about him several weeks ago. Something about them seemed awfully suspicious so I told them the same thing."

"I'll bet they know about that note Gus found on his door," Mat replied. "Either they wrote it or they know who did. Those are men to stay away from."

Mat continued his social life during the winter, going to dances in Guymon if the weather was good but attending Saturday dances around Goodwell when the weather was less favorable. Gus continued to hide out at Mat's place, newspapers his main source of information about the outside world.

By April 1918 Mat had met, danced with, and conversed with more women than he could remember. But he favored a familiar one, Rosa

Loesel, Laura and Joe's younger sister. *She's a great dancer, cute, funny, so caring, and so kind!* Her parents, Joe, Sr. and Antonia, were delighted at his interest. "Come around any time, Mat," said Joe, Sr., then added softly, "I guess that's the second time I've told you that, isn't it?"

Summer brought another good wheat crop. Mat and George's spirits were so high they celebrated by having a photographer take a picture of the wheat threshing operation on Mat's place. "You know, there's something I'd like to do for the children," George told Mat after the picture taking. "They should have a real baseball field to play on instead of just going out in the pasture. Do you know the measurements, Mat?"

Mat assured him that he did and in a few days they had laid out a baseball field in the pasture, complete with a backstop. Four straw-filled flour sacks served as home plate and the bases. Although the infield was grass-covered, it was still smooth enough that ground balls wouldn't hop too badly. "Now we'll always know where the children are," smiled George as he and Mat admired their work.

True enough. The field became a favorite playground for Mary, Katie, George, Jr., Johnny, and George III. Occasionally Mike, now fifteen, served as an umpire. Many children from neighboring homesteads joined them. They spent long days on this regulation-sized baseball diamond in the middle of land where Comanches, Kiowa, and Southern Cheyenne stalked the great buffalo herds less than fifty years earlier.

By August 1918, Gus was chafing at his isolated existence. "When do you think it will be safe for me to go back to Guymon?" he asked nearly every day.

Each time Mat would tell him to wait a while longer. "I think you need to stay out of sight until the war is over. Most people are still very hostile toward anyone German. And the newspapers are keeping them that way. Look at this article on the front page of the August 29 *Guymon Democrat.*"

As Gus began reading, a scowl quickly formed. "Listen to this, Mat. They say: 'It just makes a patriotic American feel bully to read what the Allies are doing to the Huns over in France these days. General Pershing and Foch are dancing rings and circles and semicircles around old Ludendorff. The beastly, cowardly Hun is ducking and hiding and constantly on the defensive.' Bah!" Gus shouted, throwing the paper down in disgust. "This is almost as bad as that 'Confessions of a German Deserter' story you showed me a few weeks ago."

"Feelings against Germany are still hostile, even though the Allies are winning now with the help of the American Army. Dad and Mother had some of it thrown their way earlier this month."

"Really? They're not even from Germany."

"Yes, but they speak only German and two of the stores in Goodwell won't sell to them or buy eggs from them any longer because of it. So, they've started going to Cartwright's Store, the same place I go. But ol' Cartwright has the last laugh. When I asked him about it he said he liked selling to German customers because they always paid in cash."

"Now that's a good businessman!" laughed Gus. "He'll do well."

Mat continued, "I really liked the question he raised: 'What good does it do for the wartime economy to sell to someone who just puts it on the books?'"

Mat's advice to stay in hiding was sound as there was still a risk of being lynched. In his book on sedition in the American West, Clemens Work provided chilling details of limitations on free speech during World War I. On April 15, 1918, Robert Paul Prager, a thirty-year-old German baker with socialist leanings, was lynched in Collinsville, Illinois. He was said to have made disloyal utterances to a group of coal miners. Police rescued Prager and put him in jail. However, the crowd broke in, hauled Prager to a point just beyond the city limits, and hanged him from a tree just after midnight.

A letter from Collinsville's mayor was read into the U.S. Senate record the following day. The mayor's letter characterized the murder as the "direct result of a widespread feeling within the community that the government will not punish disloyalty." Congress then hastened to pass the Federal Sedition Act of 1918. On May 16, 1918, President Wilson signed the bill into law, effective immediately.

By late June, the Department of Justice was receiving fifteen hundred letters a day related to loyalty charges. Attorney General Thomas Gregory boasted that, "Never in its history has this country been so thoroughly policed."

Herman Rhode, a seventy-four-year-old rancher from near Miles City, Montana who had emigrated from Germany in 1893 and became a U.S. citizen five years later, was convicted of sedition. The case was based on testimony from a local plumber who said Rhode responded *Ja! Ja!* to his question whether Rhode would help the kaiser whip the United States. The same witness said Rhode told him he would have no fear should the German army invade the United States because "true Germans would give certain signs which would convince the invaders that they were all right."

The jury deliberated thirty-five minutes, maybe as few as twelve, according the *Miles City Star*, in reaching a guilty verdict. A *Star* editorial that day, June 9, 1918, jumped on Rhode's testimony about "certain signs."

> To subject all nations to his will . . . [the kaiser] has subtly planted thousands of his servile subjects all over the earth. They lie like snakes in the grass stealthily watching their chance. They do not, like the brave rattlesnake, give the unintended intruder a warning that he may need to take heed to his steps, but silently watch like a

spider for a victim to be helplessly enmeshed in their net and then pounce on him.

They work and plan in secret ways and wait for a signal which shall mean the surrender of their country to the enemy who would murder and enslave their countrymen, mutilate and outrage their women and make them beasts of burden and propagation, crucify their soldiers, bayonet their babies, bomb their wounded, sink their hospital ships, steal their possessions, and lay tribute of billions on their labor forever.

Rhode's age may have saved him from a more severe sentence; as it was, the judge handed the elderly farmer with four children a four- to eight-year prison term. He served thirty-four months, making it one of the longest sentences for any of Montana's sedition prisoners.[29]

"Katie, please set the table but turn the plates upside down," said Anna as she lit a lamp.

"Upside down? Why?" asked Katie.

"We're going to have a dust storm. You don't want a lot of dust in your food, do you?" replied Anna. "Mary, wet some rags and put them around the window sills."

George came in, along with a rush of howling wind. "It's going to get very bad," he cautioned. "I see you got a lamp already lit. We'll need it before this storm ends."

"George, we've had a few dust storms ever since we've lived here. But it seems there's more of them now and they're much worse," Anna observed.

"That's true. I've heard that there were some bad dust storms around here back in the 1890s. But with the price of wheat so high there's been too much land plowed up, land that would have been better left as grazing land. We're doing well now, what with two good crops and good wheat prices. But this kind of weather worries me, especially after the dry years we've had."

"But if it's that dry why have we had good wheat crops?"

"Wheat can do well if it gets rain at the right time even if it's dry for most of the growing season. We've been very lucky."

Two weeks later, Mat rushed to George and Anna's with good news. "The war is over. Germany surrendered November 11!"

"Everywhere? Even in Austria-Hungary?" asked George.

Mat hurriedly scanned the entire newspaper article, and then shook his head. "No, as usual it doesn't mention Austria-Hungary, although it does talk about Turkey and Romania."

"I'm sure it's just a matter of time before Austria-Hungary collapses if they haven't already. They wouldn't be able to continue the war alone. I hope Joseph and Augusta are all right."

"I think this is a time to celebrate. Gus will be sad that Germany surrendered but now he should be able to move out of my place and back to Guymon."

"How are you going to celebrate?" asked Anna.

"I'm going to buy an automobile."

"Really? What's wrong with horses?" asked George, only partly in jest.

"I can get a Ford Model-T touring car for about $800. The dealer will even deliver it."

George laughed and waved his hand. "I'll stick with my horses. They're a lot more loyal than something made from iron and steel."

Mat bought the Model-T touring car. But before he could give it a fair test, he had to make a long train trip. Grandma Welsch's eyesight had seriously deteriorated the past year and eyeglasses available from the local stores were no longer of any use. Her vision had grown so bad that five-year-old George III had the duty of leading her around when she went outdoors. "There aren't any doctors here who could help her," said George. "But Anna's brother told us in his last letter that there are doctors in Chicago who can have glasses made strong enough to help her see again."

Shortly after New Years Day 1919, Mat and Grandma Welsch boarded the Rock Island for the long trip to Chicago. For both of them, it would be the first time they had seen Mathias Welsch since leaving the old country. He had moved to America a year before they did, settling in Chicago.

When the eastbound train stopped in Pratt, Kansas, Mat told her, "Grandma, Annie and her husband Frank live just five miles north of here."

"Oh my! It seems sad to be so close to them but not be able to visit."

"Yes, it is. This entire trip seems a little strange. It's been nearly thirteen years since we came out to Oklahoma from Youngstown on the Rock Island, but everything seems so familiar."

"Well, that trip must have made a big impression on you."

Mat agreed. "It was really exciting seeing this part of the country for the first time. And I had a long conversation with the conductor. He told me a lot of interesting things about it."

Finally, they reached their destination as the trip ended at the La Salle Street Station in Chicago, where Mat Welsch met them. A tall, rather handsome man, he embraced his mother and shook hands with Mat. "It's good to see my namesake, again," he said cordially. "Now, let's go to my place."

Mat Welsch lived in the upstairs of a large house on Halsted Street and worked at a nearby bakery. Once they were settled in his roomy apartment, he told his mother, "There's an eye doctor in downtown Chicago I will take you to. He treats many older patients who have cataracts and I think he can do something for your eyesight."

Grandma Welsch marveled, "Son how is it you know so much about this big city?"

"Well, I've lived here for nearly twenty years, now. It's like anyplace else. You just start exploring and soon you know the city. Chicago is easier than many places as it's laid out mostly with north-south and east-west streets. And I belong to a civic organization where I get to meet lots of people. It wasn't any problem learning the name of a good doctor for you to see."

Three weeks later, Mat and his grandmother were ready for the trip back to Goodwell. Grandma Welsch was overjoyed at the results. "This is a miracle! These glasses are awfully thick and heavy but I can see again, even with the cataracts!"

Mat Welli now knew something of Chicago, having toured parts of it with his uncle, Mat Welsch. But he was ready to go home. "It's a lot colder here than in Goodwell," he laughed. "If I visit again, I hope it's during warmer weather."

Once home from Chicago, Mat was anxious to get accustomed his new Model-T or "Tin Lizzie" as it was also known. His increased mobility enabled him to socialize far more than in the past. A trip to Guymon could be made in a fraction of the time old Chunk or even Prince had required to get him there. And a trip to George and Anna's place could be made in just a few minutes, unless the roads were impassable because of heavy rain or snow. Then, the reliable Chunk could pull Mat's buggy through the worst conditions. "I see you came over with the horse," George would laughingly say. "How come you didn't crank up the Model-T?"

"I thought ol' Chunk might feel bad if I didn't give him a turn once in awhile," was Mat's usual rejoinder.

At a Saturday-night dance in March 1919, Mat realized that he loved Rosa. *When I take her home tomorrow, I'll ask her to marry me!* After the dance ended the next morning, they drove to her parents' home.

Joe and Antonia marveled at Mat's automobile, asking about its speed and reliability. "I really like it except in bad weather. Then, ol' Chunk gets me where I need to go," laughed Mat.

"Rosa, has Mat ever let you drive it?" asked Joe.

Rosa shook her head. "No, and I don't want to. My horse Bobby goes as fast as I want to travel!"

Mat smiled at the idea. "You should give it a try, Rosa. We're out in the country where there's nothing to run into. Come on!"

"Mat, I don't know anything about automobiles. I can't just take off driving it away like a horse and wagon."

"Don't worry. I'll ride along and tell you how to work the pedals and the gear shift lever."

"Go on, Rosa!" urged Antonia. "I'll get the camera. I want a picture of this."

Rosa looked into the Model-T and saw a baffling array of levers and pedals. "Don't do anything until I crank it up," cautioned Mat as he walked to the front. It started with one turn of the crank.

"You can get in now. Slide over behind the steering wheel," said Mat. After Rosa got in, he followed, taking the passenger seat. "All right, put your foot on the left pedal. That's the clutch. You have to use it to put the car in gear or take it out of gear."

"What are the other two pedals for?"

"The one on the right is the brake. To stop, you push in on the clutch and the brake."

"What about the one in the middle?"

"That's reverse gear. We won't need it for this short drive."

"I'm already getting confused."

"Take your time. We aren't in any hurry."

"What do I do now?"

"Make sure you've got the clutch pedal pushed all the way down. Now, push the gear shift lever up and to the left, and then slowly let your foot off the clutch. I'll handle the speed with the hand throttle here on the right side of the steering wheel."

Rosa followed the instructions carefully and the car slowly inched away from the house. "That's the way, let the clutch out completely."

As Rosa drove toward the west, Antonia snapped a picture while Joe applauded and waved. She gripped the steering wheel tightly. All her muscles were tense.

"We're only in first gear. Want to try shifting into the next faster gear?"

"No, this is fine. Can we stop now?"

"We've only gone about one hundred yards. Are you sure?"

Rosa nodded.

"All right. Push down on the left pedal and I'll take it out of gear. Then I'll drive it back to the house."

The ride was over except for comments and laughter. Then Joe and Antonia went inside. "One time is enough for me!" exclaimed Rosa. "I'm going to treat Bobby extra nice from now on."

"Rosa, I'm always so happy when I'm with you. I love you. Please marry me," Mat proposed.

For a moment she was speechless. Then the words came tumbling. "Yes, Mat! I've dreamed about you asking me. I've always loved you and wanted to be your wife."

"It won't bother you that I was married to Laura?"

Rosa shook her head. "Her death was very sad but she's been gone for more than three years now."

"Well, the next time the priest is in Guymon we can have him marry us. Is that all right?"

"Oh yes, Mat! That would be wonderful."

This was welcome news to both the Loesel and Welli families. Joe and Antonia beamed at the announcement. Young Joe later exclaimed, "I guess this will keep you in the family, Mat!"

It was also well-received by George and Anna. "She's a good, strong woman, Mat. I used to talk to her some when she came down to visit Annie," said George.

Anna was especially pleased, adding, "Mat goes to all those dances and baseball games and meets so many women. I was afraid that he might favor one who wouldn't care to marry a man who already has a child. But Rosa is different. She's George III's aunt and now she'll also be his mother. This is just wonderful!"

The priest was in Guymon on Sunday, April 20. But this was Easter Sunday with a service much too lengthy to perform any marriages or baptisms. Mat and Rosa were in a quandary. "Should we wait until next month?" asked Mat.

"I hate to," she said, with intense disappointment.

"Well, the judge could marry us, even if it's a Sunday."

"That would be fine, really it would. Let's not wait another month."

The 1919 wheat harvest provided another bumper crop for George and Mat. "We seem to be blessed. The 1917 and 1918 crops were very good but this one is great!" said George.

Mat nodded. "Not everyone had the rain we had at just the right time. And with the price still at $2.21 a bushel . . .."

"I know what you mean. Don't tempt fate by boasting too much," said George.

PART THREE:

THE LATER YEARS, 1920-1938

INTRODUCTION

World War I was the first global conflict, lasting more than four years. It was also the first truly modern war, widely employing submarines, airplanes, tanks, poison gas, and machine guns. Daring pilots of the fragile biplanes fighting high above the muddy trenches had average life expectancies of about three weeks. Massed fire from the big guns, however, was the deadliest force. About 70 percent of all casualties resulted from artillery fire.

By the time it ended, November 11, 1918, most of the developed nations had committed armed forces. The casualty rates reflected the horror of modern warfare. Essentially, Europe lost an entire generation of young men with deaths totaling more than 7,000,000. There were estimates of another 6,000,000 being permanently disabled.

American forces did not enter combat until late in the conflict. Their casualties for the war totaled about 275,000. However, U.S. entry became the catalyst that turned the tide, bringing victory, a fact the Allies readily acknowledged. In April 1918 Great Britain's King George handwrote a personal greeting to the American doughboys: "Soldiers of the United States, the people of the British Isles welcome you on your way to take your stand beside the armies of many nations now fighting in the Old World the great battle for human freedom. The Allies will gain new heart and spirit in your company. I wish that I could shake the hand of each one of you and wish you Godspeed on your mission."[30]

While American troops were raw, their spirit was contagious and Allied officers were glad to have them in their armies. A prominent French general begged for them. "If you cannot send me a division," he once said, "send me a regiment. My men fight twice as well when they have American assistance."[31]

Peace negotiations following the conflict were designed to punish the Central Powers of Germany, Austria-Hungary, Bulgaria, and the Ottoman Empire (Turkey). This included war reparations, loss of colonies, and in the case of Hungary, nearly total dismemberment. New nations were established in Europe: Poland, Czechoslovakia, Lithuania, Latvia, and Estonia. Lines redrawn in the Balkans created Yugoslavia. In the Middle East, Iraq was formed from remnants of the Ottoman Empire and the idea of a Jewish state, Israel, was conceived.

Some American immigrants, many of them homesick for the place of their birth, returned to Europe after the war ended. In the year following the November 1918 armistice, more than 120,000 left the United States, for Europe. In 1920 the number was nearly 300,000. However, the years immediately following the war saw rampant hyperinflation in Europe that devastated the purchasing power of nations and their citizens. Eventually, there was serious economic depression.[32]

Postwar America boomed by comparison. In fact, the decade following the war became known as the Roaring Twenties, at least in the major cities where most of the excitement prevailed. Life in small towns and rural America remained similar to that of the nineteenth century. However, the development of radio broadcasting brought an end to rural isolation. By 1924 there were fourteen hundred radio stations in the United States and one third of all money spent on furniture was for radio receivers.

In 1929 the roar of the twenties became a cry of anguish with the stock market crash, resulting in billions of dollars in losses, leading to the Great Depression. Again, the situation was different for residents in the small towns and countryside. Few of them owned stocks and bonds. Furthermore, farm prices had been depressed since shortly after the war had ended. For residents of the Great Plains states, *hard times* would not begin until the latter part of 1931 when the bottom fell out of the wheat market and a ten-year drought began. The Dust Bowl days that followed would bring storms, disease, intense heat, and insect infestations of Biblical proportions.

America spent the 1930s dealing with the Great Depression and the Dust Bowl. During this period Japan began its aggression in Asia, Italy invaded the African nation of Ethiopia, and Germany sought to conquer Europe. Established shortly after World War I as an international body to maintain peace, the League of Nations was ineffectual. Sanctions proposed against these aggressors were ignored and those nations eventually withdrew from the League.

World War I was given a tragic misnomer, *the war to end all wars.* By the end of the 1930s the world was on the brink of an even greater conflict due largely to mistakes at the peace conference. Perhaps those mistakes following the armistice were predictable, given the political and military state of mind in 1918. The armistice was to begin at the eleventh hour of the eleventh day of the eleventh month. In spite of that general order, shortly before 11 a.m. the artillery on the Western Front once again opened fire. Each battery hoped to achieve the distinction of firing the last shot of the Great War.[33] Clearly, being *tired of fighting* wasn't synonymous with *ready to make peace.*

CHAPTER 22
OVER THE WAVES — VERSE TWO

Donau so blau,
Durch Tal und Au
Wogst ruhig du dahin,
Dich grüßt unser Wien,
Dein silbernes Band
Knüpft Land an Land,
Und fröhliche Herzen schlagen
An deinem schönen Strand.

Lyrics (rarely used) to the "Blue Danube Waltz,"
Composed in 1867 by Johann Strauss

So far, 1919 had been a good year for the family. Mat and Rosa were adjusting to married life and to parenting. They relished the added mobility provided by the Model-T, although Rosa adamantly refused to drive it ever again. Having had three consecutive bumper wheat crops, they, as well as George and Anna, were prosperous, but not overconfident regarding the future. Gus Schubert had reopened his restaurant in Guymon and was doing good business there and as a piano tuner once again. Folks attending the Saturday dances in town were again hearing his marvelous fiddle playing. But he remained highly evasive about his lengthy absence and never did explain where he spent the last eighteen months of the war.

For five-year-old George III, there was some adjustment to living in a new home with his father and Rosa. She was his aunt, now his mom, but Anna was the first mother he remembered. Besides, there were other children to play with at her place!

Anna looked out the window on a warm July morning and smiled. There was George III, already walking across the field to her home. He approached the house and quietly eased the door open. "Oh, it's you, Little Brother," she said in mock surprise, hands on her hips. "Does your mom know where you went?"

"Yes, Grandma."

"You know, when I looked out the window I didn't know if it was you or just a tumbleweed blowing across the field," she said with a broad smile. "Maybe I should start calling you Little Tumbleweed."

"No, it's just me, Grandma. I came over to play with George and Johnny."

"They're out feeding the cows. Want something to eat before you go outside? I've got your favorite treat, fresh-baked bread with butter, sugar, and cinnamon."

At George III's new home there many things to learn from his dad. "Come on, son. Let's get in the car," Mat told him one morning. Then, he said to Rosa, "Anything else you need from town?"

"Everything's on the list."

Mat cranked the Model-T and George laughed merrily as the noisy engine sputtered once but quickly came to life. Down the trail toward Goodwell they sped. About a mile from home Mat suddenly slammed on the brakes.

"What's wrong, Dad?"

"Look at that fencepost. That's the biggest rattlesnake I've ever seen!" exclaimed Mat. "And I forgot the shotgun," he grumbled, wheeling the car around and heading back to the house.

When they returned, the rattlesnake was still wrapped around the post. Mat stepped out, walked to within point-blank range, and fired. The snake released its grip and slithered to the ground. Mat fired a second shot into the writhing coils just to make certain. The trip resumed, George observed, "Good shots, Dad."

Mat nodded. "A man's never too busy to kill a rattlesnake."

"What does that mean?"

"Well, we're on our way to town but that can wait. We aren't in that much of a hurry. But the next time you meet that snake he might see you first. And you sure wouldn't want that. For all we know that's the same one that bit Uncle Gus last year. Or, he could have been the snake that spooked ol' Chunk a few weeks ago, making him throw you and Mom off."

"Yes, that was scary. I landed on the ground right beside him. It was lucky. He just crawled away! Mom doesn't like to ride Chunk very much. She says you have time to brush your teeth and comb your hair before he starts moving."

Mat smiled. "Yes, she's used to riding her horse Bobby. That horse has a really fast getaway."

"Is it because of snakes that Granddad makes Towser ride in the wagon when they go somewhere?"

"No, that's a different problem, wolves. Your Granddad used to have another dog besides Towser. His name was Bruno. One day when they were going down to the windmill to get cow chips, Bruno and Towser took off chasing some wolves. But there were too many of them and they killed poor old Bruno. Towser escaped and he got well after Grandma Welsch put some ointment on his wounds."

"I'm glad. Towser is really a good dog!"

"Well, dogs are our best friends. There's an old story the Indians tell about them: 'A long time ago Man and all the animals in the world lived together. But the Great Spirit decided this was not good, and decided to separate them. He called the two humans and all the animals together and told them of this. Then, He caused a large chasm in the earth to open up between the animals and the humans. Slowly, it got wider and wider. But just as it became as wide as two arrows are long, the dogs ran and jumped over to the other side. They've stayed on that side ever since and are still Man's best friends.'"

George grinned broadly. "That's a great story, Dad!"

Soon, they were in Goodwell, thanks to the 35 mph speed of the Model-T, a speed that could be maintained only under the best road conditions. After a quick stop at Cartwright's Store they drove to the Big Joe Lumber Company. "George, you can go look around while I get some nails and fence steeples. But be careful not to get in anyone's way," Mat told him.

George III walked down the aisles, marveling at the large stacks of lumber with their distinctive pleasant smell, kegs of nails, and myriad other building supplies. But a large display near the front of the store proved fascinating. It was two large, rectangular wooden boxes, one slightly larger than the other. The hinged lid of the smaller one was raised so customers could see its interior. George walked around, wondering and wondering. *Those might be fun to play in.*

As he continued gazing at the large boxes, an elderly man walked up. He stared for a while and then said philosophically, "Yes sir, a wooden overcoat. Sooner or later we all have to put one on." In another moment he turned and slowly walked away.

As soon as the man left, George ran to find Mat. "Dad, there's something I want to show you!"

"All right, as soon as I pay up."

George led Mat to the display. "A man called this a wooden overcoat. What does that mean?"

"Well, when somebody dies the people here at the lumber yard build a coffin and a vault for them to be buried in. That's what the man meant. We won't need one of those for a long, long time I hope. Now, let's go home."

The bumper wheat crop of 1919 became food for thought. "You know Anna, we could consider moving back to Europe now," George said one evening when all the children were outdoors.

"Really, George? Back to our hometown on the Danube River? But why?"

"Well, we've been very successful here. But it's a hard life and I'm fifty-five years old now. With what we've accumulated and what we could get for the land and this place, we would be pretty well fixed. Back home we'd be considered wealthy."

"But what about the war? I do miss Dunacseb but what would it be like now?"

"That's true. Things could still be difficult there, what with the war being over for less than a year. But it's something to think about." George smiled, but said nothing more.

School began in September but with something new. The school district had purchased Model-T school buses, which would pick up the children on regular routes. For Anna, it meant she wouldn't be heating the "mountain rock" this school term. For Mike, it was a mixed blessing. While he didn't have to take the younger children to school and pick them up each day, it meant more work at home.

Mary had completed school the previous spring, leaving only Katie and the twins, George, Jr. and Johnny, as family passengers. Katie was now in the eighth grade and the twins in the fifth. The new system worked well during the warmer months of September and October. But then road conditions became a problem. Absent any type paving, they were no better than trails during rainy weather. At times, the children had to get off and help push the bus through mud and deep ruts.

Late in November, Katie, George, Jr., and Johnny returned home from school nearly two hours late. "Why are you so late? I was getting worried," Anna asked.

"The bus got stuck really bad," they chorused. "It was so bad the driver had to walk to a house and have a man bring his horses to pull us out of the mud," added Katie.

"Johnny, why are you shivering so?" asked Anna.

"Me and George worked and worked to push the bus out of the mud hole and we started sweating. After that I started feeling so cold!"

"That's true, Mother. They kept pushing on the bus even after the other kids gave up," said Katie.

Anna touched Johnny's neck, face, and hands. "You're like ice!" she exclaimed. "Let's get you into bed right now. What about you George, are you all right?" she asked, checking his forehead.

"I feel fine."

The next morning Johnny was coughing and choking so badly he could hardly breathe. And now he had a raging fever. "Mother, do you know anything we can do for him?" asked Anna, nearly beside herself with worry.

"It's moved so fast. I'm afraid he's got pneumonia," replied Grandma Welsch. "Try having him sit up and drink some hot tea. Maybe it will help."

"George, do you know anything else that we should do?" pleaded Anna.

He slowly shook his head. "I think you and your mother are doing all that can be done."

Late the next day, November 29, 1919, Johnny's fever was even higher and he became delirious. An hour later he passed away. At age ten, he had been taken by the disease known in those days as the "captain of the men of death." In remote areas, little could be done for its victims.

Two days later he was laid to rest at the Goodwell Cemetery. On the way home George told Anna, "This is so very sad. There can be nothing sadder than looking down at the grave of one of your children. I hope I never have to do it again."

"Yes, I know how you feel."

A few days after the funeral, George again raised the subject of moving. "I think we should look into moving back to Europe," he told Anna. "I know we lost two children to diphtheria when we lived there. But wherever you live, there will be death and diseases. I just feel it would be a fresh start for all of us. And we should be able to live there comfortably. I'll write a letter to my brother Joseph and find out what life is like in Dunacseb now that the war is over."

In mid-January 1920 George was pleased to receive a reply from Joseph. "Let's sit down at the table and see what news he has for us, Anna. Better have your mother come listen too."

December 20, 1919

Dear George,

Augusta and I were most happy to receive your long, interesting letter. We are all well and the war didn't have as much effect on us as we feared it might. It's good that we are living in a small town such as Dunacseb. The Austria-Hungarian Empire collapsed at the end of the war and we aren't even part of Hungary any longer. About a year ago a new country, the Kingdom of Serbs, Croats, and Slovenes, was proclaimed in Belgrade, which is the capital. Then, three or four months later, the whole area where we live, the Backa, was made part of this new Serbian country. It's now known as Jugoslavia.

I think it's good that we are no longer part of Hungary. Hungary and Rumania went to war last summer and no one really knew why except that maybe Rumania wanted more territory from Hungary. There's also been some tension between Jugoslavia and Rumania recently but nothing quite that serious. The politicians here fight all the time but that's not surprising in a country that's made up of so many nationalities and religions. I sometimes wonder how long such a country will last. As Germans we were a minority in Hungary and now we are a minority group in Jugoslavia.

But the Danube River is still as beautiful as ever and life is good here in Dunacseb. Our field crops still do well and our garden and vineyard are better than ever. You could probably live pretty well here after having earned money in America for so many years. But George, I think it would be a gamble to leave a strong, stable country like America. There may be more changes in Europe that could make life here much less pleasant.

With best regards and Christmas greetings,

Joseph

George put down the letter, sat back in his chair, and sighed. He looked quizzically at Anna, then Grandma Welsch. No one spoke. Then he went over to the water bucket, took out a full dipper, and sipped it slowly. "Well, we need to think about this for a few days," he said, heaving another big sigh.

Anna and her mother agreed. "Maybe Mat will have some ideas when he and Rosa come over on Sunday," Anna replied.

On Sunday Mat and Rosa were shocked at first about the idea of moving back to Europe. "Why leave here at a time when we're prospering?" asked Mat.

"Remember what you once said about getting just the right amount of rain at the right time?" asked George.

"I see what you mean. Yes, the weather does run in cycles. If there's a serious drought things might not be so good. And we don't know what may happen to wheat prices now that the war's over," Mat replied, looking at Rosa. "What do you think?"

"I was born in Michigan. I don't know anything about Europe except what I've heard Dad and Mom talk about. But I'll go wherever you go."

George looked around the table, in turn meeting the gaze of Anna, Grandma Welsch, Mat, and Rosa. "Well, I'm going to be fifty-six in March. Your mother and I think it would be good to spend our remaining years in Dunacseb. We've saved a lot of money from these three bumper wheat harvests. And we should be able to get a good price for the land we own."

After a long pause, Mat finally replied, "Well, if you're going back so are we."

"Dad and Mom and Joe will really be surprised. I wonder what they'll do?" mused Rosa.

George already had the next move planned. "If the weather is halfway decent on sale day next week, the girls and I will drive the beef cattle to Guymon. We might as well start selling things off."

The following Thursday George, accompanied by Mary and Katie, arrived at Mat's place just before sunup. He had two horses hitched to the wagon with Old Red, their gentlest milk cow, tied on behind. This would be her third trip to Guymon as the lead cow. Mat stood at the pasture gate while Mary and Katie rousted the still-sleeping cattle and herded them toward the gate.

"Let's go! The sun will be up in a few minutes," urged George, climbing aboard the wagon. "As soon as Mat opens the gate, move those steers out behind us. Giddap!" he ordered, slapping Otto and Gertie's rumps with the reins. The horses stepped out at a moderate pace and Old Red quickly fell in step.

Mat opened the gate. "Heyah! Heyah!" shouted the girls. Needing little urging, forty-six mature, ornery, range-fed critters bolted through the gate. Mary and Katie stayed with them, alert for any efforts to break away. But the steers fell in behind the wagon and Old Red.

Looking around, George smiled. "This is good. Now just like always, stay at the rear of the herd, one of you on the left side, the other on the right. Be extra watchful when we come to a crossroads or fork." The sun was rising and it was going to be a beautiful day. The family's last cattle drive to Guymon, some fifteen miles distant, was off to a good start.

Hours later they arrived at the sale barn and moved the steers into a cattle chute. "What's the name on this herd?" shouted a worker as he slapped a numbered sticker on the hip of each steer.

"George Welli, from Goodwell," Mary answered.

The three of them took seats in the sales arena, watching until their cattle came through and were auctioned off. The place was packed with ranchers and homesteaders. In addition to the noise of the auctioneer and the shouts of men moving livestock through the arena, a strong smell of cigar and pipe smoke permeated the air. But it was a good antidote for the far worse smell of cow dung. "I just love how fast that man can talk!" exclaimed Katie, once again marveling at the auctioneer's rapid-fire taking of bids and calling for higher ones.

"Sold!" shouted the auctioneer. Mary and Katie took one last look at their own familiar-looking cattle being herded out of the arena to the holding pens.

"Good price. Let's go home!" exclaimed George. "But first, let's see if that woman outside still has candy for sale."

It was like the days of the old Chisholm or Goodnight trails except the "cowboys" were teenage girls who were on foot instead of horseback. And rather than celebrating the end of the drive in a Kansas saloon, they were rewarded with homemade candy and a ride home instead of having to walk another fifteen miles that day.

In March, Mat and Rosa went to Guymon for a Saturday dance. "I'll really miss not going to them when we move," Rosa said wistfully.

"Yes, I'll miss them and the dances around Goodwell, too," Mat reminisced. "We've met some really nice people out here at those affairs. I wonder what your folks are going to do. Are they going to stay here or move back to Europe with us?"

"I don't know. Mother's last letter said that they still hadn't decided. It would be nice if they came, too."

Gus was delighted to see them. "Some last dances for old-times' sake?"

"Sure thing!" replied Mat. "But we haven't sold our land yet and even when we do we'll have to stay until this year's crops are harvested."

"Well, be sure to make one last visit before you move so I can make a proper 'goodbye.' I owe you a lot for saving me from being lynched," said Gus, clapping Mat on the shoulder.

Joe Loesel came in about an hour later. "What are Dad, Mother, and you going to do about moving?" asked Rosa.

"They still aren't sure what to do. If they don't make a decision soon, we'll have to come to Europe later instead of going with you folks. Mother is for it but Dad goes back and forth, wondering if spending another year at Optima might not be the best plan."

Major events occurred soon after their trip to Guymon. On March 31, 1920, Mat deeded his 160 acres to a buyer. Several days later, George deeded his 320 acres over to a buyer. It was a seller's market as many wanted to get in on the wheat-raising bonanza. Although there were still crops to harvest, most activities and plans were aimed at the big move. "It seems odd not to be worrying about cattle prices or whether there will be enough rain to sow wheat this fall," observed George.

Following the harvest both George and Mat had family photographs taken. "I think we need to have them to show how we looked like just before moving," said George. "We did the same thing when moving from Europe in 1901."

"I remember that," smiled Mat. "But we didn't have one taken when we left Youngstown."

"No, I never thought it. Guess I was just too sick from the asthma."

Following the harvest, Mat and Rosa sold everything but what possessions they had given away or were taking to Dunacseb to the same man who purchased their land:

Livestock, Implements, and Feed
Sold by Mathias Welli to G. S. Gaither
August 1920

One team named Bert and Bess, seven years old	$300.00
One team named Rex and Mollie, four and five years old	250.00
Four colts, two years old	260.00
One mare named Bobby	50.00
One horse named Chunk, ten years old	40.00
One red cow with horns and calf	75.00
One yellow cow	65.00
One whiteface heifer coming two years old	50.00
Three pigs	30.00
One new wheat drill	125.00
One new wagon	125.00
One row binder	50.00
One buggy	75.00
Lister	50.00
Disc	25.00
Planter	15.00
Harrow	15.00
Two row cultivator	40.00

Disc plow	40.00
Knife sled	5.00
Old wagon and barge	25.00
Go Devil disc	10.00
Mower	10.00
Harness, two sets	40.00
Saddle	10.00
Single harness	10.00
Feed	100.00
Feed grinder	10.00
Total	$1,975.00

George followed suit, selling most of his farm property to the buyer after giving Joe Udry an opportunity to buy some of the animals or implements. "I could use a set of harness," Joe told him.

"Well, you can just have it if you'll take us to the train depot when we leave," George replied. Then he said to Mat, "We better go back to the bank tomorrow and finish up the money arrangements."

Early the following morning George and Mat drove the Model-T to Goodwell. Both were aware that this would be one of their last trips to town. They gazed at the passing countryside as if trying to engrave its image in their memories. Conversation was spare and a touch on the melancholy side.

"It's been more than fourteen years since we came out here with only some savings and the money Smith Brewery gave me," George observed. "There were plenty of times in those early years when I thought we would go bust. But now we're headed to the bank to make some big financial deals."

"Yes, I remember those times," Mat replied. "But there were some good times, too. And we became friends with many fine people here in the Panhandle."

"So, you're leaving us? I sure hate to see that," said the owner of the Goodwell State Bank. "You've been good customers and you've handled your finances in a fine, responsible manner. But down to business. I assume you want to withdraw all your funds?"

"We'll want cash for the trip to New York and our ocean passage, plus spending money. But we want to buy bonds with most of it," said Mat.

"U.S. bonds?"

"No, Austrian bonds," Mat replied, looking at George and adding, "We won't be coming back to America."

"Is that where you're moving, to Austria?"

"No, it's more complicated. Dunacseb, where we used to live, is now part of Jugoslavia. But Dad's brother said that the government there is in turmoil since it's a new country. So, we thought Austrian bonds might be a safer investment."

"That sounds like the next best thing to buying U.S. bonds. They're paying a handsome interest rate and we can buy them through the Kaufman Bank in Chicago. How much will you be investing?"

"I want to invest $15,000 and my Dad wants to invest $30,000" said Mat.

"And when will you be leaving Goodwell?"

"A week from today."

"Well, stop in before you go and I'll give you receipts for these purchases. Now, give me your address in Jugoslavia and the bank in Chicago will tell the Austrian government to send the bond certificates to you there. One final matter, do you understand that part of the reason those bonds are yielding such a high interest rate is because of their risk as an investment? It's not too late to invest in U.S. bonds instead," cautioned the banker.

"No, we've thought about it and we're certain Austrian bonds are best. When we need to cash them in, they should be easier than cashing American bonds," said Mat.

"You have a good point there," the banker observed, getting to his feet and extending his hand to George, then to Mat. "I'll see you next week."

The next week both families arrived at the Rock Island depot. Joe and Rosina Udry had brought George, Anna, Grandma Welsch, Mike, Mary, Katie, and George, Jr. and all their trunks and valises in one wagon. Howard White had purchased Mat's Model-T but it wouldn't hold Mat, Rosa, George III, and all their baggage. So, he and wife Georgia brought them in his wagon.

Tears were aplenty as the families said their goodbyes. "Thanks for everything, especially for being such a good friend," Anna told Rosina. "George and I will always remember those dances at your place."

"We're gonna' miss you folks," said Howard. "Here's a bag of treats for all the kids. There's even a gingerbread man for George III."

Then the train pulled out of Goodwell and all took a final look around town and the countryside. At first everyone was quiet. Soon, however, any melancholy of leaving was offset by the excited chatter of youngsters as they relished the train ride, wondering what it would bring.

Both Mat and Rosa took long looks around when the train stopped in Guymon, the town where they first met, romanced, and were married. "I guess your mom and dad and Joe will just have to meet us in Dunacseb later," Mat observed.

"Yes, they sold their land but still have to sell their livestock and goods and get moved off the place. But it will be awful nice to have them living in Dunacseb too."

The trusty Rock Island had the families in Chicago in good time, where they changed trains for the remainder of the overland trip to New York. There, they booked steamship passage on the *Pomona,* an aging vessel of Italian registry.

Once aboard, the adults were a bit dismayed. "This must have been a troopship during the war," Mat observed.

"Yes, we had much better accommodations when we came to America," George agreed.

As the ship pulled away from the dock and out into the harbor, all looked back for one last view of America. "Dad, what's that big statue?" asked George III.

"That's the Statue of Liberty."

CHAPTER 23
OVER THE WAVES — VERSE THREE

The Treaty includes no provision for the economic rehabilitation of Europe — nothing to make the defeated Central Empires into good neighbors, nothing to stabilize the new States of Europe, nothing to reclaim Russia; nor does it promote in any way a compact of economic solidarity amongst the Allies themselves; no arrangement was reached at Paris for restoring the disordered finances of France and Italy, or to adjust the systems of the Old World and the New.

It is an extraordinary fact that the fundamental economic problem of a Europe starving and disintegrating before their eyes, was the one question in which it was impossible to arouse the interest of the Four (Allies). Reparation was their main excursion into the economic field, and they settled it from every point of view except that of the economic future of the States whose destiny they were handling.

John Maynard Keynes, noted British economist, criticizing post-World War I peace treaties.[34]

The *Pomona* lumbered through the summertime waves of the Atlantic, waves that would seem small by comparison when the seasons changed, bringing surges that gave the ocean its reputation for rough crossings. George and the other adults resigned themselves to two weeks or more of boredom. Not so Mary, Katie, George, Jr., and George III. Even Mike, now age seventeen, enjoyed himself. Crossing the ocean was such a new experience and the ship was loaded with other families returning to the "Old Country."

Most of those families had lots of children. Thus, the younger members of the Welli families had no shortage of new playmates. One of their favorite events was teasing the mess steward when he made his rounds announcing the evening meal, the only one provided to those with steerage class tickets. "Dinner is served! Calling for dinner!"

"What are we having?" the children would ask.

"Macaroni and beef!" was his daily response.

"That's what we had last night!"

"That's what we're having again tonight. If you're hungry, you'll eat it!"

George marveled at the crowded ship. "I thought we would be a rarity, returning to Europe, especially so soon after the war," he told Mat.

"I've spoken to several of the men. They seem to be going back for the same reason we are. They saved the money earned in America and are taking it back to their mother countries. Several are returning to Italy where they hope to buy land."

Finally the *Pomona* passed through the Straits of Gibraltar, along the southern edge of the island of Sardinia, then to Naples, where it docked in the harbor. The passengers staying aboard for the remainder of the voyage watched in fascination as boys at the dock dived after coins some passengers threw into the water. Few of the boys came back up empty-handed. But for the young Welli children it was a sad time as they watched most of their new friends disembark.

But high spirits returned when after several hours the *Pomona* pulled away from the dock for the final leg of their journey. It passed between Sicily and the toe of Italy, around its heel, then up the Adriatic Sea to Trieste, where it docked. George and Anna wore smiles brighter than they had been in years. As the children chattered excitedly, Mat said, "Well, Rosa, this will be your first time in Europe."

She smiled, her spirits buoyed by the holiday atmosphere. "I hope that Dad, Mother, and Joe will be able to find their way to Dunacseb."

"They sold their land shortly after we sold ours. It's a shame they couldn't have traveled with us."

"I know. I think they were surprised at how quickly it went. But the man who bought their land didn't want to buy anything else. So, even with Joe's help, they had trouble selling off their livestock, wagons, and other personal items. But we should see them before too long," she said optimistically.

At Trieste they boarded a train for the next leg of the trip to Agram (present day Zagreb, Croatia) and from there to Palanka. Many of the railroad cars were in bad shape, having gone through the rigors of wartime military transport. Others were so decrepit they appeared to have been returned to service because of the shortage of rolling stock. But eager to get to the homeland, the family overlooked the rundown condition of the cars. At Palanka they disembarked to make yet another change in transportation mode, to horse-drawn wagons.

As the wagons pulled away, George looked around, thinking back to the day in 1901 when his brother Joseph had brought him and Adam Welli to Palanka from Dunacseb, thus beginning their long trip to America. "Look over there," he said to Anna, her mother, and Mat. "There's the police office. I wonder if old Chief Kleinschmidt is still around."

The remainder of the trip was filled with adult reminiscences and the excited voices of the children as they marveled at countryside that was much different from that in which they had lived. "Such strange country, Dad!" exclaimed George III to Mat.

Finally, at midmorning, the wagons arrived at the house of Joe and Augusta Welli, who were delighted to see the new arrivals. "Welcome home, George!" exclaimed Joe, grabbing his hand and shaking it vigorously. Thus began a chorus of introductions, reminiscences, and laughter.

"Mat, you were only so high when you left. Now you have a son that age," said Augusta. "Anna, I've missed you so!" she laughed, giving Anna a warm hug and kiss on the cheek. "Come in! Come in, all of you! You must be exhausted from such a trip."

After a large midday meal, the conversations turned to immediate needs. "As you asked I bought a house for you with the money you sent," Joe told George. "But the people won't be moved out until next week. Mat, there's a house nearby that's for rent where you and your family can stay if you're interested."

"That sounds good," Mat replied, then said to Rosa, "It will be just like this house, one long building."

She smiled at the idea. It would be good to have their own place.

"The war has been over for nearly two years. How are things here now?" asked George.

"Well, last June, three months ago, there was an agreement signed in Paris called the Trianon Treaty. It makes us officially part of Jugoslavia now, although that's been the case since shortly after the war ended. This part of the country is known as Vojvodina. Also, Dunacseb will now be known as Celarevo, which is a Serbian name," replied Joe.

"Bah! It will always be Dunacseb to me," laughed George. Then, turning to Mat and Anna, he continued, "Remember when we first learned that Oklahoma was going to become a state. That didn't make much difference to us, did it?"

"There's one thing that's beginning to be a problem — inflation. It's getting so our money just isn't worth as much anymore," said Joe.

"But your American money will go a long way here. Just don't cash too much of it in too quickly."

In a week George, Anna, Grandma Welsch, Mike, Mary, Katie, and George, Jr. moved into their house. A large, long house similar to all the others in Dunacseb, it also had a fine garden and orchard. It was late September and there hadn't been a killing frost so there were still fruit and vegetables in good supply.

A major attraction to the children was the large cistern well in front of the house that the entire neighborhood used. They watched in fascination the process of lowering a large bucket down into the well then cranking it back up brimming with fresh water. "Mother, why don't they have windmills here?" asked Katie.

"Because they don't have to go very deep to get water. We're close to the Danube River," she explained. Then, adding a motherly word of caution, "Don't let George, Jr. or George III lean over too far. We don't want to have to fish them out of the well!"

Mat and Rosa were equally happy with their new home. "It's one long building but it's really nice and it has all the furniture we need," Rosa told Anna and Augusta.

George III quickly found a feature of life in Dunacseb that was a source of merriment. Each morning he arose and went to the window of the front room. Mat and Rosa would hear him laughing and talking. The third morning both got up and went to see the source of his humor. "What's so funny, son?"

"Just wait, you'll see," he laughed.

Shortly, a man walked by leading a herd of pigs. He played a short, low-pitched tune on a horn he carried and several more pigs ran out from behind the neighboring houses, joining the little porcine parade as it headed out to a common pasture for the day. George's infectious laughter was quickly joined by Rosa's appreciation for the humorous scene and love of a good laugh.

Mat smiled. "I used to watch them when I was a boy. I always thought it was funny, too!"

"There's more!"

Sure enough, a few minutes later another man walked past trailed by a flock of ducks and geese. He too played a horn but it had a much higher pitch. Suddenly, ducks and geese from the neighboring houses ran out and joined this second early morning parade headed out to pasture.

George was beside himself laughing and so was Rosa. This was even funnier than the pig parade. "Mat, it was worth the trip from Oklahoma just to see this!"

"Come back tonight, Mom," said George. It's funny then too.

Just before sundown, George and Rosa watched from the window. First the swineherd walked by, each pig recognizing his home and leaving the little procession. Same with the ducks and the geese: each peeled off from the flock and went to their respective homes. Another day was done!

But in two weeks the novelty of a new home was gradually being replaced by concerns over living in a country that was politically unstable and which had an unstable economy. During a gathering of family and neighbors at Joseph and Augusta's home, one man asked George, "Why would you leave a good life in America to come back here? Don't you know there's going to be another war?"

Somewhat taken aback, George replied that this was his choice of places to retire. "But if we have to, we'll move back to America." Seeds of doubt had now been planted.

Another neighbor added to the war concerns. "This new country, Jugoslavia, is made up mostly of people who don't like each other, Serbs,

Germans, Croats, and Slovenes. Then the religions! That's another bad mix. There's Roman Catholic and Eastern Orthodox. One uses the Latin alphabet and the other Cyrillic. There are even some Muslims in parts of the country. The Paris peacemakers just drew arbitrary lines on a map of southeastern Europe. They didn't pay any attention to the people!"

But a third neighbor pointed out that the Vojvodina province, in which Dunacseb was located, received very little direction from the Jugoslav government. "We can still use the German language in church and it's the language still being used in the schools here."

"That's right," Joe replied. "I think it's because they need the wheat that we raise. There's beginning to be food shortages."

Early in October 1920, Mat and George III left the house to buy bread. But first, Mat had to change some American money into Jugoslav currency at the bank. He received five peck-sized bags. "This is too much money to carry around. We'll take most of it home before we go to the bakery," he told George.

Finally they arrived at the bakery. "We want two loaves of white bread," he told the bakery owner.

The owner shook his head. "Sorry, they aren't milling white flour any longer. There's too much waste in refining it. All we have is black bread and I've got only one loaf left."

"Well, how much for it?" asked Mat.

"Let's see how much money you have."

Mat dumped out the entire bag of currency on the counter. He and George III watched in amazement as the baker counted a stack of bills, set them aside and continued counting out additional stacks.

Finally, he placed the loaf of bread into the bag and handed Mat about twenty bills. "I guess you did have enough money," he commented with a wry smile. "For a while I wasn't sure."

"I'll carry the bag for you, Dad," offered George as they left the bakery. "Hey, it's a lot lighter now with only the loaf of bread."

"It certainly is son, much lighter. And look inside. The bread doesn't take up nearly as much room as the money it took to buy it!" Mat's demeanor changed dramatically and he was silent for the rest of the walk home. Once there he showed Rosa the bag, pointing out George's observation and saying, "We won't be staying here long, just long enough for a good visit."

"I know what you mean," she replied. "Now all you can get is black bread and there hasn't been any butter. When George wants an afternoon treat, I give him a slice of bread with lard spread over it, sprinkled with some sugar and cinnamon I brought with us. And I make him eat it indoors because other children come around wanting some too. They aren't just looking for something extra to eat. I think those poor kids are actually going hungry and that's heartbreaking to see!"

"Well, let's think about it for a few days. If we feel the same way Sunday I'll tell Dad and Mother we're going back to America."

"But where would we go, back to Oklahoma?" Rosa wondered aloud.

On Sunday, Mat told his parents and Grandma Welsch of his and Rosa's concerns. "We're afraid to stay here. The economy will only get worse. And if there is another war, Rosa and I want to be back in America."

"But where would you go, Mat?" asked Anna.

"Well, we have some ideas. I'm going to send a letter to Frank Udry and ask him to find out if there's land available in Kansas where he and Annie live. If there isn't, we'll go back out to Guymon or Goodwell."

"But how long will it take for him to look around and then send you a letter over here?" George wondered.

"We thought of that too. So, I'll tell him to send his reply to Uncle Mat Welsch in Chicago. We thought we'd leave in November, then go to Uncle Mat's place. If he hasn't received a letter from Frank, we'll just wait there for a while."

"That's a good idea, Mat!" exclaimed Grandma Welsch. "I remember how big his place was when we went to Chicago to get my new glasses."

"Well done, Mat. Looks like you've thought of everything," smiled George.

"We're very independent, what with everything being in cash or bonds. That's why we can afford to move now. But what of you and the rest of the family?"

"We'll have to think about it. We're comfortable here, even with the inflation. Besides, George, Jr. is in German school and doing well. But I'm like you. If there's another war I'd rather be back in America," George replied.

"Mother and I would rather re-cross the Atlantic in warm weather, not during the winter when it's so rough," added Anna.

"Dad, could I go back to America with Mat?" asked Mike, adding another element to the equation.

All turned toward him, surprised at first. Then, recollections of earlier times dawned on George and Anna and they began to smile. "You always did like riding with Mat down to the Texas windmill," said George, shifting his gaze to Mat and then to Anna, who recalled many other times where Mike loved to "tag along" with his big brother.

"Well, Mat, what do you think?" George finally asked. "Mike is old enough to be a big help on a farm or ranch. And there isn't much for him to do here."

"That's right, Dad," said Mike softly.

Mat broke into a broad grin. "Sure, come along with us."

Early in November, Mat, Rosa, George III, and Mike said their goodbyes and Joe took them by wagon to Palanka, where they would catch the train to Agram. "It seems strange bringing you here. It reminds me of the day back in 1901 when I brought your Dad and his cousin Adam here for their trip to America," he said, shaking hands all around.

They arrived in Agram, where they had to change trains. However, the other train wasn't due to leave until the following day. From here they would be traveling by rail across Europe to Cherbourg, France, where they were to catch a White Star liner en route to America from England. The man at the train depot directed them to an old wooden army barracks building that was used as a hotel by passengers having to stay over.

"This isn't much of a hotel," grumbled Mat as the four of them entered and saw the dimly lit interior. It was one large room about one hundred feet in length and forty feet wide, truly an old barracks building. And there were no beds or chairs and no heat or water. There was one old cook stove that passengers could use to heat food, provided they had any that required heating. All around the walls were piles of straw where passengers could put down blankets for sleeping.

"We're lucky we have to spend only one night here," said Rosa.

"But we're used to straw mattresses so this won't be too much different," laughed Mat. "We might as well get some rest."

As Mike and George III stretched out to sleep, Mat and Rosa sat talking about the remainder of the trip. Directly across the room from them, about forty feet away, a woman sat up. Rosa grabbed Mat's arm, clutching it tightly as she stared across the nearly dark room. "What is it, Rosa?" Mat was suddenly alarmed.

"That looks like Mother!" she said in a loud whisper, getting up and walking slowly across the room. Once closer, "Mother! What are you doing here?" she exclaimed, running to the woman.

"Rosa! Oh, I'm so glad to see someone I know!" said Antonia, breaking into tears.

Mat sprinted across the room. "Antonia, where's Joe and Young Joe?"

Antonia got to her feet and clung to Rosa. "We lost Joe!" she sobbed.

"But how?" Mat and Rosa chorused. By now Mike and George III had run over to see what was happening.

Several feet away someone muttered, "Shush. We're trying to sleep!"

"Grandma, what are you doing here?" asked George.

Between sobs Antonia gave them the sad news. "When our ship left Naples we couldn't find Joe. He just disappeared. Young Joe and I looked all over the ship where passengers are allowed to go but couldn't find him. And he never came to the sleeping area either."

"Did he go ashore in Naples?" asked Mat.

"We don't think so. He disappeared before our ship docked."

"Mother, do you think he got robbed?" asked Rosa in a tone of desperation.

"We're afraid that's what happened. He was wearing a money belt with most of our savings."

"But where's Young Joe? Why are you here all alone?" asked Mat.

"He went back to Naples three days ago to help the police try to find Joe. I'm waiting here until he returns. I'm so glad to see you and Rosa! But why are you folks here?"

Mat explained their reasons for leaving Europe and their plans for renewing life in America. "You say Young Joe has been gone for three days? I'm afraid the chances of them finding Joe may not be very good," said Mat sympathetically. "Rosa, maybe your mother should come back with us."

"You know you're welcome, Mother," said Rosa, taking Antonia's hand.

Antonia thought for a while and heaved a big sigh. "I think that's best. I wouldn't want to live in Europe without a husband. I'm so afraid that something bad has happened to Joe. And, and, and I'll never see him again!"

Rosa held Antonia as she broke down from days of worry and grief. "Don't worry. We'll take care of you, Mother. Just come with us. We'll take care of you." She patted Antonia on the back and held her close.

"I'll send a telegram to the Naples Police Department and have them tell Young Joe that you're returning to the United States with us and that we can be reached at Mat Welsch's home in Chicago. Is that all right?" asked Mat.

"Yes, thank you. I think that's the best thing to do," replied Antonia, somewhat more composed.

Spirits were brighter the next morning, mostly from the relief of leaving the old makeshift hotel with its gloomy atmosphere. "Well, Mike, you can start helping us right away by carrying Mrs. Loesel's trunk," laughed Mat.

But the old troop train was yet another grim reminder of the war that destroyed an entire generation of Europe's young men and wrecked its economy. The cars were unheated and without lights. Many of the windows were either broken or missing completely. Once under way, sparks from the engine flew in through the window openings. Mike and George III watched to make certain they didn't burn holes in the passengers' clothing and spent much of the trip brushing off sparks and stamping them out. The train stopped at the border of each country, where all passengers had to get off and have their passports and baggage inspected. After a few days it arrived in Cherbourg.

At Cherbourg they boarded the harbor transport jammed with passengers anxious to travel to America. It pulled out into the harbor to a White Star liner anchored there. Once its gangplank was lowered, the passengers rushed off the transport to get aboard. "Well now, this is just like a cattle stampede!" exclaimed Mat. By the time the stampede had ended, the Welli family and three other families couldn't get aboard and were forced to live on the transport for a few days. Always finding something of interest, George III was intrigued by the fact that he could step from the ship to the sidewalk in the morning but then find the sidewalk far above his head in the evening when the tide had gone out.

Later in the week, the mighty *Aquitania* stopped at Cherbourg and the families on the harbor transport were the first to board. A sister ship of the *Lusitania,* which was torpedoed in 1915, the *Aquitania* was the longest-serving Cunard ocean liner in the twentieth century. Launched in April 1913, it also served as a troop ship and as a hospital ship during the Great War. In June 1920 it was refitted for passengers, with accommodations for 597 first-class, 614 second-class, and 2,052 third-class passengers. At that time its engines were converted from coal burning to oil burning. Gross tonnage was 45,647 with four funnels and a cruising speed of twenty-three knots. It was 869 feet long and 97 feet wide.

Despite the *Aquitania's* size, the Atlantic crossing was rough, as the huge liner encountered a storm and a steady wind from the west. Still, the crossing was made in less than six days, and they docked in New York on November 20, 1920. As they approached the city Mat observed, "We're back in just three months. It sure feels good!"

The rest of the family agreed. "I'm getting anxious to see what news Mat Welsch will have for us when we get to Chicago," replied Rosa.

A few days later they arrived at Mat Welsch's apartment. "Welcome to Chicago!" he greeted them as he helped bring in their trunks and valises.

Once everyone was settled, he said, "I got your letter, Mat. And here's one for you from a Mr. Frank Udry out in Kansas."

"Thank you!" Mat ripped the letter open, hoping for the best, and scanning it quickly. "Great news! He says there's land right there at Iuka that's available, 320 acres."

Everyone was pleased. "It sounds just fine! It will be fun getting to see Annie again," smiled Rosa.

CHAPTER 24
ROCK ISLAND REPRISE

From New York we went to Chicago, where we lived for two weeks with Mat Welsch, my dad's uncle. Chicago was a very interesting place. They had trains that ran on the ground, below the ground, and above the ground. Then we came out to Pratt County, Kansas where we stayed for a while with Frank and Annie Udry, my aunt and uncle.

George Welli III, boyhood memories, 1982

The Rock Island train rumbled over the Kansas prairie at a steady, distance-eating pace toward the new Welli home in Kansas. For the fifth time since 1862 the family was making a long move. It was December 1920 and Mat Welli sat by the window thinking back to the trip west he and his father made in May 1906. *That's fourteen years ago but it seems much longer. . . . So much has happened. There are big differences. This time I'm the head of the family with a wife, young son, mother-in-law, and my brother to take care of. Start all over . . . tough but we've got some financial independence. We'll make it!*

"Coming into Pratt!" called the conductor. "Pratt, Kansas next stop!"

The train began slowing and all were alert, anxious to see this place so near their new home. "Look at all those trees at the south end of town, Mat. There must be a river there," said Mike.

"Will Frank and Annie be at the depot to meet us?" asked Rosa.

"I see. No, I have to call them on the telephone and tell them that we're here. Then they'll come pick us up," explained Mat, replying to both Mike and Rosa.

Their trip ended with the familiar lurch of the train as it stopped at the Pratt depot, a large three-story building. This stop was a bustling location on the Rock Island's "Golden State" route from Chicago to the West Coast. It was a gray, cloudy day but still warm for December. The family with their four trunks and a host of smaller grips and valises gathered inside the depot and Mat walked over to the ticket agent. "Excuse me, but I need to make a telephone call. Do you have a phone?"

"Certainly. Where do you have to call?" asked the agent.

"John Udry in Iuka."[35]

"That's long distance. I need ten cents." Seeing Mat's hesitation, he added, "Just pick up the receiver and when the operator comes on the line tell her the number you want to call."

Mat handed him a dime and lifted the receiver. After a few seconds he responded, "Number 309 in Iuka." Then he said, "Hello, this is Mat Welli. Our train got in. Yes, there are five of us with four trunks and other bags. Would you tell your brother Frank to come pick us up? OK, we'll see you then. Goodbye."

Turning to the family, Mat said "Frank and his brother John will be here in about twenty minutes." Then with a broad grin he said, "That's the first time I've ever used a telephone. It's really handy!"

Soon, a Model-T truck and a Model-T sedan pulled up at the depot and Frank Udry and his brother came in. For a while there was a barrage of greetings, laughs, questions, and exclamations. Frank and his brother were strikingly similar in appearance. As they began loading the truck with the baggage, Frank told them, "Annie is sure looking forward to seeing all of you again."

The little caravan headed north toward Iuka and Frank Udry's place just outside town, pulling up to a large farmhouse with a windmill and outbuildings. Two dogs ran out to check over the newcomers. But Annie's greeting was even louder, filled with exclamations and much laughter. "It's so good to see you all, and especially my dear friend Rosa! And little George, you've grown so much! Are you hungry? I'm making an extra big dinner for us."

When the baggage was unloaded, John Udry took his leave. After the huge, almost holiday-style meal, Frank told them, "We should show you what your new hometown looks like." With Frank, Mike, and Mat in the front seat and Annie, Rosa, Antonia, and George III in the back, the trusty Model-T clattered off to tour Iuka.

Iuka was first settled in the spring of 1877 by settlers who came by covered wagon from Iowa. More settlers followed the first group, many of them Civil War veterans from Iowa, Illinois, Indiana, Ohio, and Pennsylvania. They called the new settlement Ninnescah, after the river some six miles to the south. A town company was formed on July 28, 1878, but it was discovered that there was another Kansas town named Ninnescah.

According to historian J. Rufus Gray, "A man named Charlie Dunn had the honor of supplying the new name of Iuka. Iuka was the name of an Indian chief in Mississippi who found relief from his rheumatism and other afflictions in a mineral spring at that state. He now lies buried under a bank building in Iuka, Mississippi. Union soldiers from Illinois fought in a battle at Iuka, Mississippi, and returning north gave the same name to new towns in Kentucky, Illinois, Arkansas, and Kansas."[36]

The Model-T passed through streets lined with neat-looking houses and a town center which had a drugstore, the Iuka Co-operative Grain Exchange, Iuka State Bank, Kansas Flour Mills, the Midland Lumber Company, offices for two more grain companies, and the railroad depot. "I saved the most important for last. Here's Taylor's Department Store. You can get anything you want from needles and thread to canned goods, hardware, shotguns and rifles, or farm implements," said Frank, stopping so they could get a good view of the large business establishment.

The newcomers were impressed. Mat turned around in his seat and told Rosa, "Looks like there's everything we need here." At that time there were about ninety residences and surrounding farms along with thirteen businesses in Iuka.[37]

"There are many more stores in Pratt but it's five miles away," added Frank. "There's one more place to show you, the schoolhouse."

As they pulled up to the two-story brick building, Annie said, "George, you'll like your teacher. Her name is Ina Kutz and she's just a marvelous woman."

The next day Frank took Mat to a house just southeast of town to meet Charles Tillery, who was giving up the lease on 320 acres of wheat land adjacent to the south edge of town. A tall, thin, amiable man, he was happy to meet someone interested in taking over. After showing them the acreage, he explained, "I want to give up wheat farming and just raise horses. I have enough land around my new house for pasture and raising oats and fodder."

"What kind of horses are they?" asked Mat, always interested in new equine information.

"Tennessee Walking Horses. They're a fine, all-purpose horse for both light work and riding. But they're best known for their smooth gait," replied Tillery.

"The difference between them and other breeds must be like the difference between riding in a buggy with springs and an old farm wagon on a road with lots of ruts," suggested Frank.

Tillery laughed. "That's pretty close to how it is. Now, Fred Apt, the man who owns these 320 acres, lives in Iola, Kansas. That's in the far southeastern part of the state. He's a very intelligent, agreeable man. We give him one third of the crop sales and he pays the property taxes."

"Sounds fair. I need to visit the bank here and get established financially. I suppose we would close the deal there," replied Mat.

Frank took Mat to the Iuka State Bank and introduced him to Frank Young, the head cashier, then left for Taylor's Store. A tall, distinguished-looking gentleman, Young asked the purpose of Mat's visit.

"We've just moved here and need to get started wheat farming. I want to take over the half-section that Charles Tillery is farming for Fred Apt. Most of my funds are invested in Austrian bonds. But the price has dropped and I hate to sell them and take a loss."

"I see. Have you ever borrowed money from a bank before?"

"Yes, at the First State Bank in Goodwell, Oklahoma."

"Let me go make a telephone call and then we'll see what we can do."

Mat sat meditating. *I'm glad I paid them so promptly when I borrowed money for building the new house after the tornado!*

In a few minutes Frank Young returned, beaming. "There will be no problem, Mr. Welli. Now, just how much will you need to get started?"

Shortly after Christmas, the family was settled in the house located on the Apt property. It had two large bedrooms, a good size kitchen area and living room, and all the necessary outbuildings. Mat and Rosa slept in one bedroom, Grandma Loesel and George III in the other, and Mike had a cot in the living room. Mat had a new Model-T sedan for shopping trips in Iuka and the longer trips to Pratt. When school resumed in January, George III was enrolled in the first grade and began the daily half-mile walk each way. Most of their social life was visiting with the Udrys. Frank was becoming as good a friend to Mat as Annie was to Rosa.

"I'd better write some letters," said Mat. "The first will be to Dad and Mother letting them know we're settled now. Then, a letter to Uncle Mat in Chicago and I should write ol' Gus and Howard White and let them know we're back in America. George, you can mail the letters on your way to school tomorrow."

Rosa laughed. "Gus will really be surprised. I'd love to hear what he'll have to say about this news!"

Late one evening in January 1921 there was a knock on the door. Rosa opened it and saw her brother, Joe Loesel, but he was alone. "Mother, Joe is here."

Antonia hurried out of the bedroom, still holding her rosary. She hugged Joe but tears formed before he said anything. "You're by yourself, Joe?" she asked fearfully, fingering the beads.

Everyone gathered as Joe sat down. "I stayed in Naples for two weeks hoping to find some sign of Dad. The police showed me each body in the morgue during that time, but I didn't see him. They also showed me all the items in their lost and found room. Finally, we decided that he must have fallen or was thrown overboard."

For a while no one spoke. Finally, Antonia gave a huge sigh. "That's awful news but it's the news I was afraid you would bring."

Rosa put her arm around Antonia and kissed her lightly on the cheek. "Mother, you have a home with us."

"She's right. You certainly do have a home here," added Mat. "But Joe, what will you do?"

"I can get back on with the Rock Island, even if it's a job as a common section hand. I thought I'd get a room near the depot in Pratt. What about your folks, Mat? Are they going to stay in Europe?"

"They were leaning that way when we left. But if there's a new threat of war or if the economy worsens I think they'll come back to the U.S."

This was the beginning of times known as the "Roaring Twenties." But most of the "roaring" was happening in the larger towns and big cities, especially those farther east. And while business was booming and the stock market soaring, prices for grain and livestock were still in the slump that began when the Great War ended.

In rural areas and smaller towns such as Iuka and Pratt, life continued to be more like that of the nineteenth century. County fairs, circuses, rodeos, baseball games, dances, and the family sing-along to a piano or other instrument were the most common entertainment. Movie theaters drew well, but movies with sound were still several years away. Additionally, church and school functions and those of veterans' organizations such as the G.A.R., the VFW, and the newly formed American Legion provided opportunities for a community get-together.

The *Pratt Tribune* for May 28, 1921 carried an article headlined "DECORATE HERO GRAVES MONDAY — Legion, G.A.R. and Their Auxiliaries to Remember Sacrifices made by Their Comrades and Friends — PARADE AND ADDRESSES."

Iuka also continued its traditional observance, which began in 1885. On May 30 Mat told George III, "Put some clean clothes on. We're going to church this morning."

"But this isn't Sunday."

"No, but it's Decoration Day. They have a big program here in Iuka that will last all day long. It will be at the Christian Church and the cemetery in the morning. Then, there will be a basket dinner and another program in the afternoon."

Shortly before 10 a.m. the family arrived at the church, sitting down in a pew near the front. After a few minutes the pianist began playing "America the Beautiful." As the congregation joined in song, an armed color guard marched in, placed the flags in holders, and returned to the rear of the church. A man with a large bass drum took a seat in the front pew, along with young girls who had brought flowers and placed them by the flags.

Mat touched Rosa on the shoulder, smiled, and motioned toward George III, who was sitting on the edge of his seat, fascinated by the ceremony.

A young boy walked to the front of the church and nervously cleared his throat. "Four score and seven years ago," he began, and then recited President Abraham Lincoln's Gettysburg Address from memory. George III looked at Mat and smiled.

After the principal speaker made his patriotic address he sat down and Charles Tillery went to the podium. "We will now conduct the Roll Call of the Dead," he announced solemnly.

Jay Tremaine, the man with the bass drum, stood and attached it to the harness he was wearing. Two of the flower girls walked to a large fan-shaped stand, each with a handful of small American flags.

"We begin the roll call with veterans of the Civil War," said Tillery, pausing to look at the drummer and the flower girls, then back to his list. "Mark D. Updegraph. Mark D. Updegraph."

After the second calling of the name, Jay Tremaine gave the drum a resounding beat. *"BOOM!"* Immediately, one of the flower girls inserted a flag into the top of the fan-shaped stand.

"Benjamin Adamson, Benjamin Adamson," called Tillery.
"BOOM!"

"Henry Copeland, Henry Copeland."

"BOOM!"

"M. J. Goodwin, M. J. Goodwin."

"BOOM!"

And so it went through the entire list of deceased Civil War veterans: "A. W. Young . . . John Eden . . . Simpson Parks . . . Jacob Baker . . . Aaron Harlan . . . C. B. Williams . . . John Helsel . . . Elmer E. Deardorff . . . George Barker . . . William Webster . . . Wilbourn H. Wilson . . . William B. Clark . . . William B. McArthur . . . Frederick C. Beach . . . Elmer H. Brown . . . J. W. Moore . . . James W. Flood . . . John Carr . . . George Helsel . . . John Q. A. Shives . . . Royal H. Tremaine . . . Pomory Williams . . . Henry A. D. Berg . . . George C. Toland."

Tillery looked up from his list and said, "Now, veterans of the Great War: Frederick Harlan . . . Maurice Helsel . . . This concludes the roll call."

The congregation stood and began singing "The Battle Hymn of the Republic." During the song the color guard retrieved the flags and the flower girls picked up their bouquets, following the men outside the church where all, including the drummer, formed up. Once most of the people were out of the church, the drumbeat began. The armed color guard, followed by the drummer and the flower girls, began the march to the Iuka Cemetery. Falling in behind were several men who appeared to be in their seventies or eighties.

Once the family was loaded into the Model-T, Mat as well as other drivers followed the somber march. After a quarter mile, Mat saw that one of the elderly men had stopped. "Sir, would you like to ride the rest of the way?"

"I most certainly would!" the man exclaimed. After Mike helped him into the car he said, "Thank you for stopping. I used to be able to march all the way to the cemetery. But it's getting so halfway is all I can manage with that Confederate bullet still in my leg."

In late August, Mat received a letter from Europe. "It's from Dad. This should be very interesting," he told Rosa. After everyone had gathered, he began reading.

Dear Mat and Rosa,

We have decided that we cannot stay in Europe and will be returning to the United States next month. Your Mother and I had hoped to spend our final years here where we were born but things just aren't good for doing that. Inflation seems to get worse every week, not just here in Jugoslavia but in other parts of Europe, too. We've heard that it's especially bad in Germany and that makes me worry about there being another war. We've also heard that in Budapest, Hungary the schools had to close last winter for lack of heating fuel. There have been so many refugees coming to Budapest that they are living in railroad cars. The last we heard about five thousand cars were being used.

If your mother and I were the only ones in the family, we would probably stay here. But we have to think about Mary, Katie, and George, Jr. They will do better growing up in America.

We will arrive in New York in late September and then go to Chicago to spend some time with your Uncle Mat. Then we'll come out to Kansas. Please see if there's land available near you that I could farm.

We pray that this finds all of you well.

George

Mat handed the letter to Rosa and looked around at the others. "Well, I hope we can find a place for them. I'd better check with Frank Young at the Iuka Bank. And I'd better start reading the newspaper every day."

CHAPTER 25
OVER THE AIR WAVES

I don't hold with furniture that talks!
Early "objection" to radio broadcasts

Late in September 1921, Mat drove his Model-T sedan and Frank
Udry his Model-T truck to the Pratt railroad depot. When the Rock
Island arrived, off stepped George, Anna, Grandma Welsch, Mary,
Katie, and George, Jr. After nearly a year the family was together again.
"Welcome to Kansas!" exclaimed Mat. "It's good to have you back."

"It's really good to be here. Jugoslavia and much of Europe seem
to be heading for even worse times. We just had to leave," George said
with a frown.

"Yes, there were articles in the newspaper several months ago about
the threat of another war," Mat replied.

For two weeks Mat and Rosa's two-bedroom house was packed with
family, despite having the three boys, Mike, George, Jr., and George
III, stay with Frank and Annie Udry. But Mat had been diligent about
finding a place for them to live. "There's a quarter of land with a house
just a couple miles southwest of Pratt that's for sale. It has a windmill
and all the other buildings you'll need to get started. But there's one

thing it doesn't have, electricity. I'll take you and Mother to see it tomorrow."

After looking the place over, George said, "I think I'll cash in some of my Austrian bonds. I'd rather just buy it outright and not owe anything. As for electricity, we haven't had it since we lived in Youngstown. So we'll get along without it for now."

On June 22, 1922, shortly before the wheat harvest, Rosa gave birth to a girl. "What should we name her?" asked Mat.

"Mother said that if it's a girl she would like to have us name her Laura."

Mat swallowed hard. "Yes, I remember. After your sister, right?"

"Yes, she thought it would be a kind thing to do. It's fine with me if it's all right with you."

Mat nodded. "All right. That's what we'll name her. She should have a middle name, too. I think Louise would be good."

One evening in the summer of 1923, there was a knock on the door and Rosa went to answer. When she opened it, there stood Gus Schubert! "Why . . ."

"Shhh!" said Gus, placing his finger over his lips. "Is Mat here?" he whispered.

"Sure, but he went to sleep in his chair," Rosa whispered in return. "He'll really be surprised to see you!"

Gus walked into the living room and over to Mat's chair. "I got nothing left but ham and beans this time of day!" he said loudly.

But Mat continued sleeping.

Gus shook him by the shoulder and repeated the old catchphrase. Mat awoke, sat up straight, and did a double-take. "Gus? Gus, what are you doing here?"

Mixed with jokes and laughter reminiscent of the old days and updates on the family situation, Gus told them, "I just moved to a town up north of here named Ellinwood. I decided to quit the restaurant business. So I sold it and old Coalie, came to Kansas, and bought myself a Model-T."

"What did the Model-T cost you?"

"Just under $300."

"What will you do in Ellinwood?"

"I'll tune pianos. I'm still good at it and a lot of people there have them," Gus laughed.

"Can you stay with us for a while?" asked Rosa.

"I need to leave tomorrow afternoon and get back home for some tuning jobs." The next day Gus told them as he drove away, "Buy yourself a piano. I'll keep it in tune for you. No charge!"

"If we move to a bigger place, we should buy a piano. It will give Laura and George something more to do," Mat told Rosa.

November 1, 1923 Rosa gave birth to a son they named Mathias John, popular names in both the Welli and Welsch families. However, tragedy struck just a few weeks later on December 28. "Mat, the baby won't wake up!"

Mat checked Mathias, looked sadly at Rosa, and took her into his arms. "He's gone, Momma. The little guy is gone."

Rosa sobbed, clinging to Mat. "Should I have Annie and Frank come over and be with us?" he asked.

"Yes, it would help."

Frank Udry took care of final arrangements for young Mathias, sparing them the heartbreaking task.

By 1923 there were 550 radio stations in the United States and listeners bought 1.5 million radios. The following year the number of stations had increased to fourteen hundred and purchases of radios amounted to one third of all money spent on furniture. Music was truly becoming the "background noise" of the day.

Early in 1925 Mat joined the avid radio audience. But this was more than a new piece of furniture. It represented contact with the rest of the world for the entire family, a contact not provided by newspapers until after the fact. From the speakers poured music as entertainment and, equally important, weather and farm market information. Upon coming in for the noon meal Mat would quickly turn on the radio to hear the current prices of wheat and cattle and get some idea of what the next day's weather would bring. At times he grew frustrated at the early weather prediction efforts. "Aha! They said it would rain today but it's clear as a bell! Maybe they should have the guy giving the livestock futures predict the weather too," he would laugh.

But the radio was also educational. "George, does your geography book have a map of the United States?" Mat asked one Saturday evening, turning on the radio.

"Yes, Dad. It's right here at the front of the book."

"Well, sit down and let's see how many states we can listen to tonight."

Rosa took a chair near the radio as did her mother, Antonia. "This sounds interesting. How far away will we be able to hear?"

"I think it depends on the weather. If there's a storm near the station or near us there will be a lot of static and we won't be able to hear it very well. But it's a clear night for us so we'll see what we can pick up." Mat turned the dial and tuned in a station. "Sounds like it's kinda' far away . . .."

"This is station KDKA in Pittsburgh," said the announcer after several songs had been performed by a live vocal group.

"Do you know where that is, George?" asked Mat.

"I think it's in Pennsylvania. Yes, here it is on the map."

"Well, put it on your list of states," said Mat as he spun the dial, stopping when a strong signal came over. This time they listened a while longer to a station that eventually identified itself as WSM in Nashville, Tennessee. "Did you find it on your map?"

"Yes, Dad."

They didn't listen long to the next station, despite its strong signal. "It's right here in Kansas but Frank Udry told me this Dr. John Brinkley is just a quack," Mat grumbled. "He sells fake medical advice to old men!"

Spinning the dial again he picked up music that caught both his and Rosa's ears. "What do you think of this, Momma?"

"It sounds great, just like some of the music we use to dance too!"

Mat laughed. "Yes, but I think Gus Schubert could give their fiddle player a run for his money! The next time he comes down I'll tell him about this program."

Later, the program identified itself as "The National Barn Dance coming to you over WLS in Chicago." They spent the remainder of the evening listening to the station. "This was fun," smiled Rosa when they finally turned off the radio. The entire family, including Rosa's mother, had been entertained. Antonia didn't understand English but enjoyed the music immensely. And George III went through a drill on U.S. geography while compiling his list of stations listened to and the states in which they were located. Two months later, in March 1925, they heard the inauguration of President Calvin Coolidge as radio assumed an even greater role in bringing newsworthy events to the public.

The family grew in size that summer. On July 10, 1925, Rosa gave birth to another daughter. "I want to name her Mary but make it longer," she said after the doctor had left.

"Well, Mary is a good family name. I have a sister named Mary and my dad's mother was named Mary," Mat replied. "How about Marylou?"

"That has a nice sound," said Antonia.

"Then that's what it will be," smiled Rosa.

In the summer of 1926 Mat ran into Charles Tillery at Taylor's Store. "Mat, I have a business deal for you," he said as they loaded purchases into their cars.

"Really, what have you got?"

"I've bought a house in Iuka that we're going to move to. I'm going to keep a couple of riding horses and sell off the others. Would you be interested in buying the house and land where we live? Would you also like to buy the broodmares from my herd? There are a couple of other breeds besides the Tennessee Walking Horses now."

Mat paused for a moment, considering the proposition. *The house is larger and more modern than the one where we live. Our family has gotten larger. There's good pasture land for grazing and best of all I'd love to raise horses!* "That sounds like an interesting proposal, Charlie. Let me talk to the folks at the Iuka State Bank."

"We'll be happy to make a loan to you, Mat," said Frank Young.

"We certainly will," seconded Verne Taylor. "I like the way you do business. You pay off your farm loans promptly and we don't even have to send you a notice about the due date."

Several weeks later, the family had moved to the new place with a house that quickly became home. In addition to his own string of eight work and riding horses, he now owned twenty broodmares. "All right, Son, we'll raise our own tractors," Mat told George III, now twelve years old. Then he added somewhat wistfully, "But some day real tractors will replace these old friends of ours."

Shortly after New Year's 1927 Mat was deeply engrossed in his newspaper, not missing a detail. "Hmm, Momma, listen to this," he said to Rosa.

"Some big news in the paper?" she asked.

"Yes, Zenith has come out with a new radio. Here's what it says: 'The New 1927 Radio is here. Zenith makes the first and most important announcement in radio for 1927, the New Zenith Model 17. Not a camouflaged, so called Light Socket Radio set, but a truly custom-built radio, designed to operate without wet or dry batteries, chargers, acids or water. Just plug into the light socket, that is all. No attachments to worry over. Always full power. The tone is incomparable.' Here, take a look at the picture," he said, handing her the newspaper.

"It's handsome — like a small piano."

"That's true. It is nice to look at. They call this the Spinet Model. But the best thing is that it operates on electricity instead of a battery."

"Really? Well, that's good. I'm always worrying about Laura and Marylou fooling around with the battery on this one. But how much would it cost?"

"It doesn't say but I'm sure it will be well over $100, maybe closer to $200. But radio gives us lots of entertainment, information, and even helps educate the children. And having one that you just plug in would be a big improvement over our old one. It looks like something you'd use to send out an SOS aboard some cargo ship." Mat looked off into the distance momentarily and then smiled. "We'll ask Annie to come over next Monday and look after the kids while you and I go to Pratt and shop for a radio."

In late June 1927 Mat received a telephone call the day he finished harvesting the wheat crop. It was his dad.

"Mat, Grandma Welsch passed away a few minutes ago."

"Did she get sick from something?"

"No, she just couldn't get out of bed this morning. Said she was too old and tired. When Anna took a glass of water to her a few minutes later, she was gone."

Mat swallowed hard. *Grandma Welsch? That wonderful grandma who always loved hearing me play the harmonica?*

"I thought that since you speak English you should make the final arrangements," George continued.

"How are Mother and the rest of the family?"

"It's a sad day. We're all very sad around here now." George's voice was down to a whisper.

After the funeral service, Mat comforted Anna. "She lived a good long life, Mother. From 1847 to 1927. And she did a lot of good things, too."

"I know," sobbed Anna. "But it just seemed that she would always be with us."

"Yes, I felt the same way. But look at George III, that fine son of mine. I'll always remember that Grandma helped bring him into the world."

Anna smiled through her tears. "That seems so long ago, Mat. But she helped bring you into the world too. That's . . . "

"Thirty-six years ago," he said, finishing her calculation.

Mat and Rosa smiled proudly as the graduation ceremony ended. It was May 1928 and George III had completed grade school. Norris Tarman, the principal and teacher for grades five through eight, approached them. He was a tall, lanky, serious-looking man.

"Good evening, I'm glad you could come to our little graduation exercise. I wanted to know if you plan on having George go on to high school."

"We thought we would suggest it to him," replied Mat.

"That's good! But I'd say it more strongly," said Tarman. "George is one of the best students I've had in a long time. I was tempted to have him skip a grade two years ago but thought it better for him to stay with his own age group. He should definitely go to high school and maybe even college if you can afford it. Please urge him to continue his education."

George III needed no urging and was excited by the idea of going on to school. In September 1928 he entered Pratt High School as a freshman. Mat bought a 1921 Model-T Coupe for him to drive to and from school.

Mat looked out the living room window and saw Charlie Tillery pulling into the driveway. *I wonder what he's got to talk about. One thing's certain, it's always interesting!* "Come in Charlie and have a chair," he greeted him.

"I can't stay but a little while, Mat. Just got to ask you a favor."

"Sure, what would it be?"

"Well, 1928 is an election year and I'm running for mayor of Iuka."

"You've got my vote," Mat chuckled.

"Thanks but I'm running unopposed so getting elected won't be a problem. What I want to ask is whether you would run for the vacant position on the city council?"

"Now that's something I never would have thought of. Really? For sure?"

"Yes, several of us think you would be a good addition to the council. In the years you've lived here you've become well thought of."

Mat thought for a few seconds and smiled. "All right. You can put me on the ballot!" *Life keeps getting more interesting.*

George did well his first year in high school and when school was out in the spring of 1929, Mat decided to reward him. "How would you like to take an airplane ride?"

"Sure thing!" George was excited at the idea.

"We wanted to do this closer to your fifteenth birthday in March but the air show at the Pratt Airport was cancelled because a storm damaged several of the airplanes. But there's going to be an air show next Saturday and they'll be offering rides."

On Saturday they drove to the airport, located north of Pratt. "Lots of cars, Dad," George observed. "And just look at all the airplanes!"

"Many people are here to see the airplanes and watch the parachute jumps. I'm curious to see how many want to go for a ride," said Mat as they approached a ticket booth. "What plane is giving the rides? And how much does it cost?"

The man pointed toward a large Ford Tri-Motor aircraft near the edge of the runway. "That one over there. It's one dollar."

Mat looked at Rosa. "Do you want to go too?" he asked with a broad grin.

"Absolutely not! But I'll snap a picture of the plane when it takes off."

"Just one ticket for the boy," said Mat. He laughed aloud when handing the ticket to George. "Momma, this will be kind of like the picture your mother took that day in Oklahoma, the one when you drove the Model-T for the first and last time!"

They watched as George confidently walked out to the airplane, handed his ticket to the pilot, and waved to them. In a few minutes it taxied onto the runway with its load of sightseeing passengers. Shortly, it came rushing back, all three engines roaring. Rosa took a picture just as it lifted off the runway, banked, and headed south toward Pratt. After several minutes' absence it flew back over the airport, heading north toward Iuka. "Looks like George is getting his money's worth," chuckled Mat.

And then the ride was over, George ecstatic over the experience. "That was lots of fun, Dad! Thanks!"

"Did it make you feel like Charles Lindbergh?"

"Well, a little bit. Now I can better imagine what it must have been like flying over the Atlantic."

On the ride home Mat said, "George, you've experienced all forms of transportation: horses, trains, ocean liners, automobiles, and now an airplane. Maybe in a couple of weeks we'll go to the rodeo they always have in Sun City."

"Where's Sun City?" asked Rosa.

"It's southwest of Pratt, down in Barber County."

Although farm prices were still depressed following their downturn when the Great War ended in 1918, family life was now comfortable with the more difficult years of the early 1920s behind them. Mat relished the addition of horse-raising to his means of making a living. For young Laura and Marylou this meant there were often colts frisking about the pasture in springtime that they loved watching.

Mat and Rosa enjoyed the almost idyllic small-town life in Iuka. Frank and Annie Udry were frequent visitors. On Sundays, both families often drove to George and Anna's home a few miles southwest of Pratt. As the oldest grandchild, George III had spent many summer days at their home when still a young boy.

Old times from the days in Oklahoma were occasionally revisited when Gus Schubert and Joe Loesel both visited Mat and Rosa. These days provided a nearly endless source of laughter and camaraderie for the three old friends.

Back in the house for the noon meal in late October 1929, Mat turned on the radio. When it finished warming up, he heard ". . . heavy selling pressure has forced the price of wheat down twelve cents a bushel! There has been an avalanche of selling orders!"

Mat plopped down in his chair beside the radio and turned up the volume as the announcer continued. "On Wall Street stocks are being dumped in panic selling. U.S. Steel has dropped $9.50 a share and

Johns-Manville is down a whopping $40 a share! American Telephone is down $21!"

"Oh no!" exclaimed Mat, leaning forward in the chair.

"Mat, dinner is ready," called Rosa from the dining room.

"We'd better listen to this for a while, Momma. Wheat prices are way down. And so is the stock market. I'm afraid there's big trouble ahead."

Rosa came into the living room and listened for a few minutes. Finally she urged him to the table. "I understand falling wheat prices but not much of the other news. But one thing I know for sure. You must eat, Mat. Groceries are cheaper than medicine!"

Mat grinned at her impeccable logic. "All right, Momma. That's always good advice for George, Laura, and Marylou so I guess it's good advice for me too."

When the newspaper was delivered that evening, Mat quickly checked the headlines. There had been some recovery but the news was still bad: "Sharp Breaks (in) Wheat Prices — After dropping twelve cents, prices rallied but still closed five cents lower." He quickly read another headline: "A Near Stock Panic Today — The most terrifying panic of selling since the war scare of 1914, dealt a crushing blow to the leading stock markets throughout the country today and was checked only by prompt reassurances from the country's leading bankers. During the early afternoon, the ticker quotations were an hour behind the floor transactions . . .."

Mat dropped the paper and stared at the front page. It was dated October 24, 1929, a date that would later become known as "Black Thursday." The news was truly bad; however, the worst was yet to come.

CHAPTER 26
HARD TIMES

This problem of unemployment is the most torturing that can be presented to a civilized society. . . . One may even be pardoned for doubting whether institutions based on adult suffrage could possibly arrive at the right decisions upon the intricate propositions of modern business and finance. . . . You cannot cure cancer by a majority vote. What is needed is a remedy.

Winston Churchill, member of Parliament, 1930[38]

Early Sunday afternoon, Mat and Rosa, along with George, Laura, and Marylou, drove to George and Anna's farm just southwest of Pratt. As usual, Frank and Annie Udry's Model-A was already parked near the windmill. Rosa beamed. "Oh, it'll be good to see Annie!"

As they got out of the car, Mary and Katie ran out to escort them inside past the gauntlet of barking dogs. "Hello, everyone! Come on inside, they won't bite."

Rosa turned to the dogs, shook her finger, and scolded them in a foreign-sounding gibberish. "That wouldn't even pass as bad German, Momma. But it always seems to quiet them," laughed Mat.

Once inside, there was the usual chorus of greetings and exchange of humorous remarks, the type shared by close family. When the adults were settled, Mary and Katie invited George, Laura, and Marylou out to the kitchen. "Do you kids want some treats to eat?" asked Mary enthusiastically.

"Yes, come on out to the kitchen. We just got through baking cookies," said Katie with a broad smile. "Oh me! You girls are growing up so fast. And George, you're getting so tall, almost as tall as your dad!"

"Where are Mike and George, Jr.?" asked George III.

"They went pheasant hunting, out at the west end of the pasture," Mary replied.

"George, take some cookies for them and for yourself," offered Katie as he prepared to join his uncles in the hunt.

But the older adults' conversation quickly became more serious than those of previous family gatherings. "The markets were really bad last week," Mat began.

"I'm afraid we'll be seeing wheat prices go much lower. With the stock market down too, it's going to make everyone cautious," Frank replied.

"Well, if times are going to get tough, I'm glad we're in the United States. It would be much worse in Europe. In his last letter, Joseph said that people are getting more concerned all the time about what will happen. If the economy here goes bad, you can multiply the loss for Jugoslavia and the other countries over there," added George, Sr.

This triggered more introspection as the families analyzed respective financial situations and expressed relief at the level of their self-sufficiency. They enjoyed a level much above that of many others in the United States.

"I think we're lucky not to be in debt," observed Annie. "If hard times really are ahead, the farmers who mortgaged their land to buy new cars, machinery, and things for the house may have trouble keeping the bankers satisfied."

"That's for sure. All my machinery and cars are new but they're paid for, even the new Model-A Roadster I just bought for George III," replied Mat. Then he said to his dad, "But these Austrian bonds we own probably won't stand up to hard times, will they? The price is still about half what we paid for them."

"I sold most of mine when I bought this place, and the machinery and livestock to get started again. But I'd hate for the ones I have left to become worthless. Sometimes I wish we'd listened to the banker in Goodwell and bought U.S. bonds."

"Well, you could own Jugoslavian bonds. They would be an even bigger risk," added Frank with a wry smile.

The afternoon wore on, most of the conversation dealing with the stock market, potential unemployment in the big cities, wheat prices, and the 1930 crop prospects. Finally, just as it was nearly time to leave, in walked the three hunters. "Did you get some pheasants for tomorrow's dinner?" asked Anna.

"Yes, three of them," replied Mike, greeting Rosa and Annie and shaking hands with Mat and Frank.

Mat remained standing as Rosa went to get their coats from the bedroom. "George, Laura, Marylou, we have to go now," said Mat.

"I hate to see you leave so soon," said Anna.

"We've got cows to milk, Grandma," replied George III, giving her a parting hug.

"Yes, and they won't wait, will they? But thank goodness we have the cows and the chickens for milk, cream, butter, and eggs. The orchard and the garden always help out too."

"And hogs and steers for fresh meat," added Rosa. "If hard times come, I'll can more fruit and vegetables than I usually do."

Annie related a final aspect of rural self-sufficiency. "You know, some days when we go to the store, the money we get for the cream and eggs we bring in pays for a lot of the groceries."

On "Black Thursday," October 24, 1929, nearly 12,900,000 shares traded when the market took its major downturn. Stocks were down again on Monday with more than 9,000,000 shares traded, one third of them during the final hour of trading. October 29 became "Black Tuesday" as stock prices collapsed when 16,410,030 shares were traded. The *Pratt Tribune* headline for the following day read "RALLY IN PRICES — STOCK MARKET" but the hope was futile. The rally was attributable to bankers stepping into the market and buying in order to add some stability. "Rally at Close Cheers Brokers; Bankers Optimistic, to Continue Aid," stated the October 30 *New York Times*.

By November 1 stocks had lost nearly $16 billion in value. The Ford Motor Company announced price reductions on models of cars and trucks in full-page newspaper ads, including the November 1 *Pratt Tribune*. "The Ford Motor Company believes that basically the industry and business of the country are sound. Every indication is that general business conditions will remain prosperous. We are reducing prices now because we feel that such a step is the best contribution that could be made to assure a continuation of good business throughout the country," read the ad. The Town Car was reduced from $1,400 to $1,200, the Roadster from $460 to $440, the Taxicab from $800 to $725, and the Model-A Panel Delivery Truck from $615 to $590. Similar reductions were announced on sixteen other models.

Mat was encouraged by the wheat prices. They had finished three to four cents higher in late October. *Maybe things will stabilize.*

But financial collapse in the United States would trigger the Great Depression. Stock prices had been inflated to unrealistic levels. As the prices fell disastrously, corporations, utilities, insurance companies, banks, and thousands of individuals lost the huge amounts of money they had invested. Insurance companies and banks then began to fail and millions of people lost their life's saving. Corporations went out of business or cut production in order to survive, resulting in widespread unemployment.

The United States, with fields capable of growing food for the world, natural resources of every kind, a gigantic industrial machine, and a large, competent labor force, became a nation where most of its citizens were reduced to poverty. Crops rotted in the fields while millions went hungry. Fresh milk, direly needed by young children in the cities, was poured out on the ground. Many of the population suffered through cold, heatless winters while coal mines shut down and public power companies went bankrupt. There was a crying need for industrial products of nearly every type but factories were closed. By 1932, unemployment had reached a level of more than 13 million.

Their built-in self-sufficiency from diverse farming, doing without extravagances, along with being debt-free, enabled the Welli and Udry families to get through 1930 and 1931 and remain nearly as secure as middle-class residents of the larger towns and cities. By this time they had acquired "state of the art" farm machinery, including the all-important combine, which eliminated much of the labor cost in harvesting wheat.

"Keep that Case combine in good repair and grease the fittings two or three times a day and it will last for years," Mat proclaimed. He received no argument from his dad or Frank Udry.

"The next implement dealer who tells me I need a more modern combine will get no further business," laughed Frank. "We only use the darn things ten days a year and the rest of the time they just sit."

"The same goes for that radio we have. It's good for several more years."

On March 10, 1931, Rosa gave birth to another daughter. "Momma, we should name this little girl after you," Mat urged. And the new baby was named Rosa Mae.

Mat continued to listen to every radio newscast and maintained his voracious reading of the daily newspaper and numerous magazines. *National Geographic* was a favorite and he frequently recommended articles to George. "Look! There's an article about Admiral Byrd in this month's issue."

Mat read an ad for the Literary Digest Book of Marvels[39] that was very enticing and ordered a copy. The book was a treasure-trove of cutting-edge scientific, medical, industrial, historical, and geographical information for the time and was written for a general readership. "We got to get this even though it's a bit of a luxury, Momma. It will have lots of good information for George and later on for the girls."

When the book was delivered a few weeks later, Mat quickly called, "George, come take a look at our new book." They admired the handsome, nine-by twelve-inch tome of 128 pages. It had a dark maroon cover with a feature that made it a very personal item.

"Look, Dad, it has your name engraved in gold!"

They began paging through it. "Listen to this introduction, George, 'We often hear it said that the age of miracles is past. This is an obvious mistake. We have but to look about us to realize that the greatest age of miracles is just beginning. Anyone who is familiar with the history of scientific progress in the past third of a century can cite offhand at least a score of achievements that are nothing less than miraculous.' Hmm, it lists twenty scientific, medical, and industrial achievements. I can't argue with any of these!"

"Nice picture of a tri-motor airplane. Is it a Ford, like the one I rode in?"

"No, it says it's a twelve-passenger Fokker, flying the regular route between Kansas City and Los Angeles for Western Air Express."

Father and son spent the late afternoon scanning through the new book. Mat was intrigued by all the dinosaur pictures. "Here's a picture of that place in Mongolia where Roy Chapman Andrews found the dinosaur eggs several years ago!"

George was most excited by the explorers. "Look at that, Dad. Two full pages on Admiral Peary and Admiral Byrd!"

But an article about "television" on page eighty-six really stoked the imagination. "It says that this is only an experimental success right now. But I think it means that some day when we turn on the news we'll be able to see the announcer as well as listen to him," said Mat.

George was even more enthused. "I think I'll read the whole book before school starts this fall. It could help me in chemistry."

"Who teaches that class?"

"J. Rufus Gray. He's very good. I had him for physics last year. I liked C. S. Wood too. He taught general biology when I was a sophomore."

"You guys have to move so Laura can set the table," laughed Rosa. "My goodness, this has been like listening to a couple of scientists or explorers!"

As they got up Mat asked, "What about writing? Do you have any classes that require it?"

"We do some writing in English class but not very much."

"Do they have a course in journalism?"

"Yes, but I don't remember who teaches it. There's a school newspaper called *The Mirror*."

"I think you should sign up for that class too. Good communication is very important and you would get some practical writing experience there."

"Supper's ready! Come to the table!"

During 1930 and 1931, life for residents of the Southern Plains had remained relatively comfortable when compared to living in a major city and being unemployed. The wheat crops were good in both years. Although it turned dry in mid-1931, farmers remained optimistic, despite the dip in wheat prices to $0.25 a bushel, a level that for them would become a legendary symbol of the Great Depression. This was a price about $2.00 per bushel less than the market prices of 1917-1918, when the one of the victory slogans was "Food will win the war!"

"Plant it in the dust and your granaries will bust!" was the conventional wisdom of the early 1930s. It expressed hope that eventually there would be sufficient rain to raise a crop. However, the last few days of August 1931 produced a tremendous dust storm with strong southwest winds and temperatures in the upper nineties. Late in September, comparisons were being made to the hot, dry days of the early 1890s when the ground was baked so hard that shod horses struck sparks when walking. It was so dry in those days that the Rock Island Railroad brought a "rainmaker" to Pratt, but to no avail.

In September 1931 George III was back at Pratt High School for his senior year. "Well, Dad, I'm taking journalism and I'm on the *Mirror* staff."

"Really? That's good. Who teaches it?"

"Miss Pauline Weitz is the instructor."

"What are you doing for the school paper?"

"I'm the sports editor."

Mat did a double-take. "Editor? Really? Does that mean someone works for you?"

"Well, Carl Ayers is the assistant. I volunteered to be the editor so he offered to be the assistant. Carl is on the football team so that means I'll be doing all the writing. But having someone from the team to check with on football terminology and strategy will be great."

"Yes, I can see where it would be good to have an expert to consult. Hear that Momma? Our son is the sports editor for the school newspaper."

"What will you be doing?" asked Rosa.

"It means I'll be going to all the football games and some of the early season basketball games, even those away from home. I'll take notes at the games and then compose articles for the *Mirror* when it comes out each week. I'm the sports editor for the first semester. Someone else will do it the second semester."

The lead for George's first article read, "Coach Fred Lighter says prospects for the upcoming gridiron season are fair." The sportswriters for the *Pratt Tribune* and the *Pratt Union* also took Coach Lighter at his word and did nothing to elevate football fans' hopes. However, the repeated gridiron victories, several of them overwhelming, soon showed this caution to be unjustified. Some fans began to compare the team with the glorious gridiron warriors of 1928.

As the traditional Thanksgiving Day game with Liberal, Kansas High School approached, Pratt High School had an unblemished record.

October 2	Pratt 19 – at Haviland 0
October 9	Pratt 51 – Greensburg 0
October 16	Pratt 46 – at Kingman 0
October 23	Pratt 24 – Dodge City 0
October 30	Pratt 45 – Stafford 0
November 4	Pratt 10 – St. John 0
November 13	Pratt 25 – Great Bend 0

"George, Pratt High hasn't even been scored upon this season. But I haven't seen any mention of that in your articles or in the Pratt newspapers," Mat observed.

"I don't want to jinx them," laughed George. "Next Thursday is the final game out at Liberal. The Rock Island is going to add five special cars to their westbound train. The team, the band, and the fans and I will be leaving early in the morning and get there about one o'clock for the 2:15 kickoff."

"Will you be staying overnight?"

"No, the train leaves Liberal right after the game and will have us back in Pratt by ten o'clock."

George sat in a steady rain that turned the playing field into a sea of mud. "It wasn't pretty. The rain and mud kept the Pratt Greenbacks from doing anything spectacular, except win by a 12-0 score over the Liberal Redskins," began his article. It ended with, "But we have an undefeated team that was also unscored upon for the entire season!"

Mat frowned after opening the May 11, 1932 *Pratt Tribune*. "Kansas Outlook Down — Means Better Wheat Prices — Kansas to have an 87,202,000 bushel crop (in 1932). The forecast, due to unfavorable prospects in the Great Plains region, is regarded as a bright spot in the world wheat situation and will tend to reduce many of the existing surpluses."

"And that's supposed to be good news!" he exclaimed, shaking his head. Then another item caught his eye. "Hey everyone, come listen!" He stood up and began reading as the entire family gathered around. "'*Mirror* Again Ranks High — Pratt High School Paper Wins First in Class 3 in K. S. C. Contest. The *Mirror*, Pratt High School newspaper, placed first in class three of the 15th annual high school newspaper contest of the Kansas State College journalism department.'"

Mat skipped down in the article, paused briefly, and then began reading aloud, "'Class three is composed of schools with senior high enrollments of 101 to 300. The newspaper has received several honor ratings this year, recently placing in the excellent class in the National Scholastic Press Association contest conducted at the University of Minnesota.' This is really great, George. And the best part is that all your names are listed. Look everyone. It says, 'George Welli, sports editor!'"

George laughed. "Having that great football team to write about must have helped quite a bit!"

Rosa took the paper and translated it into German for Antonia, who beamed upon hearing the good news about her oldest grandchild. "Well done, George!" she told him. "You've grown up to be a tall, strong, handsome young man and you have a good mind too. I'm so proud of you!"

Two weeks later, the family attended the Pratt High School commencement exercises, watching proudly as George received his diploma. Afterwards Mat told him, "Times are a bit hard now and I'm afraid that a drought is setting in. But we can afford to have you attend Wichita Business College next year. You need to learn something that could help you get into banking or some other business. Farming is okay but it's awfully unpredictable when you have to rely on the weather so much."

Late in July, Mat came home from an Iuka City Council meeting and announced, "They want me to run for the Iuka Township Board this fall. The chair position is open."

Rosa was curious, but pleased. "Really? They must think very highly of you. Who else is on the board?"

"Bill Geissler and George Helmke. They're good men and it should be fun to work with them, as they both like to joke. George is a veteran. He served in the Great War."

In November 1932 Mat stayed close by the radio listening to the election news. "Well Momma, it looks like we are going to have a Democrat for president. Franklin Roosevelt seems to be winning."

"What about you? Are you going to be on the township board now?"

"No one ran against me so I'll be the winner. My job will be a heck of a lot easier than Mr. Roosevelt's. I have to supervise road maintenance and oversee the election board in Iuka Township. He has to pull this country out of a depression."

George III completed the year-long course at Wichita Business College and returned home in the fall of 1933. However, far too many banks had closed because of the Depression and job openings were practically nonexistent. So he entered a farm partnership with Mat. "With you around full time we may be able to acquire some more land," Mat told him.

Sure enough. "Mat, I'm the agent for the Lemon family and they have 320 acres just north of town that's available," Frank Young told them when they visited the Iuka State Bank. Thus, George III became a wheat farmer rather than a banker.

Given the dry weather throughout 1933, road maintenance crews had relatively little work, except for light grading of the many miles of roadway in Iuka Township. In times of heavy rainfall, the roads became deeply rutted from traffic, no matter how light, and needed to be graded quickly. During dry weather, however, the need to grade or put down new gravel was infrequent.

Early one Monday morning in late October, Mat's telephone rang. "Three longs and one short. That's our ring," said Rosa, walking briskly to the large, wooden telephone mounted near the dining room window. After lifting the receiver, she said, "Oh yes, he's here. It's for you, Mat. He sounds awfully excited."

"This is Mat. Really? How big? Really? Really! Well, don't do anything more until I get there!" Turning to Rosa, "It's the boys down at Gust Seidel's sandpit. They were loading up gravel and ran into some bones, really big ones!"

"But what could they be?" Rosa was incredulous.

"I don't know but I'd better take a whiskbroom, some flour sacks, and some gunnysacks along with me." Mat's mind whirled at a fast pace. *A long-dead buffalo? Some prehistoric monster? Here in Kansas I can see it might be a buffalo. But a prehistoric animal?* He climbed into his 1928 International truck and hit the starter. The engine roared to life and he waved to Rosa as he began the three-mile drive to the gravel pit.

"Well, boys, what have we found?" he asked eagerly of the three men standing near the back of a small truck.

"Right here, Mat. You can see it looks like a socket bone," said one. "I hit it with my shovel when we were loading up the truck."

"But the socket for what kind of an animal? And how big?" wondered the other two.

Mat dropped quickly to his hands and knees and began using the whiskbroom to sweep away untold years of accumulated sand and gravel. "It's too big to be a buffalo bone. Buffalo bones aren't much bigger than those of cattle. The socket in this bone must be nine or ten inches in diameter!"

After some time the socket bone, nearly three feet in length, was fully exposed. Mat then began probing the surrounding area with a stick. "Whoops! There's another one!" he exclaimed gleefully. Using the same slow procedure they finally unearthed it. "A shoulder blade maybe?" Mat surmised.

Finally, they gave up finding additional bones. "Thanks for calling me, you guys. I think these are probably the bones of some prehistoric animal. I'll take them to school so the children can see them." Then he carefully wrapped them, first in the clean flour sacks and then in the gunnysacks for additional padding.

Once home, he showed them to Rosa, George, and the rest of the family. "I think we should put these bones in the Iuka School for a few days so the children can see them."

"We could also take them down to Pratt High School. Some of the professors might know what kind of animal they're from. J. Rufus Gray and C. S. Wood could tell us," George advised.

"That's a good idea. Then, they could go on display at the grade school, maybe the newspaper office, and maybe even the display cases at the courthouse."

Rosa laughed long and hard. "It's good to see my two scientists are back. Now, please move those old bones so Marylou can set the table for dinner!"

Late in January 1934[40] *The Pratt Tribune* published a front-page article about the discovery:

BONES FOR ALL TO SEE

Mat Welli Plans to Place Bones of
Pre-Historic Monster in Courthouse

When the shovel of a member of a sand-hauling crew struck a hard object in a sandpit on the Gus Seidel farm southeast of Iuka last fall, the workmen had jammed into something about two million years old. It was the hip-bone of a mastodon, which had lain there buried for centuries.

Mat Welli, Iuka Township officer who was directing the hauling of sand to the roads in that township, immediately became interested and it was removed carefully. The hip-bone was in an almost perfect state of preservation. In addition, the shovel of the man uncovered most of the shoulder blade of the huge animal in the same pit.

The bones were carefully preserved by Mr. Welli, who sent them to the Iuka School for the pupils to see. Later they were brought to the schools here where classes could speculate their age. The bones are now in the *Tribune* office where they may be seen. Later Mr. Welli intends to place them in the glass cases at the courthouse.

The hip-bone and the shoulder blade were found about seven feet under the surface of the ground. Care was taken in further digging in the hope that perhaps more of the prehistoric animal, that was much larger than an elephant, could be found.

Some time before, a tooth weighing a pound and a half had been found in the Luders pit a mile west of the Seidel pit. This is in a perfect state of preservation and only recently was taken by Dr. Lee Hamilton to a dental convention.

While Mr. Welli is intensely interested in these prehistoric findings, he values them chiefly for their interest to school children and hopes the schools will make full use of them.[41]

CHAPTER 27
DUSTY SKIES

Swirling Dust Envelops West
From Black Hills to Panhandle
Front-page headline, *Pratt Daily Tribune*, **March 20, 1935**

Because of wheat shortages in Europe during World War I, plowing up grassland, even some better left for cattle grazing, became a key initiative of President Woodrow Wilson's administration. The patriotic slogan "FOOD WILL WIN THE WAR, WHEAT IS NEEDED FOR THE ALLIES!"[42] had an even stronger appeal in view of the government's price guarantee of $2.21 per bushel. This was nearly double the average price in years before the war. At $2.21 it was foolhardy not to be patriotic. The farmers of the Great Plains harvested 74 million acres of wheat, which was a 38 percent increase over the period 1909-1913.

When the war ended in 1918, Europe still needed food imports. By 1919 wheat lands in Kansas, Colorado, Nebraska, Oklahoma, and Texas had been expanded by plowing up an additional 11 million acres of native grassland. The wheat farmer was now far more than just an individual trying to support his family. *He had become a major factor in international commerce.*

This bonanza attracted even more investor-sod busters. These individuals were known as "suitcase farmers," a derisive label that would later become one of contempt. As most of the new ground went into wheat production, there was a severe glut on the market by 1931 due to that year's record-breaking crop. On September 30, 1931, the *Pratt Union* reported a wheat market price of $0.26, *nearly two dollars a bushel less than the 1917 price.*

Other signs were even more ominous. One third of what was to become the Dust Bowl region, 33 million acres, was now bare cropland, extremely vulnerable to high winds during drought conditions.[43] The rains stopped in the summer of 1931, beginning a decade-long ecological disaster. The Soil Conservation Service compiled a frequency chart of all dust storms large enough to be classified as regional in their extent.[44]

Year	Storms
1932	14
1933	38
1934	22
1935	40
1936	68
1937	72
1938	61
1939	30
1940	17
1941	17

The Welli and Udry families endured both intense heat and dust storms in 1932 and 1933. The drought continued for a fourth consecutive year as Pratt County, Kansas received only half the normal twenty-six inches of annual rainfall. In June 1933 there were fourteen days of 100 degrees or higher, with a temperature of 111 reached on June 4. July temperatures reached 100 degrees thirteen times. August was relatively mild, with temperatures reaching 100 degrees *only* seven times. And usually the driest month, August provided 4.31 inches of the mere 13.11 received in 1933.[45]

"You know, I've always said that we're all gonna' end up shoveling coal for the Devil but this is way too soon!" quipped Frank Udry shortly after New Year's Day.

"True, but maybe 1934 will be better," Mat replied grimly. "We really need rain. I saw in the paper that we had less than half our normal rainfall in 1933."

On a cool, early spring day in March, Rosa heard a knock. "Why, hello Gus! It's so good to see you!"

"Thanks! It's good to see you again, too."

"Come on in and sit down. Mat's in the bathroom shaving. He should be out in a few minutes. It's a nice cool morning and we all slept a bit late. I had to rush to get Laura and Marylou off to school. Mat, Gus is here!"

Gus strolled into the living room. "Well, a piano. When did you get it?"

"Who wants to know?" asked Mat with a broad smile, extending his hand.

"We bought it from some folks here in town. Their kids are gone now so there was no one to play it," replied Rosa.

"Want me to tune it while I'm here?" Gus walked over and struck a few chords. "It's not too far out of tune. It wouldn't take long and there's no charge for old Oklahoma friends. Who plays it?"

"Laura and Marylou and maybe Rosie when she gets older," Rosa replied.

"What about George III?"

"He's happy playing his harmonica, says the piano would take more time than he has available," said Mat. "George has a job now working for the Panhandle Eastern."

"The pipeline company? What's he do, help lay the lines?"

"No, he works at a monitoring station in a small tin building just north of Iuka. Has to read the pressure gauge and call in the reading to headquarters every two hours."

"All day long?"

"And night. It's twenty-four hours a day. He also has to open a valve every once in a while to let excess moisture blow out."

"How does he do it? I mean how can he get enough rest, and meals, and clean up?"

"Well, it's only a mile away, so he can come home eat and clean up and still get back before it's time to call in the next reading."

Gus smiled grimly. "That's an awful job. It's a good thing George is young. How much does it pay?"

"Only $100 a month but he's just going to be doing it in March, April, and May. After that he and I will be getting ready for the wheat harvest. He takes his harmonica and the newspaper with him out to the pipeline shack. You know what? I didn't hear you drive in."

"Got a new Ford V-8. It's really quiet compared to the old Model-A I had. Come on outside, I'll show it to you."

As Gus predicted, the piano tuning was relatively easy. After he finished Rosa looked at the clock, went to the radio, turned it on, and adjusted the dial. Mat smiled. "It must be time for our favorite program."

After the radio warmed up there was a brief pause and then, "The Texas Playboys are on the air!" called the announcer. Lively fiddle and guitar music poured from the speakers. Rosa laughed and turned up the volume.

Gus listened closely. "Very good!" he exclaimed when the theme song ended.

"Let's sit and listen," said Mat. And for the next half hour they laughed, tapped their feet, and sometimes clapped their hands to the infectious music of Bob Wills and his Texas Playboys.

"That's great music. I haven't heard them before. What station is that?" asked Gus during a commercial for Playboy Flour.

"It's on station KVOO down in Tulsa. Rosa found it a few weeks ago. We like it 'cause they play mostly dance music. And it's happy music compared to some you hear on the National Barn Dance or from Nashville. What with the hard times and the drought we can always use some cheering up," Mat replied.

They listened and smiled throughout the program. Even Bob Wills' song introductions added to their merriment.

"You know me. I love to listen to good fiddle playing. I'll have to see if I can get that station up in Ellinwood," said Gus. "Speaking of radio programs, do you ever listen to Father John Coughlin, Mat?"

"Isn't he that Catholic priest whose program is on Sunday afternoons? I've heard of him but I've never listened."

"You might want to tune in. He knows politics and he's a really good speaker and always sounds like he knows what he's talking about."

"Well now, the president has a very tough job trying to bring us out of these hard times. It might be good to hear what someone else thinks about whether things are gonna' get better."

The next morning Mat and Rosa walked with Gus out to the car as he was leaving. "It was good to see you again, Gus," said Mat, extending his hand. "Come back anytime. Oh, the piano, are you certain you don't need something for tuning it?"

"No, not at all. And like I said, it wasn't that far out of tune."

"Well then, much obliged until you're better paid," laughed Mat.

Gus chuckled. "You know, I've been hearing that expression quite a bit since hard times hit us a few years ago."

"So have I. Let's just hope the worst is over," called Mat as Gus began backing out of the driveway.

For Mat and other wheat farmers, things had improved somewhat. Wheat prices rebounded from the 1931 low of twenty-five cents to nearly seventy cents a bushel. However, the stage had been set for a natural disaster that would add immeasurable suffering to the effects of the Great Depression. The drought continued and with it temperatures consistently 100 degrees or higher, which baked the parched soil even more.

"I hate to do it but we'll have to sell off most of our horses," Mat lamented one evening late in July 1934.

"Oh, must we?" asked Rosa.

"Things are getting bad, aren't they?" George III's observation quickly following Rosa's question.

"We have to before we run out of feed. We'll keep Pet as a saddle horse, Dick and Deacon as a wagon team." Mat cleared his throat before adding softly, "They're practically part of the family. But it's so bad in western Oklahoma the government is shooting livestock that are starving and dying of thirst. They shot 600 head just the other day to end their suffering."

George III looked closely at his father. "I heard in Pratt today that they're going to ship a thousand cattle from Pratt County to the slaughterhouses because there isn't enough feed."

"Well, I'm glad we're keeping some horses," said Rosa, her voice matching the melancholy tone set by Mat. "It just wouldn't be the same without a few of them around."

George smiled. "Dick and Deacon are well matched, really well matched. Remember the time when we were in the field waiting for the hired man to bring out the wagon?"

Mat laughed. "Momma, I don't know if you remember this story or not. But when we got worried and came back to check on him it was easy to see the problem. He had Dick hitched up on the left side and Deacon on the right side. They wouldn't budge!"

"Oh, that's right. They're supposed to be hitched with Deacon on the left and Dick on the right," laughed Rosa. "I love horses. They can tell when things aren't the way they're supposed to be. Horses are smarter than you think!"

Their conversation continued long into the night, well past their regular bedtime. But it just wouldn't cool off. Shortly before midnight Mat took a flashlight to check the outdoor thermometer. "Well, now I sure wish I hadn't looked at the thing. It's still 100 degrees!"

"Thank goodness Laura, Marylou, and Rosie are sleeping. I guess at their ages you can sleep through anything," replied Rosa

"Grandma's sleeping too. The heat doesn't seem to bother her very much either," added George.

The next day's newspaper verified Mat's reading. The temperature reached 111 degrees at mid-afternoon and was still 100 degrees at midnight. By 6 a.m. the temperature was a comparative cool 83 degrees. The headlines read, "Pratt Spends a Restless Night — At Midnight, Official Mercury Stands at 100 Degrees, Making Sleep Difficult."[46]

The year 1934 would become one of the hottest and driest in Kansas history. Only 22.75 inches of rain fell in Pratt County, about 4 inches less than average. This was the fifth consecutive dry year. But as often happens, the rainfall was received at the right time for planting wheat in September.

In December 1934 George, along with buddies Paul Tillery and Bub Maynard, drove the twelve miles from Iuka to Byers to watch Byers High School's basketball team play Cullison High School. But this night the girls' teams squared off before the boys' teams did. "Well, we get to see a doubleheader," George observed.

The girls' game began as a nip-and-tuck affair but Byers pulled away in the second half, winning 31-22. "George, you're the old sports writer. How would you write up this game?" laughed Paul and Bub.

"The play of the Byers guards made all the difference. When the ball got to the Cullison end of the court they were constantly harassed and had to make hurried shots. How was that, boys?"

In 1934 women's basketball was a half-court game for the players. Each team had two guards and a defensive center. In addition, there were two forwards and an offensive center. When a defensive player got control of the ball she could dribble only as far as half-court, and then had to pass to an offensive player beyond the line.

"Come on, George. I saw how you were watching that one Byers guard. What's her name again?" kidded Bub.

"Esther Swafford," offered Paul, still chuckling.

George continued his sportswriter's description of the game. "The crowd marveled at the aggressive, dogged defensive play of Byers guard Esther Swafford. Standing no more than five foot two, she literally stuck to the opposing forward like the proverbial glue, frequently intercepting passes from the other team's defensive players before their offensive players could even react." Then, looking squarely at Paul and Bub, "That little Byers guard may be just the gal for me. I've got to meet her!"

"How are you going to do that, just call her up on the telephone?" Paul asked.

"No, it's better to meet in person. Guess I'll be going to lots of Byers basketball games."

"Good thinking, George," smiled Bub. "That way she can see what a tall, dark-haired guy you are. She won't dare turn you down when you ask her out!"

On New Year's Eve, a major dust storm hit western Kansas and the Oklahoma Panhandle. "One of Worst of Season," declared an Associated Press headline. Such storms had begun affecting Pratt County the previous October, each seeming to increase in intensity. When the first one blew in from the southwest, Mat told George, Sr., "It's tempting to joke that the land we sold at Goodwell is coming to Kansas to catch up with us. But that's awfully close to being the truth so it ain't very funny."

"I know what you mean," his dad replied glumly. "I wonder how our friends out there are holding on with all these storms."

"We're a little better off but not by much. I saw in the paper that 1934 was one of the hottest on record around here and that it was the fifth straight year of below-normal rainfall. Things have to be even tougher out there." Mat brightened a bit and continued, "Maybe 1935 won't be as hot as last year."

It was Byers High School's last home game of the season and George III was at the gym early. So far, every time he wanted to approach Esther Swafford after a basketball game she was with a group of other teenagers. *Isn't she ever alone?* But tonight his luck changed as he nearly bumped into her when she was coming into the stands to watch the boys' game. "Hello, nice game you played!"

She peered up at him. Nearly six feet tall, George towered over the diminutive guard. "Oh, why thank you. I've seen you at most of our games. Do you live around here?"

"I live at Iuka. My name is George Welli."

"Where do you go to high school, at Preston?"

"No, I went to Pratt High School, graduated three years ago."

"Oh, the big school," she laughed.

"I was wondering if you would like to go to a movie with me some time."

"Oh, really?"

"Yes, as a matter of fact there's a new Gold Diggers movie coming to the Barron Theater next week."

Esther smiled. "Is Dick Powell in it?"

"Yes, he's in it and so is Gloria Stuart. This one is called 'Gold Diggers of 1935.'"

"I just loved 'Gold Diggers of 1933'! Ruby Keeler is my favorite actress. But most of all, I'm just mad about Dick Powell's singing."

"Well then, does this mean you'll go with me?"

"Yes, George, it does."

For George the next week seemed to pass slowly. *Will the weekend never get here?* On Saturday he washed and polished his 1931 Model-A Roadster until it gleamed in the sunlight, and then drove to the Swafford farm just south of Byers.

"Come in, George!" invited Esther. "George, this is my dad, Charlie Swafford, and my mother, Ona."

George shook hands and smiled the proper smile when meeting a girl's parents for the first time. "It's a pleasure to meet you, Mr. and Mrs. Swafford."

"Mat Welli must be your father. He's the township trustee at Iuka," commented Charlie.

"That's right. And he was on the city council for a while too."

"I read an interesting story about your dad in the paper last year. It was the one about finding those big mastodon bones down at the sandpit."

"George, these are my little sisters, Betty and Doris," said Esther. "I've also got an older brother named Wendell but he went to St. John with some friends a little earlier."

Then George, accompanied by Esther for the first time, retraced the twelve miles back to Iuka and continued on the last five to see the movie in Pratt. The film far exceeded their expectations.

"Oh, that was even better than the first Gold Diggers movie!" exclaimed Esther as they left the theater. "I loved Gloria Stuart. She was just darling! So cute! And Dick Powell's singing was as beautiful as ever. I can't get that song out of my head!"

"You mean the 'Going Shopping' song?"

"Yes, wouldn't it be fun to have so much money that you could just walk into any of those expensive stores and buy whatever you wanted?"

George laughed. "Even a $12,000 diamond bracelet, the one that made Gloria Stuart's mother faint when she saw the bill?"

"Especially that! It's so nice to see a show that makes you forget the hard times and the dust storms. And that 'Lullaby of Broadway' dance number, those dancers were so gorgeous! I'm going to have to buy sheet music for some of those songs in the movie the next time I go to town."

"Oh, do you play piano?"

"Yes, quite well."

"Well, for now how about a hamburger at Dick's Bar-B-Que? They still make the best burgers in Pratt. I ate there a lot when I was in high school."

The evening was beautiful, with a bright moon overhead. But just over halfway to Iuka the night suddenly turned pitch black. "George, did your headlights burn out?"

"No. It's dust settling in, probably from out west. The headlights can't penetrate but just a little way. We'll have to open the side windows and watch the edge of the road to make certain we don't end up in the ditch."

George slowed the Model-A to a crawl as he alternately looked out the left window and the windshield. Esther gazed out the passenger's window to gauge the distance of the roadster to the right side of the road. "Lucky for us that we're just a couple of miles from Iuka," said George. "I think we should stop at my folks' place. You could call your folks from there and let them know you're safe."

"Yes, that's what we'd better do. It would take all night to drive to Byers at this speed."

Finally, the welcome sight of the street leading to Mat and Rosa's home came into view. "Look's like we're going to make it safely," said George, much relieved. "This dust is so thick. It seems as if each storm is worse than the one before."

After a few more minutes of moving at a snail's pace they arrived. "Hello, everyone," called George. "The dust is so bad I brought Esther home with me. It's not safe to drive up to Byers."

After making introductions George told Mat, "It hit us just as we were about halfway to Iuka. It's really bad out there."

Rosa laughed. "George, you bring home company before I've had time to dust! What will Esther think of me as a housekeeper?"

Esther looked up at the fog of reddish dust in the air. It was especially noticeable around the light fixtures as beams reflected off the dust particles. "Well, Mrs. Welli, it might not look as dusty at my folks' place but that's only because we have gas lights instead of electricity," she observed diplomatically.

The spring of 1935 became a cauldron of endless dust storms. At one point in March-April, the wind blew constantly for twenty-seven days. But residents in the towns and out in the country simply swept out their homes and continued their lives. For Mat and George III and other farmers and ranchers, additional care for their animals was necessary. Cleaning the faces, nostrils, eyes, and ears of their three remaining horses was done after each storm. The work team of Dick and Deacon were snow white, but after a dust storm they often resembled Pet, the gray Thoroughbred. All three came to welcome the treatment.

While not as tranquil as the 1920s, life continued in Pratt County. When summer came, George III joined the Iuka softball team as a much-needed high-speed pitcher, earning numerous victories as the team moved into the playoffs. Now Esther could admire his athletic prowess.

Mat continued to read avidly and listen to the radio, often with an eye to the humorous aspects of news, especially sports. "Son, take a look at this write-up in the sports section. Better yet, read it aloud," he told George.

George glanced through it, grinned broadly, and began reading, "'Sept. 27 — Pennant To The Cubs — Sportsman's Park, St. Louis — (AP) The sensational Chicago Cubs came to the end of their glorious baseball road today by slugging the great Dizzy Dean into submission with 15 hits and clinching the National League pennant with their 20th straight victory, a 6-2 triumph over the St. Louis Cardinals.'[47] I can see what you mean, Dad. Whoever wrote that got a bit carried away with the drama. Maybe he's a Cubs fan!"

George and Esther continued dating and were seen nearly every weekend at the Barron or Kansas movie theaters in Pratt. Movies with lots of singing and dancing were her favorites. George's choices were the westerns of Buck Jones, Ken Maynard, and Tim McCoy along with every W.C. Fields movie or short comedy.

"I don't understand why you don't like John Wayne movies very much," said Esther after seeing a preview.

"Oh, he's all right but he's kinda' young. He has a ways to go before he's in Buck, Ken, and Tim's league."

The two grew ever closer until both recognized that they were deeply in love. "I want to marry you, Esther," he told her on Valentine's Day, 1936.

"I love you too, George. Yes, I'll marry you. But should we have a wedding or just go somewhere and get married?"

"Going away sounds best. These are hard times, but our families would feel obligated to spend money they really couldn't spare if we had a wedding. I think we should just go down to Oklahoma early next month and have a minister in Cherokee or Alva marry us. Then, I'll go back to work for the Panhandle Eastern to earn a little extra money. And I think we need to have some place lined up where we can live before we tell anyone else that we're married. That was a long speech for me. How did it sound to you?"

"Wonderful! We can just tell our folks not to plan on having a wedding. "

EPILOGUE

For ten years the drought, intense heat, and dust storms came, creating disasters of Biblical proportions. The early drought years reduced bare cropland to nearly desert-like conditions. And the intense heat in 1933 and 1934 helped make the blitz of dust storms in 1935 inevitable. Entire sections of the Great Plains, from South Dakota's

Black Hills to the Texas Panhandle, a distance of about six hundred miles, became boiling infernos of mammoth dust storms.

Northern areas of the Great Plains did not escape. Early in May 1934, a huge dust storm deposited 12 million tons of dust over Chicago, and then moved eastward to Buffalo, Boston, New York, Washington, and Atlanta. Even ships 300 miles out in the Atlantic found dust on their decks. The radio and newspapers called it "Kansas dirt," but it was actually from Wyoming, Montana, and North Dakota.

Newspaper reporters in the Great Plains states ran out of superlatives in describing the onslaught of nearly constant storms. "Worst of the Season, Worse than Last Week's, Worst in History, No End in Sight," became commonplace headlines.

Trains were derailed by the drifted dust. Often the railroads had to use snowplows to clear the tracks. At times, travel by automobile was impossible.

Some wheat that sprouted after receiving sparse rain was killed by static electricity created by the dust storms. That which remained was often attacked by hundreds of thousands of hungry jackrabbits, animals that thrived during drought conditions. Dust settling on lakes and streams made it impossible for fish to get oxygen and many died. Poultry men in eastern Colorado reported that dust storms blew feathers off their chickens, killing hundreds of them.

Many farmers and ranchers lost their cattle herds when water and feed supplies ran out. Valuable pure breeds were shipped east out of the drought area, but many others were shot by federal government marksmen to end their suffering. In February 1935 the government ended its cattle buying programs, announcing it had purchased more than 8.1 million head in the drought states, paying an average of $13.50 a head.

Dust pneumonia became a serious problem. In Dodge City and surrounding Ford County, Kansas, one third of all deaths in 1935 were caused by it. The year 1936 brought even more record-breaking heat and with it, another plague, grasshoppers by the millions that could fly one hundred miles in a day. They devoured all vegetation in their path.

Despite the hardships, about 75 percent of Great Plains residents stuck it out through the long, onerous decade. Those who moved were primarily families who had lost all means of sustaining themselves. Their self-sufficiency was depleted.

Some of those remaining on the land could be called incurable optimists. On March 16, 1936, the Associated Press reported that Western Kansas residents were hopeful that this spring's dust storms would not be as severe as those of last year. They based their optimism on the fact that the anniversary of "Black Friday" (March 15, 1935) brought a storm much less severe than the one a year earlier. Visibility was about one block in this (current) storm. Three days later it was reported that residents of Sharon Springs, Kansas were elated upon receiving .08 of an inch of rain overnight, the first precipitation of any type since September 6, 1935.

But the term "incurable optimist" doesn't truly reflect the courage and staying power of the hardy souls living on the Southern Plains. A young Texas songwriter named Cindy Walker wrote the song "Dusty Skies," which vividly defined *hard times* as known by those residents during the long, onerous, and heartbreaking decade of the Dust Bowl. It was recorded by Bob Wills and his Texas Playboys Western swing band in 1941 and added to their repertoire.

The poignant lyrics were especially appealing to Dust Bowl victims, many of whom had become loyal Bob Wills fans when he began his radio broadcasts. Thus the song accurately sums up the heartbreak experienced by so many, but who nevertheless refused to give up hope.

CHAPTER 28
BROKEN BONDS

Hitler? Adolph Hitler? Bah! All he's going to do is make the rest of the world hate Germany more than it already does!

George Welli, Sr., March 1937

George III and Esther just married in Cherokee, Oklahoma the previous Friday, March 6, 1936, turned into the driveway of Charlie and Ona Swafford's home south of Byers. "Well, what do you think they'll say?" asked George.

"They weren't very surprised when we told them what we were going to do. But Mother may still be a little disappointed that we didn't have a wedding here at the church."

But their apprehension was unfounded. "Welcome to the family, George!" exclaimed Esther's dad as the two shook hands.

"Thank you, Mr. Swafford."

"Well, just call me Charlie from now on."

"First names for me too, call me Ona," said Esther's mother.

"We're not going to tell anyone else that we're married until we have a place to live," said George. "I'm buying a house with forty acres from the McManus family that we'll move into next week."

"That's right; you mentioned that the other day. Where's it located?" asked Charlie.

"It's in the very northwest corner of Iuka, just across the road from the half-section of land I'm farming."

"Where will you stay until then?" asked Ona.

"Well, George is going to be working for the Panhandle Eastern again, so we'll just live in that little gas house for a few days until we can get moved into our place," laughed Esther. "We'll go over to George's folks' place to clean up. Right now I need to pick up a few of my things."

"Don't bring too many. That gas house is already cramped," laughed George.

"What's your house like?" asked Charlie.

"It's big!" Esther exclaimed. "It has a huge kitchen, a dining room, a parlor, and four bedrooms. There's also a big barn, a windmill, and all the other buildings you need on a farm."

"My goodness! It sounds much bigger than this place," Ona observed with a smile.

Then it was off to Iuka where Esther was welcomed into the Welli family. "Back from Oklahoma already?" joked Mat. "George is a very lucky man to have such a pretty wife," he added.

Rosa was equally happy for them, as was her mother, Antonia Loesel. "You did well, George," Antonia told him in German. "Your dad and I think she's just so beautiful. And she reminds us a lot of your own mother. She's smart, friendly, and independent."

Dust storms continued the same pattern in 1936, beginning in late February and increasing in intensity throughout the spring. This year they seemed just as strong but much more frequent.[48]

Year	Storms
1932	14
1933	38
1934	22
1935	40
1936	68
1937	72
1938	61
1939	30
1940	17
1941	17

Despite the dust storms, both Mat and his father remained optimistic. In late June, wheat prices were about one dollar a bushel, more than four times higher than the 1931 low of twenty-five cents. Mat bought a new Zenith radio. This one was a tall console model with a large, round black tuning dial above the speaker area. It received AM broadcasts and two shortwave bands. "This is all the radio I'll ever need," he told Rosa. "This is absolutely the last one I'll buy."

Rosa laughed. "That's what you said about the spinet model. But I have to admit, this one picks up all the stations really well. Bob Wills and his Texas Playboys sound great!"

At Mat's urging, his dad bought a battery-powered radio and put up a wind charger that would recharge the battery. "This is the quickest way to get the news and the farm market reports nowadays," Mat told him. "Mike, George, Mary, or Katie can listen and then translate the news into German for you."

"I think you're right," George replied. "Guess it's time to move into modern times even though we still don't have electricity out here. Besides, from what they read me out of the newspapers, there are lots of things going on in Europe these days to keep up on."

In late June 1936, there was a new threat. Grasshoppers had become so thick in parts of eastern Kansas that they entered homes and began feeding on clothing and upholstered furniture. Even more ominous, it was reported that fields had been stripped of from 50 to 95 percent of vegetation. The hordes were moving westward with alarming speed.

One morning in mid-July Anna ran into the house. "Mary, Katie! You girls get some towels! Right away!"

"What's wrong, Mother?"

"Grasshoppers, lots of them, are eating the garden. Get some towels we can swat them with!"

The trio, each armed with a large towel, ran out to save their beloved garden. *Making garden* was a family phrase that bespoke pride of accomplishment after long hours of hard work. Now their efforts were being threatened by a horde of pests!

"Shoo!" screamed Anna, swatting her towel at hoppers already feasting on carrot, turnip, parsnip, radish, and beet tops. "Mary, you get the ones eating the corn. Katie, you go after the ones on the tomato vines!"

They worked with a will, swatting vigorously at the ravenous hoppers. But more and more of the swarm dropped down for the feast, making a scene of absolute buzzing turmoil. At times it was as if they were working inside a cloud.

"Aieee! Ouch! Some of them went down my dress!" screamed Katie.

"They're getting in my hair, Mother," complained Mary.

"There are more of them coming all the time. We'll have to go inside, girls." As Anna spoke, a grasshopper flew into her open mouth. Dropping her towel, she plucked it out. "Inside, girls. We can't save the garden."

Once indoors, they began searching their hair and clothing for more of the ravenous insects and squashing the ones they found. For more than an hour they waited inside until the horde moved on toward the west.

"Well girls, let's go see what they left us," said Anna, as she cautiously opened the door. Except for a few strays, the hoppers were gone. The trio walked out to their beloved garden expecting the worst, and finding it. The garden was totally denuded of vegetation, with only the wooden row markers showing where flourishing plants once thrived.

Anna was philosophical. "We could replant some of the fast-growing vegetables and still have something for late summer and fall."

"Mother, look at our peach trees!" exclaimed Katie, running over to the orchard. "Oh no!"

Anna and Mary quickly joined her to check the damage. "They ate our peaches!" exclaimed Mary.

They walked around the two peach trees, both of them void of leaves. "Look. They got the peaches, too. All that's left are the pits hanging from the stems!" exclaimed Anna.

Katie began sobbing, then Mary and finally Anna. The sight of their orchard, robbed of both leaves and fruit, was too much to bear. The bare, lonely peach pits still hanging from the trees represented the final indignity.

The afternoon newspaper reported that a horde of grasshoppers had dropped in on the Pratt sewage disposal plant that morning. The building's exterior became covered with insects that eventually found their way inside.

So far, 1936 had seen extensive dust storms, drought, and grasshopper plagues. On July 17, two days after the grasshopper invasion, the temperature in Pratt was 115 degrees, the first time the thermometer had reached that level in twenty-five years. Kansas was about to become the nation's hot spot for the rest of the summer.

In 1933 there had been thirty-four days of 100-degree-or-over weather in Pratt. This worsened in 1934 with fifty-two such days, followed by 1935, with its mammoth dust storms and thirty-one days of triple-digit heat. But 1936 brought even more heat of three-digit intensity. The all-time record for Pratt was broken on August 13 when the thermometer pushed a fraction of a degree past 115.

The newspapers and radio brought news of heat-related deaths in Kansas and neighboring states. In mid-August, a doctor in nearby Blackwell, Oklahoma found ten clinical thermometers in his office broken, their limit being "only" 110 degrees.

Early in the morning of August 28, the long summer heat wave was broken by a cold front, which passed through Pratt. By noon the temperature was 72 degrees. The previous day had been the fifty-fourth day of 100 degrees or above for the summer.

Newlyweds George III and Esther found relief from both the hard times and the heat at the movie theaters. "Air Cooled" read newspaper ads for both the Barron and the Kansas theaters during the torrid summer months. Enjoying a good movie in a comfortable theater was one thing. Adding to the pleasure was finding the outside air much cooler than earlier in the day. Sometimes, however, patrons would have to sit through both showings to ensure finding cooler air outdoors.

"George, you're *still* laughing at that crazy movie?" asked Esther on the way home from seeing "Poppy," starring W.C. Fields.

"I've seen almost every movie and comedy short he's made. But this one will be one of my favorites. The part where he sells the bartender a 'talking dog' by throwing his voice is just great. When the dog says, 'Just for selling me, I'll never speak again!' it just floored me. And Fields' answer, 'He's a stubborn little fellow. He'll probably keep his word,' actually made my sides hurt from laughing."

"I could tell. You were louder than anyone else. He's really a funny man but I don't always understand his humor. You do good impressions of him, getting better all the time."

"His voice is part carnival barker, part sneer, and part whine. W.C. comes through as a real rogue and scoundrel!"

"What's your favorite line from all his movies?"

"Hmm, I saw him in a comedy about three years ago. The title was 'The Fatal Glass of Beer' and it took place up in the Yukon. Several times in the film he opened the cabin door, looked out, and said, 'And it ain't a fit night out for man or beast.' Right after saying that, he'd get hit in the face with a big bucket of snow. Another time he said, 'I think I'll go out and milk the elk.' Then they showed a whole herd of reindeers running around. This was really a strange comedy."

"I never saw it. It sounds like one where I'd need you to interpret!"

Esther found a new favorite when they saw "Follow the Fleet," starring Fred Astaire and Ginger Rogers. But she was quiet after leaving the theater, so quiet George asked, "Didn't you like the show?"

"Oh my, yes! But I'm still spinning from watching them dance that last number, 'Let's Face the Music and Dance.' They were so good it almost made me cry."

"Yes, that song was kind of somber, wasn't it?"

"But it was excellent, just beautiful. There were lots of great songs. I really liked Ginger Rogers singing 'Let Yourself Go.' And the comical dance they did to 'I'm Putting All My Eggs in One Basket' was so much fun. This may be a movie where I buy sheet music for two or three songs!"

Late in 1936 there were optimistic reports predicting an end to dust blowing in Kansas's southwestern counties. They were based on the belief that much less acreage was bare land, further, that deep furrows "listed" in the bare land would prevent it from blowing.

However, continued drought proved the predictions wrong. At Guymon, Oklahoma there had been only ten inches of rain for all of 1936. January 1937 provided only .28 inch of moisture. As a result, the dust storms began early, February 8, covering the Texas and Oklahoma Panhandles, northeast New Mexico, and southwest Kansas, extending eastward to Pratt.

The storms blew almost continually throughout the region until February 20, 1937, when from two to five inches of snow covered the entire Dust Bowl area. Herbert Clutter,[49] the Finney County, Kansas farm agent, said the moisture wouldn't solve the erosion problem but would provide a "breathing spell" and permit listing operations that would save a lot of the wheat crops. Intense dust storms were regular events throughout the spring, continuing until early June.

After Gus's suggestion in 1934, Mat became a regular listener of Father John Coughlin's radio broadcasts. Lately, however, he was becoming uneasy over the direction they were taking.

The broadcasts began in 1926 and reached nationwide popularity by the mid-1930s as did his weekly magazine, *Social Justice.* Because of the Great Depression, his conspiracy theories appealed to many average, middle-class Americans, who turned to him for support and advice. Initially a staunch supporter of President Franklin D. Roosevelt, Coughlin became disenchanted with his programs.

"I wish I hadn't started listening to this guy," Mat grumbled early in March 1937, turning off his prized, like-new Zenith.

"Father Coughlin sounds angry and disagreeable. Is that why?" asked Rosa.

"It's a bigger problem than that. When I first started listening to him three years ago, he seemed to make sense. It sounded like he just wanted to help ordinary people. But he's been getting more radical all the time. Now he sounds like a Nazi, like he's turned into a henchman for the German Reich. Last month he wrote an article in that magazine he puts out, *Social Justice*, claiming that President Roosevelt tried to pack the Supreme Court with additional justices because he wants to be a dictator."

"The last time Gus was here your conversation got really loud."

"Gus is back to being the same old Gus that we knew twenty years ago during the war. I think we have Father Coughlin to thank for that."

"Meaning . . ."

"Yes, in Gus's opinion, Germany can do no wrong. He keeps talking about how Adolph Hitler has taken the Germany economy out of the Depression. Based on that, he says Hitler has done a better job than President Roosevelt!"

"Is it true?"

"Hitler has taken them out of the Depression but he did it mostly by rearming and breaking the peace agreements made after the war. A year ago he moved troops into the Rhineland. He ignored the League of Nations when they complained and they didn't do anything about it. And he started asking for Germany's former colonies back. Gus is coming down from Ellinwood on Friday. I hope we can keep the conversations away from the economy, Germany, and Father Coughlin!"

On Friday Mat greeted Gus warmly and entertained him with jokes he and Frank Udry had recently heard at the Pratt Elks Club. Friday evening was spent joking, reminiscing about old times in Oklahoma, and discussing the wheat crop and whether there would ever be an end to the dust storms.

But on Saturday a front-page article about the Spanish Civil War set Gus off. "See now! Spain is about to be taken over by the Communists. Those weaklings in London and Paris should just let the German and Italian battleships blast the insurgent positions at Barcelona and Valencia. That will give General Franco the kind of help he needs!"

Mat could feel the hair rising on the back of his neck and his voice grew louder. "No, Gus, those ships are there to enforce the men-and-arms embargo." Suddenly he could see that Gus was far more radical than he had ever been twenty-some years ago. "Gus, we're Americans. You've been a citizen for how many years?"

"Since 1910. What does that have to do with it?" Gus's tone was challenging, no longer jovial, just barely polite.

"Adolph Hitler is going to start another war. We're going to have to fight Germany again in order to remain a free country! Have you forgotten that you almost got lynched for supporting Germany twenty years ago?" Mat saw Rosa freeze at the kitchen door, then retreat back to its relative calm. He was glad the girls were outside playing.

"There's more freedom in Germany than there is in this country with its New Deal, better known as the Raw Deal!"

"How in the world can you say that, Gus?"

Gus picked up the newspaper and read the headline, "Can't Agree on 3.2 Beer." Then he slammed the paper down. "In Germany you can get anything you want to drink. Anytime! Here in Kansas we still can't get anything to drink. At best, maybe we'll get 3.2 beer in a few months. Now tell me that we have more freedom here than they do in Germany!"

"Well then, why don't you just go back to Germany? Better than that, I'll pay your way back if you'll promise to stay!"

Stunned, Gus sprang to his feet. "Maybe that's just what I'll do!" he snarled. He walked quickly to the door, slamming it loudly as he left.

Mat remained in his chair, still shaking from anger.

Rosa tiptoed out of the kitchen. "He's gone now?"

"Yes! I hope I never see him again!"

The next day the entire family was at George and Anna's farm for the usual Sunday gathering. Anna took the women out to show them this year's garden, some of which was already planted. George, Sr., Mat, George III, Frank Udry, Mike, and George, Jr. went out to the pasture to see the new cattle. Mat vowed not to be the first to bring up politics.

However, when Frank Udry brought up the subject of Germany Mat didn't hold back and told them of his argument with Gus the previous day. "What really made me mad was his claiming that they have more freedom in Germany under Hitler than we do in this country!"

George, Sr. turned, an incredulous look on his face. "Hitler? Adolph Hitler? Bah! All he's going to do is make the rest of the world hate Germany more than it already does!" His voice, always deep, was guttural and his fists were clenched.

"More than it already does, Granddad?" asked George III.

"Their submarines made them lots of enemies during the Great War when they sank unarmed ships. And they also used poison gas." George, Sr. looked grim. "More freedom indeed!"

"And early in the war they invaded Belgium, which was a neutral country," added Frank Udry.

"If there's another war those Austrian bonds we own won't be worth much," George, Sr. grumbled. "I should have sold all of them in 1921, not just enough to buy this place. That banker in Goodwell who said we should buy U.S. bonds knew what he was talking about."

"That's true," agreed Mat. "But the price has been running about one-quarter to a third of what we paid for them. I keep hoping the foreign bond market will improve. If they ever get back up to half of what I paid maybe I'll sell."

Once the family was back inside, Mary, Katie, and Esther went to the kitchen. Shortly, they returned with a large birthday cake and Anna called for everyone's attention. "March 14 is a special day. The boy we used to call Little George, Little Brother, or sometimes, Little Tumbleweed is twenty-three years old. Happy Birthday, George!"

Katie and Esther began singing the birthday song and one by one they all joined, in English except for George, Sr. and Anna, who sang in German. They applauded as George III blew out all the candles the first try.

As it grew later, the guests began departing. Mat, Rosa, along with Laura, Marylou, and Rosie were the first to leave, after lengthy goodbyes. Then Frank and Annie Udry left after Frank's characteristically abrupt "We go."

Finally, George III and Esther said their goodbyes to George, Sr., Michael, George, Jr., Mary, and Katie. Then they walked over to Anna. "Thank you so much for the birthday cake, Grandma," said George III, giving her a hug.

"You're welcome, Little Tumbleweed," she laughed. "You've done so well. You're educated, have a big place of your own, and a fine, lovely wife who's going to have a baby very soon. You know what? If it's a boy, John or George would be a good name for him."

On the way home, Esther asked, "What was your grandmother saying to you?"

"She was congratulating me on how well I've done."

The 1937 wheat harvest brought a good yield and prices ranged from $1.19 to $1.36. Therefore, disposing of the Austrian bonds remained a low priority for Mat and his dad. It had become a revolting subject, a reminder of a bad investment. Worse, it was also a reminder that the move back to Europe had been a mistake.

But George, Sr. took comfort from the fact that they now lived in Kansas. "Sometimes when I worry about the drought and dust storms here I remember that we could still be living out at Goodwell," he told Mat.

"That's a good point. We lived out there for fourteen years and maybe we could have survived. But I agree. It would have been much tougher than here in Kansas," Mat acknowledged.

The drought continued through 1937 and, with it, more grasshopper plagues. Early in July in Yuma County, Colorado, it was reported that bodies of grasshoppers crushed from passing cars had made the roads slippery and hazardous. However, reports in October and December claimed that the Dust Bowl area had been reduced to one third its former size.

Once again, the reports were overly optimistic. The dust storms returned with a vengeance and much earlier, beginning in mid-January in 1938. "The dust storms came earlier, the soil's still dry as powder, and they're predicting grasshoppers to be five or six times as bad this year!" grumbled Mat. "Beside that, wheat prices are down almost fifty cents a bushel from a year ago! What else can go wrong?"

On Friday, March 11, 1938, Mat's attention shifted to reports Germany had invaded Austria. "GERMAN TROOPS MARCH INTO AUSTRIA" screamed the headlines. The next day's news was just as ominous: "Hitler Proclaims Union of Germany and Austria Before Cheering Throng."

"Mat, what does this all mean?" asked Rosa.

"Well, Momma, Hitler has declared *Anschluss*, meaning that Germany and Austria are now united. I'm worried what that means to us financially. On Monday, I'd better go see Frank Young at the Iuka bank."

"You mean our Austrian bonds . . ."

"Yes. Austria no longer exists. Unless Germany assumes the obligation to pay them off, they'll be worthless."

On Sunday, March 13 the news Mat heard on the radio was even more dismaying. "Right at this moment Austria is no longer a nation but is now officially a part of the German Empire. Austria and Germany are being welded together under one command, one army, one policy, one economic compact."

"Frank Young had bad news, Momma," grumbled Mat upon returning from the bank the next day. "He says that since Austria no longer exists, its bonds are worthless. And he said it's very unlikely that Germany will make good on them."

"That's thousands of dollars lost!"

"Yes, $15,000 for us and about $5,000 for Dad. But we haven't seen the money since 1920 when we bought them at the Goodwell bank. Let's see if there's any more news on the radio," Mat said glumly, sitting down in his chair drawn up close.

Shortly after it warmed up, he heard: "This is Edward R. Murrow speaking from Vienna. It is now nearly 2:30 in the morning (March 15, 1938) and *Herr* Hitler has not yet arrived. But many people are in a holiday mood. They raise the right arm a little higher here than in Berlin."

"Yes, they're happy making the Nazi salute in Vienna, now. But I think Hitler is going to lead them all into war. Then how happy will they be?" Mat growled.

Mat's concern over war intensified upon seeing the next day's newspaper. "Austria Just Another State," he read aloud. "Bad things are happening already. Just like in Germany, Jews can no longer vote.

Some Jews are being made to scrub the streets, just like in Germany." After reading quietly for a while he practically exploded. "Momma, there's nothing but bad news in the paper today. Besides the news from Austria, it says that 'Nineteen Billion Dollars Have Been Spent (the) Past Five Years For Relief In U.S.' Wheat prices are going to stay low and another bad dust storm hit Liberal. I think I'll just go to bed early tonight!"

The next day he was in better spirits and more philosophical, even though the news was grim. On the radio and in the newspapers he was told of similarities to the war scare of August 1914. "Maybe we didn't invest wisely when we left Oklahoma but we did the right thing by coming back to America. All of our children speak English and they're all going to go to high school, maybe even college like George did. We've had some truly hard times financially and we've had drought for seven years now. But I shudder to think we could still be living in Dunacseb!"

"That's true," replied Rosa. "What do you think your Uncle Joe and the rest of the family there will do?"

"It will be tough for them, maybe even worse than in 1914," said Mat, walking over to the telephone.

"Who are you calling?"

"I'd better talk to Dad. He always has good advice and when he sees nothing can be done about a situation, he knows how to live with it."

Outside, the wind was sweeping over the Southern Plains with an intensity that could mean only one thing. Reports for the next day would describe the worst dust storm of the season sweeping in from the northwest, following the previous day's severe duster from the southwest.

EPILOGUE

This was a family that experienced hardship, hard times, personal tragedies, and financial loss. Nevertheless, they succeeded in achieving the immigrant's dreams of becoming valuable, productive Americans.

It was an independent, thrifty, self-reliant family that persisted in the face of adversity. They did without, made do, and did for themselves. In bad times they closed ranks and supported each other.

Despite the hard times and tragedies, they maintained an attitude of wit and good humor. At many family gatherings, musical instruments were broken out so that all could hear and perhaps sing the old tunes that had become family favorites. And if the musicians seemed slow to perform special favorites, the listeners wouldn't hesitate to call out "Play 'Buffalo Gals' . . . play 'Golden Slippers' . . . play 'Sidewalks of New York' . . . play 'Over the Waves,' or . . . please play 'The Beer Barrel Polka'!" However, the request most often heard was "Play 'Red Wing'!"

This was a family that refused to blame others, thereby spurning the victim label. Perhaps without realizing it, they followed the counsel of a man who would become our twenty-sixth president.

> *"Far better it is to dare mighty things, to win glorious triumphs, even though checkered by failure, than to take rank with those poor spirits who neither enjoy much nor suffer much, because they live in the gray twilight that knows neither victory nor defeat."*
>
> **Theodore Roosevelt, April 10, 1899**[50]

NOTES

Chapter 1.

1 Historians would later refer to this battle as the "Gettysburg of the West."

Chapter 2.

2 *The Columbia-Lippincott Gazetteer of the World*, 1952 edition, has the following: "Bernau, (town) population 12,984, Brandenburg, East Germany, 13 miles NE of Berlin; cotton and silk milling, glove manufacturing. Formerly noted for the beer brewed here. Has a 16th century church and 15th century town walls. The town was chartered in the year 1232." Unlike many small European towns and villages, Bernau still exists and bears the same name. It's a tourist attraction, having its own web site, www.bernau.com.

3 Sue Clarkson. *History of German Settlements in Southern Hungary.* 2003. pp. 1-4; http://www.cefha.org/banat/gi/history/bhistory. html

Chapter 3.

4 Geoffrey Wawro. *The Austro-Prussian War; Austria's War with Prussia and Italy in 1866.* 1996. pp. 53 & 56. Cambridge, UK: Cambridge University Press.

5 Ibid., pp. 49-53

6 Ibid., pp. 11-12.

Chapter 4.

7 Geoffrey Wawro. *The Austro-Prussian War; Austria's War with Prussia and Italy in 1866.* 1996. pp. 125-126. Cambridge, UK: Cambridge University Press.

8 Gordon A. Craig. *The Battle of Königgrätz; Prussia's Victory over Austria, 1866.* 1964. p. 166. New York: J. B. Lippincott Company.

Chapter 6.

9   Oscar Jászi. *The Dissolution of the Habsburg Monarchy.* 1929. pp. 226-31. Chicago: The University of Chicago Press.

10 Edward Crankshaw. *The Fall of the House of Habsburg.* 1963. The Viking Press.

11 Richard J. Evans. *Rituals of Retribution: Capital Punishment in Germany, 1600-1987.* 1996. Oxford University Press.

12 *Oxford History of the Prison: The Practice of Punishment in Western Society.* Edited by Norval Morris and David J. Rothman. 1995. New York: Oxford University Press.

Chapter 7.

13 Oscar Jászi. *The Dissolution of the Habsburg Monarchy.* 1929. p. 233. Chicago: The University of Chicago Press.

14 http://www.ohiobreweriana.com/library/holdings/smith.shtml

Chapter 8.

15 Youngstown Historical Center of Industry & Labor
    http://ohsweb.ohiohistory.org/places/ne09/

16 Howard C. Aley. *A Heritage to Share: The Bicentennial History of Youngstown and Mahoning County, Ohio.* 1975. p. 169. Published by The Bicentennial Commission of Youngstown and Mahoning County.

Chapter 10.

17 J. Evetts Haley. *Charles Goodnight, Cowman and Plainsman.* 1936 P. 383. Norman: University of Oklahoma Press.

Chapter 11.

18 Johnny Gimble and Bob Will. "All Night Long." 1949. © Gardenia Music/Saran Music/Lew-Bob Songs. (BMI)

Chapter 14.

19 Pauline Hodges, PhD, Editor. *RECOLLECTIONS OF NO MAN'S LAND Memoirs of Fred Carter Tracy.* 1998. P. 76. Goodwell, OK: No Man's Land Historical Society.

Chapter 16.

20 http://memory.loc.gov/ammem/dihtml/diessay0.html
An American Ballroom Companion, Music Division,
Library of Congress

Chapter 17.

21 Meirion and Susie Harries. *The Last Days of Innocence; America at War, 1917-1918.* 1997. pp. 32-34. U.S. Publisher, New York: Random House.

Chapter 19.

22 National Archives, regimental returns, various U.S. Cavalry regiments.
23 *Optima Optimist.* Optima, Oklahoma. June 15, 1915.
24 Jules Witcover. *Sabotage at Black Tom; Imperial Germany's Secret War in America – 1914-1917.* 1989. pp. 12-25. Chapel Hill, NC: Algonquin Books.
25 "The Black Tom Explosion," by H. R. Balkhage and A. A. Hahling. *The American Legion Magazine*, August 1964.
26 Jules Witcover. *Sabotage at Black Tom; Imperial Germany's Secret War in America – 1914-1917.* 1989. pp. 321-327. Chapel Hill, NC: Algonquin Books.

Chapter 20.

27 Meirion and Susie Harries. *The Last Days of Innocence; America at War, 1917-1918.* 1997. pp. 293. U.S. Publisher, New York: Random House.
28 H. Wayne Morgan and Anne Hodges Morgan. *Oklahoma: A Bicentennial History.* 1977. p. 101. New York: W. W. Norton & Company, Inc.

Chapter 21.

29 Clemens P. Work. *Darkest Before Dawn; Sedition and Free Speech in the American West.* 2005. pp. 168-173; 204-205. Albuquerque: University of New Mexico Press.

Introduction — Part 3.

30 John Clark Ridpath, LL. D. Ridpath's History of the World, Volume X, The World War. 1923. P. 3724. Cincinnati: The Jones Brothers Publishing Company

31 Ibid., P. 3935.

32 Mark Wyman. *Round-Trip to America; The Immigrants Return to Europe, 1880-1930*. 1993. pp. 109-24. Ithaca, NY: Cornell University Press.

33 Many years ago I went through U.S. Army basic training with the Sixth Infantry Division at Fort Ord, California. When the training was over, each newly minted GI received a commemorative book. Much like a high school annual, it included our pictures, training photos, and historical information about the division. One historical photo made a lasting impression. It portrayed a howitzer on the Western Front with this caption: "'Calamity Jane,' a 6th Division Artillery piece, fired the last shot of World War I at 10:59 on the morning of November 11, 1918." As the years passed, however, I've questioned how that last shot could have been identified on a 400-mile front stretching across western Europe.

Chapter 23.

34 John Maynard Keynes. *The Economic Consequences of the Peace*. 1920. pp. 226-227. Harcourt, Brace and Howe.

Chapter 24.

35 Iuka, pronounced "eye-YOU-kuh."

36 J. Rufus Gray. *Pioneer Saints and Sinners*. 1968. p. 46. Pratt, KS: Pratt Rotary Club, publishers.

37 Iuka-Byers Telephone Directory for 1917.

Chapter 26.

38 Winston Churchill, M.P. *Parliamentary Government and the Economic Problem*. June 19, 1930.Romanes Lecture, University of Oxford.

39 Henry Smith Williams, M.D., LL.D. *The Literary Digest Book of Marvels*. 1931. New York: Funk & Wagnalls Company.

40 "Bones for All to See," *The Pratt Tribune*, circa 1934 (Exact date not available).

41 At the time *Play 'Red Wing'!* was published, the mastodon bones were still on display at the Pratt County Historical Society.

Chapter 27.

42 See Chapter 21 for World War I poster.

43 Donald Worster. *Dust Bowl; The Southern Plains in the 1930s.* 1979. pp. 89-94. New York: Oxford University Press.

44 Ibid., pp. 14-15.

45 "1933 One of Hottest on Record," *The Pratt Daily Tribune.* January 1, 1934.

46 "Pratt Spends Restless Night," Ibid., August 1, 1934.

47 "Pennant to the Cubs," Ibid., September 27, 1935. Author's Note: The Cubs lost the World Series to Detroit four games to two.

Chapter 28.

48 Donald Worster. *Dust Bowl; The Southern Plains in the 1930s.* 1979. pp. 14-15. New York: Oxford University Press.

49 "Heavy, Wet Snow Blankets Whole Dust Bowl Area," *The Pratt Daily Tribune.* February 20, 1937. Author's Note: County farm agents served as expert advisors to farmers and ranchers on various agricultural matters. Herbert Clutter and his wife, Bonnie, were murdered by Perry Smith and Dick Hickcock on November 15, 1959. They were tried, found guilty of murder, and executed by the State of Kansas in April 1965. The case was chronicled in Truman Capote's book *In Cold Blood.*

50 Theodore Roosevelt. *The Strenuous Life.* April 10, 1899. Speech before the Hamilton Club, Chicago.

About the Author

Stan Welli is a freelance writer from the Chicago Area. He graduated from the University of Kansas in 1962 with a B. S. in business administration.

Printed in the United States
94346LV00004BD/1-63/A